Funny Things Can Happen
on Your Way through the Bible

2.0

Lord, with what care hast thou begirt us round!
Parents first season us; then schoolmasters
Deliver us to laws; they send us bound
To rules of reason, holy messengers,
Pulpits and Sundays, sorrow-dogging sin,
Afflictions sorted, anguish of all sizes,
Fine nets and stratagems to catch us in,
Bibles laid open, millions of surprises....

George Herbert (1593–1633), *Sin* (excerpt)

Indeed, the word of God is living and effective, sharper than any two-edged sword, penetrating even between soul and spirit, joints and marrow....

(Hebrews 4:12)

Funny Things Can Happen on Your Way through the Bible

2.0

Humor and Wit in the Catholic and Orthodox Canons

CHARLES D. BARRETT

With a Foreword by John M. Bullard

"The Lord who sits enthroned in heaven laughs..."
(Psalm 2:4, NEB)

RESOURCE *Publications* · Eugene, Oregon

FUNNY THINGS CAN HAPPEN ON YOUR WAY THROUGH THE BIBLE, 2.0
Humor and Wit in the Catholic and Orthodox Canons

Copyright © 2013 Charles D. Barrett. All rights reserved. Except for brief quotations in critical publications or reviews, no part of this book may be reproduced in any manner without prior written permission from the publisher. Write: Permissions, Wipf and Stock Publishers, 199 W. 8th Ave., Suite 3, Eugene, OR 97401.

Resource Publications
An Imprint of Wipf and Stock Publishers
199 W. 8th Ave., Suite 3
Eugene, OR 97401

www.wipfandstock.com

ISBN 13: 978-1-62032-907-8

Manufactured in the U.S.A.

Unless otherwise noted, texts from Scripture in this work are taken from the *New American Bible with Revised New Testament and Revised Psalms* © 1991, 1986, 1970 Confraternity of Christian Doctrine, Washington, D.C. and are used by permission of the copyright owner. All Rights Reserved.

Other translations cited are indicated by the following abbreviations:
New English Bible–NEB; New Jerusalem Bible–NJB; King James Version–KJV; Revised Standard Version–RSV; Authorized Version—AV; New Revised Standard Version—NRSV.

Grateful acknowledgment is made to Annie Vallotton for an excerpt quoted in the Preface from her interview with Paula Taquet-Woolfolk, published on Graham Kennedy's *The Bible Illustration Blog*, September 18, 2008. The excerpt is used by permission of Mr. Kennedy.

An index of topics and types of biblical humor, their location in Scripture, and their treatment in this book is available from the author's blog, grinnbarrett.com.

In the spirit of the Second Vatican Council this book is dedicated to the extension and strengthening of the ties linking Christianity's three great families in conversation and common cause.

"The Lord who sits enthroned in heaven laughs..."
(Psalm 2:4, NEB)

"Anybody who created mankind must have had a sense of humor...."
—Diana Trent, "Waiting for God" (BBC Sitcom)

Contents

Foreword • ix
Preface • xi
Introduction • xv

PART ONE: The Book of the Original Covenant

1. Torah • 3
2. History • 62
3. Wisdom and Poetry • 103
4. Prophets • 142

PART TWO: The Book of the New Covenant

5. Gospels • 169
6. Acts of the Apostles • 223
7. Letters of Paul • 232
8. Letters General and Catholic • 251
9. The Apocalypse • 262

Notes • 269
An Eschatological Appendix • 277
Appendix 2 • 279

Foreword

"Do you suppose God has a sense of humor?" asked the Jewish friend of his rabbi. "Of course; he made you and me, didn't he?" came the reply. And a reasoned reply it was. Anyone who has read and studied the Bible will recognize copious examples of humor both stated and implied in the Old and New Testaments and in the Apocrypha. They range from the hundreds of puns and plays on words in Isaiah to whole books, like Jonah, Tobit, and the speeches in Job. Jesus himself uses that grim sort of humor, seen in parables, metaphors, and similes in the Gospels, which drives home a lesson and makes it stick in the mind.

Holy Scripture is a two-sided collection of writings. It is recognized as divinely inspired; that is to say, the worshiping communities that base their faith and practice on Holy Writ have attributed its origins to divine inspiration, however that expression is understood. On the other hand, it is a perfectly human book, put together by human effort and reflecting human society and individual human concerns. Recognition of the dimension of humor brings into clear relief the Bible's humanity.

As one who modestly dabbled in this field myself, back a half-century ago in graduate school days at Yale, I am immensely gratified to read the delightful work of my colleague Dr. Barrett, found here. With detective cunning he has searched the Scriptures and identified humor all over the place. Adroitly he has used what he finds to sharpen the theological import of the passages. Indeed, his purpose is to enhance the theological message of Scripture by focusing on the dimension of humor. In doing so he has superimposed on that message his genius for poetic retelling of the stories, clarifying their theological implications and touching base with the greatest Christian theologians. In this he goes far beyond earlier treatments of the topic by such writers as Elton Trueblood, Webb Garrison, and Jacob Klausner.

This book and its prequel are unique in their exploration of humor and wit in the Bible. They are a boon to all who preach, teach, and write in the light of Scripture.

John M. Bullard, PhD
Albert C. Outler Professor *emeritus* of Religion
Wofford College

Preface

For over three decades one of my main goals as a college teacher was to instill in undergraduates an appreciation for the theological and literary riches of the Bible. Since many of the students taking my courses did so to meet a requirement, capturing and holding their attention entailed looking for imaginative ways to read the text. One of the most effective of such ways involved examining the abundance of wit and humor—the numerous puns, barbed epigrams, and jokes—in Scripture.

After my retirement a decade and a half ago I began, first for my own amusement, then for use in study groups, to jot down, in prose and homely verse comparable to the commoners' Hebrew and Greek of the original texts, as many instances of biblical humor as I could recover or discover anew. The first result was *Funny Things Can Happen on Your Way through the Bible: Scriptural Oddities and Odd Thoughts about Them in a Book of More Rhyme than Reason,* the prequel to this volume, which focused on translations in the King James (largely Protestant) tradition.

In the initial volume I concentrated first on the obviously humorous episodes and stories in the scriptural accounts, then moved on to broader genres and even entire vistas of comic shade and tone—for example, the dramatic stories of Joseph, Moses, the Judges, David, Jesus, and the Apostolic mission, all of which feature the ironic twists and turns of comedy and occasionally even farce. The extended treatment of these and similar narratives in that first book was the obvious result of this discovery. I invite readers to read that first foray into biblical humor as background for and elaboration on the one made here.

The perspective taken in that first volume was obviously and consistently Protestant. My objective in this follow-up project is to escape that perspective and represent as best I can the angles of vision of the other two-thirds of the Christian family. I'm certain I can't entirely succeed at this and request forgiveness and charitable correction from those whose faith I misrepresent.

I hope too, dear reader, that, despite the rickety Rube Goldbergesque verse in which many of them are presented, the samples of biblical humor and wit presented herein will be enough to convince you that we have in Scripture a trove of eyebrow-raising, rib-tickling, and soul-enriching insights into the meaning of our shared pilgrimage.

I wish you joy, laughter, and an enriched experience of Scripture's humorous dimensions as you read. Permit me now to close with a prefatory *apologia* for what you are in for.

> I must admit, with a frustrated sigh,
> that nothing resembling
> a modern poet am I—
> no bard for whom each work's a daring solo,
> a *coup triomphant* or *creatio de novo*.
>
> I hate to use the crutches of rhythm and rhyme
> but lack the knack of inventing my own time.
> So here I am: a reluctant non-modernist,
> an incorrigibly out-of-step recidivist
> returning recurrently to my life of crhyme.
>
> A "crhyme," short for "criminal rhyme,"
> is so named because time after time
> it makes look ridiculous what could be sublime[1]
> and breaks virtually all of poetry's laws
> in a shameless pursuit of tehees and guffaws.
>
> So send on your posse
> from the True Poets Union
> to read the riot act to a manifest looney'un
> whose dream is to be hanged with the very same noose
> Union members sought to use on O. Nash and T. Seuss.

P. S. to the Preface: Getting the Most from this Book

My thoughts in what follows are footnotes to Scripture. In many cases they will make little sense unless you read the biblical texts they comment on. In every case they will make more sense when you read the accompanying texts. It will help greatly if, when reading them, you imagine the vocal inflections and body language that may have adorned their original oral form.

Wherever I have felt that careful reading of an entire story or lesson is important to my comment on or paraphrase of it, I have included the text. More commonly I have reproduced only the "triggering" or "punch-line" excerpts from the pertinent narratives. I urge you, dear reader, *in all cases,* to read and reflect on the larger narratives before reading what I consider humorous in or about them. Doing so thoughtfully may soon have you agreeing with Annie Valotton, the contemporary Dutch artist who illustrated the American Bible Society's Good News Bible, when she says, "Laughter is the king, and saves one's life! You especially need humor! Too many people read the Bible with a severe face! I say no, the Bible is not that! The Bible is life, and it is wonderful!"

A Note on Inclusive Language

In this book I have tried to be faithful both to a sense of obligation to history and valued traditions, on the one hand, and to the contemporary cries of conscience for inclusiveness on the other. In theology, the point at which doing this poses the greatest problem is in the use of the divine name. From their moments of origin, the Hebrew and Christian faiths have had to fight the pagan practice of treating God or the gods as sexual beings. In my view, the early Church's use of masculine pronouns and nouns ("Father," "Son") was a matter of linguistic convention, not a surrender to pagan or patriarchal sexism. Today's translator is obliged to preserve the intention of the texts, not their form. In the absence of an inclusive pronoun, I have accordingly tried, wherever straightforward, clear language will permit, to avoid the use of pronouns when referring to God. When doing this would require awkwardness or a distracting redundancy, however, I have used TL as the pronoun substitute for The Lord, changed the traditional poetic "He" to "(S)He" and retained the traditional "Him," "His," etc., trusting the use of the capital to remind readers that no reference to gender is intended.

Epiphany 2013

Introduction

In George MacDonald's enchanting story *The Princess and the Goblin*, a mine boy named Curdie uses rhyming verse to counter-terrorize subterranean goblins who are maliciously undermining the mine shafts in which he and his fellow miners work. "The chief defense against them was verse," MacDonald writes, "for they hated verse of every kind, and some kinds they could not endure at all. Although there were certain old rhymes which were very effectual, yet it was well known that a new rhyme was even more distasteful to them, and therefore more effectual in putting them to flight."[2]

In a day when prosaic academic readings may tend to undermine the rich shafts of poetic meaning that run the length and breadth of the biblical text, MacDonald's tale strikes me as a parable suggesting a fitting antidote to such a subverting tendency. Though the scholars so engaged may not intend it, insensitivity to the original intent of the biblically based religious traditions could be a major effect of prosaic ("historical," theology-free) ways of reading Scripture. Returning to an imagination-engaging, verse-inspiring take on Holy Writ may be the most effective way communities of faith can counter the threat to such a sensibility.

Such a way of reading Scripture is one of this book's main objectives. In a humbler, cruder way, what's found here joins the Church's great hymnodies in trying to express faith's multi-dimensional insights and spare them the reductionist reaming-out inflicted by reason-based, "history"-seeking methods employed by fundamentalism and modernism from opposite ends of the spectrum.[3] Engagement of the imagination (both mine as writer and yours as reader) is a major goal here. The cockeyed versification my imagination has produced may lack the sober gravitas of academic language, but if it opens up new (or recovers old!) ways of understanding the texts, that price may be worth paying. And—here lies the rub—it may also prove an expeditious way to move closer to the *religious* (theocentric, faith-driven) and *revelatory* (truth-disclosing) intentions of those who gave us the Bible.

Given the dignity of psalter and hymnody, the use of verse to express Scripture's religious and revelatory intentions may be easier to justify, however, than the use of humor toward those ends. In the introduction to this book's prequel I attempted to answer the major philosophical objections— chiefly, the charges of irreverence and irrelevance— to the search for humor in holy writ. Here let me go a step further to argue for humor's practical usefulness as an aid to understanding. When, for example, we see in the first three chapters of Genesis a crescendo of jokes culminating in the drum-roll punch line "Dust you are, to dust you shall return," we can make out in these chapters the most perceptive and penetrating sketch of the human condition ever penned. Learning that the word *adam* in Hebrew is a common noun meaning "humankind" before it is used as a proper name frees us to see the Adam-Eve story as a parable for/comment on human history as a whole instead of a quaint description of the foibles and quirks of a couple of primitive individuals. In the text's play on words connecting *adam* ("humankind") to *adamah* (Hebrew for "from the earth") Joke One in the narrative recalls us all to our humble roots— brings us down to earth, if you will. Joke Two then leads us through the animal park with Adam on a frustrating and futile search for a mate. After this joke pays us the compliment of distinguishing us from the lower animals, the next (Eve's brush with the serpent) makes this compliment the source of our next embarrassment, as the very lowliness of the lowly reptile flatters Eve (and, in her, us) into worshipping God's image in ourselves instead of the God whose image we bear. This embarrassment leads us, in Joke Four, to hide from God in the woods, thus responding to His judging call with the non-verbal equivalent of "Nobody here, Lord—nobody but us trees!" And, finally, as the irony dawns on us that our pursuit of divine status has served only to prove our dust-bound nature, we hear our Maker and Judge, in the punch line of the Meta-joke, declare as much (Genesis 3:19).

Scripture thus alerts us in its opening chapters to humor's usefulness as a way of showing us how we look to God. In the course of this book I hope to prove that reading Scripture at large with an eye for its humor can continue to have such an effect. The spirit I hope one finds expressed in the book is captured well in a quatrain by Victor Daley that was a close runner-up in the contest to serve as one of the book's epigrams:

> *Then Peter kindly said, "Laugh more, groan less;*
> *That heaven is dull is simply Satan's rumour;*
> *The ways of God are ways of pleasantness,*
> *and well He loves a saint with wit and humour.*

—Victor Daley, "A Vision of Sunday in Heaven," Stanza 28

A Word about the Apocrypha

The major difference distinguishing the canons of the Catholic and Orthodox traditions from the Protestant lies in the former collections' inclusion of a group of books commonly called the Apocrypha.

"Apocrypha" in the broadest sense refers, sometimes pejoratively, to "writings of unknown ('secret') origin." The history of the specifically Roman Apocrypha was a rocky one. The Church's premier translator St. Jerome (producer of the Latin Vulgate, which became the Roman Church's authorized version for more than a millennium) declared these writings sub-canonical but then included them in the Vulgate as "deutero" (secondarily) canonical. Elucidating Jerome's position, Cardinal Cajetan, a contemporary of Martin Luther, wrote: "these books (and any other like books in the canon of the Bible) are not canonical, that is, not in the nature of a rule for confirming matters of faith. Yet, they may be called canonical, that is, in the nature of a rule for the edification of the faithful, as being received and authorized in the canon of the Bible for that purpose . . ." (Cardinal Cajetan, "Commentary on all the Authentic Historical Books of the Old Testament," cited by William Whitaker in "A Disputation on Holy Scripture," Cambridge: Parker Society [1849], p. 424).

Though the treatment of the apocryphal writings here follows the order of the Catholic canon (with Orthodox additions where appropriate) in distributing them among the fully canonical books of the Hebrew Bible, it is possible to find them in separate compilations published independently or between the Old and New Testaments in Protestant Bibles. My guide as to order has been the collection found in *The Apocrypha. The Authorized Version.* London: Oxford University Press, n.d., which includes the intertestamental works in the Catholic and Orthodox canons and some others as well.[4]

Part One

The Book of the Original Covenant

The Garden and the Desert

Adam/Eve lived in the Garden of Innocence,
with slight need for the arts of penitence,
but Moses, residing in the Wilderness of Sin,
needed thorough instruction therein.

In Eden the animals were for naming
and were candidates for Adam's mate;
in the desert of Sin they needed taming
and weren't considerable even for a date.

The innocent shepherd, Abel,
brought a lamb, in thanks, to the Lord's table
but Aaron, as a descendant of Cain,
offers his to remove guilt's stain.

Eve found in a serpent
the source of our downfall;
Moses found in one
an amazing cure-all.

As the jewel in creation's crown
Eve had no direction to go but down.
As shepherd of the thoroughly corrupt
it was Moses' job to lead them up.

1-Torah

Genesis

The Seven Days of Creation
(Genesis 1:1—2:3a)

The creation epic in Genesis 1 describes the cosmic grandeur of the Creator's work. The believer can also read it, however, as a list of very personal gifts from an exquisitely thoughtful Lover.

> On the first Day of Creation
> my Lord gave to me
> the light that enables my mind to see.[1]

> On the second Day of Creation
> my Lord gave to me
> a world sufficiently chaos-free
> to aid the light in helping me see.

> On the third Day of Creation
> my Lord gave to me
> a plant-bearing Earth portending my birth,
> and a world sufficiently chaos-free
> to aid the light in helping me see.

> On the fourth Day of Creation
> my Lord gave to me
> sun-, moon-, and star-light, engend'ring time and sight,
> a plant-bearing Earth portending my birth,
> and a world sufficiently chaos-free
> to aid the light in helping me see.

> On the fifth Day of Creation
> my Lord gave to me
> fish that entice me to swim and birds inspiring me to fly
> in the depths of the sea and the heights of the sky . . .

sun-, moon-, and star-light, engend'ring time and sight,
a plant-bearing Earth portending my birth,
and a world sufficiently chaos-free
to aid the light in helping me see.

On the sixth Day of Creation
my Lord gave to me
horses to ride and cows that moo—
pretty soon, the entire zoo—
then, later on that same day,
the gift of my own life
and, soon after, that of a wife,
a mate with whom to work, laugh, play—
fish among whom to swim and birds among whom to fly
in the depths of the sea and the heights of the sky,
a plant-bearing Earth portending my birth,
sun-, moon-, and star-light, engend'ring time and sight,
and a world sufficiently chaos-free
to aid the light in helping me see.

On the seventh Day of Creation,
the Lord conferred on me
an invitation to enjoy the creation,
joining TL and the celestial staff
in a Day of rest and restoration,
of festive celebrations and occasions to laugh:
A Day when I might review and the Word renew
the gifts of life and a winsome mate
with whom to work, play, and procreate,
enjoying while we so do
—horses to ride and cows that moo,
—visits with animal friends in the zoo,
—fish among whom to swim and birds with whom to fly,
—the plant-bearing earth that portended our birth,
—sun-, moon-, and star-light, engend'ring time and sight,
—a world helpfully chaos-free . . .
and the light that enables me
God's grace in all things to see.

Perspective

The First Laugh's on Literalists who are not Literal Enough
(Genesis 1:1-19)

The Bible abounds with wit and humor, but its readers often have a hard time realizing that's true because written messages lack the vocal inflections and body language, such as a smile, shrug, or raised eyebrow, that mark face-to-face speaking.

If God both "laughs" and sometimes intends to inspire laughter through Scripture, as I think God does, that laughter must be bittersweet when sober, literal reading that fails to take body language and voice inflection into account suppresses the Word's life-giving spirit.[2] It must grieve God especially to see what happens when people read the scriptural account of the world's creation as if it were an article in *Science* magazine. In response to such literal interpretations, I think that the Creator's commentary on Genesis 1:1–2:4a might go something like this:

> My Notes make it clear that I am a poet, not a composer of prose.
> This is but one of the things—surely one of the dearest things!—that the invention of Limit and the effort to communicate with limited beings have moved me to become.
>
> Poetry gives words room to breathe.
> It enables them to expand and contract, inhale and exhale, enriching old meanings and taking on new.
>
> The prosaic often becomes stale, static, sterile. Poetic words resemble my Word in their occasional power to bring a dead matter to life.
>
> How amusing I find it, therefore, when prose-bound mortals fail to comprehend the distinctions, laid out in my Notes on Creation,
>
> between my Time and theirs and
> between the Space I encompass and the space that encompasses them.
>
> In making Night and Day I made Time.
> In fashioning a Firmament I made Space.

Not Time and Space as mortals know them,
but Time and Space as I know them,

Time not as measured motion . . .
or as the convenient numbers of a clock
or the handy layout of a calendar
or the learned pages of a history text.

Space not as motion's measuring rod
or as points beyond the arrows of a compass
or the helpful legend of a map
or the useful orientations of an atlas.

Time rather as the distinction between Day and Night,
the Already and the Not Yet,
the Uncreated and the Created.

Space instead as the distinction between Heaven and Earth,
the Always-Present and the Sometimes-Here,
Spirit and Body.

Time and space as my tools of creation
and only derivatively, on loan,
as tools mortals may use to explore and learn about our shared world.

In my Notes I left them broad hints of these differences.

I make it clear there that my creation of Day and Night, Heaven and Earth, came long before, across an infinite logical chasm from, the creation of the suns and moons by which they reckon duration and distance.

Could I give any clearer indication that their thoughts are not my thoughts, that their science has only remote connections to my pre-science and omniscience?

Could I make it any clearer that the laugh's on literalists who are not literal enough to see the plain meaning of my account of the Creation?

A Case in Point
(Genesis 1:27)

So God created man [Hebrew: A*dam*] *in his own image . . . , male and female created he them.*

Can this be right?
Was Adam a Hermaphrodite?
Not all the evidence is in:
Gen. 2:22 too makes our head spin—
for wouldn't the makings of a bride
imply a potential woman inside?

Though strict literalism would suggest it's so
it pays to ask what literalists know—
suppose "Adam" is a synecdoche,
a part standing for a whole, a unit for a class;
then a *stricter* literalist line could lead us to opine
that "Adam" doesn't mean one person but humanity *en masse*.[3]

What's God's Image Look Like?
(Genesis 1:26-27)

Do we deserve a medal
for being bipedal—
for not being, like other animals, lingually dumb,
or for enjoying the use of an opposable thumb?

If we let Holy Writ say its bit
here seems to be the essence of holy wit:
"Instead of attributing merit to what we inherit
we'll resemble God more if we
accept His gifts in humility."

If in God's Word we're to see what God would have us be,
then all inordinate pride will have to be crucified,
and unless we can concede our dependence and constant need,
continued likeness to God can't be guaranteed.

God's Image is Where?
(Genesis 1:26, 3:19)

"'Reduce yourself to dust, and you can avoid sex.' This is a verbatim conclusion drawn on "Morning Edition: Science Friday," NPR 1/29/10 @7:45 a.m. by Ira Flato, Flora Lichtman (Videographer), and Paul Sherman, Professor of Animal Behavior, Cornell U.:

> The tiny bdelloid rotifer (two dozen of whom can ride a grain of salt) is a self-reproducing (purely female) half-a-millimeter worm-like creature whose natural habitat is water. It is called a rotifer because it takes nourishment from its environs through a fan-like rotor organ on its head. In turn it is itself a favorite food of certain waterborne fungi. Its defense against such fungi is to dehydrate itself to a dust-like particle and starve out the fungi, who can't survive dehydration. Thus, unlike other self-reproducing via single sex organisms, it survives its predators' assaults by extended periods of dryness (three weeks or so seems to do it) until, blown by the wind to a new "home," it is rehydrated by rain or dew, free of parasite fungi. This remarkable power to survive as dust makes the bdelloid almost unique among single-sex reproducers. Dust is in effect not its fate but its redeemer and its liberator from dependency on a second sex.
>
> —ETVradio.org, 1/30/10

God is the model of self-sufficiency,
sui generis or self-causing,
boundless in efficiency,
in endurance never falt'ring or pausing.

Though we believe it would likely be vain
to seek such traits at the *bottom* of Being's chain,
tireless science, breathing defiance,
pushes us hard to look again.

After searching for the epitome of *creaturely* self-sufficiency
science offers us the bdelloid, a creature roughly the size of a void.
Among the wonders of nature
that you might contemplate, you
would be hard put to find another creature of such a kind.

Virtually self-creating, the bdelloid skips all the rites of mating;
then, unlike Eve and Adam, who find in dust their death

(their loss of Heaven's gift of breath)
the bdelloid finds in dust a way to keep the grim reaper at bay.

Thus, though it's decidedly odd
and not something one would expect,
might we be surpassed in mirroring God
by this self-regenerative, death-defying fleck?

Satisfaction
(Genesis 1:31)

God looked at everything he had made, and found it very good.

After all vacuums and nooks are filled
by His marvelous creative Act
the Creator seems more thrilled
with the Value than the Fact.

The Proof? Having shown (S)He could make,
then fill, sea, earth, and air,
God's said to exclaim, "Everything's Good!,"
not just "Everything's There."

Perspective

Who Laughs Last? God and the Philosophers
(Genesis 1:1-2:24; 1 Corinthians 1:20-25)

Where is the wise one? Where is the scribe? Where is the debater of this age? Has not God made the wisdom of the world foolish? 1 Corinthians 1:20

Divine Perfection could change only by becoming imperfect, so in the minds of Plato and Aristotle, drafters of Western philosophy's first major systems of thought, the notion that the Divine Being could change was ludicrous. The act of creating would entail such change, disturbing the divine serenity, so their systems assumed the universe was uncreated—that it, like the God or Mind of the cosmos, is an eternal feature of the cosmoscape. If God even contemplates it, (S)He does so in such a way that no whit of the divine character is changed.

The classical philosophers' disdain for the notion that God could change took root in early Christian theology and still has a strong following in orthodox theologies. Yet the notion of an absolutely changeless God has only the slenderest sort of basis in Scripture. The Bible seems far better acquainted with a God who can change dramatically, an idea of deity many philosophers and theologians would consider an uproarious joke.

The God of the Bible not only changes but moves. This shows up in biblical humor. In most of the Bible's wit as well as its woe, God assumes a less cosmic, much lower and local role than the one (S)He plays in the Great Hymn of Creation in Genesis 1. It cannot be otherwise, for—though the span of God's creation is vast, to mortal eyes boundless—any narrative about it that's understandable by mortals must be local. Even for God, exposure to creaturely otherness must mean exposure to locality!

For the Omnipotent One, a move from Everywhere to Somewhere must seem no move at all. Yet entering into a Somewhere with focus and intensity makes that Somewhere a very different thing—as different as the boiling water in a kettle is from the icy waters of a mountain lake, or as the heat of battle is from the battle map of a headquartered general.

According to Genesis 2 and 3, the Somewhere God first entered in becoming "local" was a land where the hot and dry collide annually with the cold and damp, and great rivers serve as life-affording arteries to the corpse of an arid earth. In this desolate Mesopotamian morgue, God's Word brought life for these rivers to nourish, a Garden for them to water.

It is here that the divine-human comedy described in Holy Writ begins. The divine wit we see at work in the First Act of this comedy is more sublime but not necessarily more profound than that found in the simpler, humbler events described later. It is in events of this earthier sort that we find most of the Bible's humor. How sad it is that many thinkers of the philosophical but non-Socratic sort are too sublimely caught up in superterranean climes to perceive the implications of such events for theology. The notion of a God who enjoys His creation and laughs, gracefully not meanly, at its stumblings and pratfalls, is one of those implications.

The Price for Adam's Labor
(Genesis 2:20-24)

The LORD God then built the rib that he had taken from the man into a woman.   22

> Was it because Adam wasn't glib
> that God made use of his rib
> to fashion a creature who could ad lib
> and compose lullabies
> beside Cain's crib?
>
> It's funny how the male anatomy
> suits field or fact'ry better than academy
> while the female is more at home
> at a teacher's knee
> or pondering a thoughtful tome.
>
> We aren't told how much strain
> our race's father had to sustain
> birthing our fair mother Eve,
> but that it took a toll on his brain
> is easy to believe.

Eve's Song, or Sometimes I Feel like a Motherless Child . . .
(Genesis 2:22)

Yahweh God fashioned the rib he had taken from the man into a woman, and brought her to the man.   (NJB)

> How'd Eve fare,
> having no mother there—
> no model to follow as she gave her children care?
> No provider of cooking lessons
> or ears to hear girly confessions?
> No source of maternal advice
> distinguishing naughty from nice?
> No counsel about projects to start—
> and, worst of all, only a man
> to whom to pour out her heart . . . ?

The Original Sin
(Genesis 3:1-7)

Now the serpent was the most cunning of all the animals that the LORD God had made. The serpent asked the woman, "Did God really tell you not to eat from any of the trees in the garden?" The woman answered the serpent: "We may eat of the fruit of the trees in the garden; it is only about the fruit of the tree in the middle of the garden that God said, 'You shall not eat it or even touch it, lest you die.'" But the serpent said to the woman: "You certainly will not die! No, God knows well that the moment you eat of it your eyes will be opened and you will be like gods who know what is good and what is bad." The woman saw that the tree was good for food, pleasing to the eyes, and desirable for gaining wisdom. So she took some of its fruit and ate it; and she also gave some to her husband, who was with her, and he ate it.

"[A] new species, never made by God . . . sinned itself into existence."

—C. S. Lewis[4]

The more we forage in the tale of sin's origin,
the easier it becomes to see that sin's original cause
goes beyond disobeying laws
to challenge God's creative sanity
and create a different humanity.

Can anything be more original than
a creature who can alter its Maker's plan
by producing something new—
taking a path pure righteousness
won't let its Creator pursue?

Lest we overlook God's act of daring,
His radical audacity in sharing
His very image in our creation, consider the implication:
God's granting us freedom to create
makes us, in creating, God's First Mate.

Has the outcome of this gamble led God to rue
creating such a rebellious crew?

Clearly our wanton mutiny requires the Creator's increased scrutiny,
and His good-from-evil feat of salvation
may outstrip His all-from-nothing creation.

Pioneering
(Genesis 3:1-6)

When Eve stole the forbidden fruit
from the temptation-laden sapling,
might we say she committed the first kidnappling?

Welcomed she'd been,
with no danger of committing sin,
to any other plant, from root and flower to fruit.

But we can imagine the Tree's cry
when Eve dared the proscription to defy—
spitting, as it were, in God's eye.

The act was not something nonviolent, like a threat or extortion;
tearing *this* fruit from its life support
was a potential-defying abortion.

An Invention beyond Intention
(Genesis 3:6)

The woman saw that the tree was good to eat and pleasing to the eye, and that it was enticing for the wisdom that it could give. So she took some of its fruit and ate it. (NJB)

Was the tree an oak?
No. Acorns wouldn't be "good to eat"
and indeed might have made Eve choke.

Was the tree an elm?
No again;
an elm's bitter fruit could overwhelm.

How 'bout an aspen?
Aspen fruit's strong lemony taste
would have left Eve raspin.'

But if it was a fig, that just might be big:
though eating too many might cause her grief,
the fig could offer Eve a sheltering leaf,
and, no matter how her woes might grow,
help her invent the fashion show.

The Struggle Goes On . . .
(Genesis 3:1-5)

'Tis the oldest of stories,
yet constantly new:
presented true and false choices,
we rarely choose the true.

Even today the reptilian soul
coils about our spine,
vying for control
of both will and mind.[5]

Thus, hard as it is for the modern mind
to entertain harsh views of humankind,
history can still make us believe
we're all victims of the serpent who fooled Eve.

Apples
(Genesis 3:6)

As from Eve's seducer to Steve's we've evolved,
has the problem of navigating life's course been resolved?
Eve's led us to a selfish unitarian I from a loving triune God;
has Steve's done more than expand that I–
by attaching it to a phone, a pad, or a pod?

The Point of the Tale
(Genesis 3:8-24)

"Who told you that you were naked?" he [God] asked. "Have you been eating from the tree I forbade you to eat?"   11 (*NJB*)

Omniscience can hardly be predicated
of a god who needs to be updated;
such power to know hardly seems a feature
of one who learns the latest from a creature.

Yet the point of this story is not in its theology;
it's a tale, instead, of a called-for apology
and a call to future responsibility
from those who've forsaken God for a tree.

Image and Reality
(Genesis 1:26; 3:6; Exodus 20:4-5 a)

Then God said: Let us make human beings in our image, after our likeness. Let them have dominion over the fish of the sea, the birds of the air, the tame animals, all the wild animals, and all the creatures that crawl on the earth.   1:26

The woman saw that the tree was good for food and pleasing to the eyes, and the tree was desirable for gaining wisdom. So she took some of its fruit and ate it; and she also gave some to her husband, who was with her, and he ate it.   3:6

You shall not make for yourself . . . a likeness of anything in the heavens above or on the earth below or in the waters beneath the earth;   20:4-5a

An ancient tale by the fabulist Aesop
hints at how Narcissus became a fabulous fop:

A little dog bearing a treasured bone
reached a roadside pond in which its image shone.

Coveting the bone clutched in the water-dog's teeth
Rover lunged and snapped at the image beneath.

Sadly, in pursuing the fictitious bone,
the pup only managed to lose its own.

The biblical counterpart to great Aesop's art
is the tale of naive Adam and Eve his mischievous madam.

Both media offer tales of elemental morality
that draw back the curtains on human reality.

Father Adam and Mother Eve bore a far greater treasure,
a Gift-Image whose value lay quite beyond measure.

In the Genesis account of their first scrimmage with God
they squander this greatest of gifts, this Image of God.

Both the fable of Aesop's Dog and the account found in the Genesis log
tell us that, whatever your locality,
pursuing a treasure's image may mean losing its reality.

The Hardest Law to Break
(Genesis 3:8b)

. . . the man and his wife hid themselves from the LORD God among the trees of the garden.

Hiding among trees
beats bending knees,
or so Adam and Eve
seem to believe.

When their future looks hollow
the law they're moved to follow
is the deepest in all creation:
the formidable law of self-preservation.

Unlike other laws of God or the snake
this one's almost impossible to break;
at issue is not just their pride;
here they're out to save their hide!

Wanted
(Genesis 4:1)

The man had intercourse with his wife Eve, and she conceived and gave birth to Cain. (NJB)

Eve so wanted Cain
that her birthing pain,
down payment on her fine,
couldn't her confidence shake
or her joy undermine.

Blinding maternal love
makes him her lifelong turtle dove,
so there's no way she can see
how one day she'll be haunted
by a poster echoing her heart
in declaring him "Wanted."

Cain's Offerings
(Genesis 4:1-17)

In the course of time Cain brought an offering to the LORD from the fruit of the soil, while Abel, for his part, brought one of the best firstlings of his flock. The LORD looked with favor on Abel and his offering, but on Cain and his offering he did not. Cain greatly resented this and was crestfallen. So the LORD said to Cain: "Why are you so resentful and crestfallen? If you do well, you can hold up your head; but if not, sin is a demon lurking at the door: his urge is toward you, yet you can be his master." . . . Cain said to his brother Abel, "Let us go out in the field." When they were in the field, Cain attacked his brother Abel and killed him. Then the LORD asked Cain, "Where is your brother Abel?" He answered, "I do not know. Am I my brother's keeper?" The LORD then said: "What have you done! Listen: your brother's blood cries out to me from the soil!" Therefore you shall be banned from the soil that opened its mouth to receive your brother's blood from your hand. If you till the soil, it shall no longer give you its produce. You shall become a restless wanderer on the earth." Cain said to the LORD: "My punishment is too great to bear. Since you have now banished me from

the soil, and I must avoid your presence and become a restless wanderer on
the earth . . .   3–7, 9–14

> The grain you offered me,
> my dear Earth Mother,
> I offered Another.
>
> When thy offering and mine
> did not suffice
> I sought a greater sacrifice.
>
> Through my father and mother
> thy Lord and mine
> had offered me a brother.
>
> What these three
> offered me
> I sacrificed, O Earth, to thee.
>
> Now I stand bereft:
> banned from you and family,
> I've nothing left.

The Brothers a la Mother Goose
(Genesis 4:1–16)

Abel became a herder of flocks, and Cain a tiller of the ground. . . . Cain said to the LORD: "My punishment is too great to bear. Look, you have now banished me from the ground. I must . . . be a constant wanderer on the earth. Anyone may kill me at sight." Not so! the LORD said to him. If anyone kills Cain, Cain shall be avenged seven times. So the LORD put a mark on Cain, so that no one would kill him at sight.   12b, 14–15

> Abel kept sheep, Cain loved to farm;
> Cain got upset, and Abel came to harm,
> leading God to banish
> Cain from his farm.
>
> Cain said, "Hear me, Lord: This is more than I can bear;
> you've cut me off from that for which I most dearly care.

Is there a place on earth where I can find a home,
or am I condemned to pine, endlessly, as I roam?"

The Lord declared to Cain, "I'm giving you a mark;
you should be and do okay as long as you don't park.
Don't think that what I've done means that I don't care.
I've taken away your farm but I give you 'everywhere.'"

Life from Abel's Angle
(Genesis 4:1-17)

Abel became a keeper of flocks, and Cain a tiller of the soil. In the course of time Cain brought an offering to the LORD from the fruit of the soil, while Abel, for his part, brought one of the best firstlings of his flock. The LORD looked with favor on Abel and his offering, but on Cain and his offering he did not. Cain greatly resented this and was crestfallen. 2b–5

I was the younger but the more daring.
Cain preferred farming, I a life more mobile.
The farmer's job of earth-caring
seemed to Cain the more noble.

What's planted is predictable
—steady and reliable;
the shepherd's life, on the other hand,
seems edgy and less viable.

The farmer's life is waltz-like,
following a seasonal rhythm;
sheep, leading a life erratic—urgent, risky, never static—
need a shepherd always with 'em.

Seasons come and go slowly
for the plowed, then fruitful, field;
life's pace is more urgent for a flock—
dependent on each day-in-the-wild's yield.

The gods of the farm dwell in land and rain
and grace takes the form of ripening grain;
the Shepherd of shepherds is the flock's God
and grace comes through oases and TL's protecting rod.

God accepted my lamb but rejected my brother's grain,
leading him to envy, then slay me in disdain,
reducing Mom and Dad's parenting job
to that of raising Cain.

Questions for Abel
(Genesis 4:1-4)

Next she gave birth to his brother Abel. . . . 2a

No mention of a laugh marks your biograph.
You were the good boy, your mother's joy,
born second, after one who again and again
gave her inexpressible pain.
But did you ever actually laugh,
helping her smile through the rain?

Were you, like a later younger son,
one who'd take your inheritance and run,
leaving behind the security of the farm
and running the risk, to your parents' alarm,
of the wider world's threats of grievous harm?

Was it for you an adventure
to go where the Lord sent you
and rely totally on the resources
divine grace lent you?

You eschewed—no sober, sodded life for you!—
being married to Mother Nature
and waiting to see what the weather would do:
whether it would help a crop come through
or instead upset and deflate you.

You played, it appears, the jester in Nature's court,
refusing to let the weather act as spoilsport
or let waiting on a harvest lull you to sleep—
prepared always to tend and escort,
wherever the Lord led, His sheep!

Did you live such a life,
though your story mentions no laughter
and ends in your shocking demise,
that, when your mother recalled your laugh, her
buoyed spirit would dry her eyes?

Missing Links
(Genesis 4:17a)

Cain had intercourse with his wife. . . .

The missing link for Darwin and Co.—
the ultimate, "pinnacle" primate—
is the one from whom a new species could grow,
the hinge on humankind's gate.

The missing link for Adam and Co.
is not the prime but the second mate—
could Cain find anyone other
than a younger sister to date?

The first question's a matter for paleontology,
with little meaning for authentic theology.
The second, it should be easy to see,
is an unsolvable mystery.

Unless the Source of the first one decides
to provide us a second Bible (and (S)He's not liable),
we'll have to put to rest our psychic strife
about the provenance of the first son's wife.

What about the Fish?
(Genesis 6:5-7)

So the LORD said: I will wipe out from the earth the human beings I have created, and not only the human beings, but also the animals and the crawling things and the birds of the air, for I regret that I made them. 7

To treat the Bible as a book of science is to run into all sorts of unsolvable riddles. Reaching this realization hardly requires a degree in physics or geology. As the following crhyme indicates, a bit of imagination suffices:

>Did the Lord's start-again wish
>include a new beginning for fish,
>requiring the Ark to house an aquarium?
>Or would the tanks in some on-board niche
>contain only Noah's wine and rum?
>
>Noah's story, it's not hard to see,
>reads less like science than poetry,
>teaching us, on the question at hand,
>few facts about water or land—
>just that humans must at times share hegemony
>with whales and other sovereigns of the sea.

Was Eight Enough?
(Genesis 7:7)

Together with his sons, his wife, and his sons' wives, Noah went into the ark because of the waters of the flood.

>If any of the eight
>had been late,
>who could the widow(er)
>have found to date?
>
>"We're all in the same boat"
>was ne'er fore or aft so true,
>and if the ark hadn't stayed afloat,
>what would the world've come to?

These questions, of course,
will only leave us at sea
if we take the story
quite literally.

Quoth the Raven
(Genesis 8:1-13)

At the end of forty days Noah opened the hatch he had made in the ark, and he sent out a raven, to see if the waters had lessened on the earth. It flew back and forth until the waters dried off from the earth. Then he sent out a dove, to see if the waters had lessened on the earth.   6–8

"I guess I was among the most brazen
of the fugitives in the haven;
in any case I was first to leave
and, much as Noah and my mate might grieve,
I was determined not to return.

"I'll take my chances, matey;
that cramped hold drove me crazy;
I'll the waters skim
'til I find a barren limb,
so don't make my fate your concern.

"Push come to shove,
let the old man send a dove,
a symbol of peace, not an omen of death,
to scout a planet
'most out of breath.

"As a card-carryin' raven
I'm not sure this world's worth savin';
and even if I could see, freed from Noah's Barge,
what lies in the depths for me,
I couldn't afford the carrion charge."

Life in the (D)Ark
(Genesis 8:19-22)

Then Noah built an altar to the LORD, and choosing from every clean animal and every clean bird, he offered holocausts [burnt offerings] *on the altar.* 20

> Life must have gone on as usual in the ark
> and a good bit must have happened in the dark;
> for, when Noah needed animals to sacrifice,
> it's not part of the story that he took an inventory
> or even had to look twice.

Noah found Grapes (a la Mother Goose)
(Genesis 9:20-27)

Noah, a man of the soil, was the first to plant a vineyard. He drank some of the wine, became drunk, and lay naked inside his tent. Ham, the father of Canaan, saw his father's nakedness, and he told his two brothers outside. . . . 20–22

> Noah found grapes in the eyes of the Lord
> but mere grape juice left him jaded and bored;
> soon, after mastering the art of making wine,
> he drank it in his tent 'til his nose began to shine.
>
> Noah stayed, stone drunk, inside his tent.
> Son Ham got curious, and in he went.
> Finding Noah lying in a state of shame,
> he went out and told all, ruining Noah's name.

The Other Metamyth
(Gen 12:1-9)

The LORD said to Abram: Go forth from your land, your relatives, and from your father's house to a land that I will show you. . . .   1

When Mike Nichols' movie *The Graduate* came out in the 1960s, a review in *The New Yorker*[6] panned it for not following Aristotle's classic pattern for telling a story, especially a comedy—a pattern expressing a dramatic unity sustained through a beginning, a middle, and an end. This classic pattern has sometimes been illustrated by reference to an adolescent's pilgrimage from being sick of home to leaving home to becoming homesick and returning home. The *New Yorker* review pointed out that Benjamin Braddock, the graduate whose story the movie tells, leaves home but shows no sign of becoming homesick or of returning home for the happy ending that defines classical comedy. The movie's plot has a beginning and a middle but no end—Benjamin simply wrecks a wedding, then rides off with the bride of a romantic rival on a passing bus (the movie's *deus ex machina*) to escape her wrathful family and the rest of the wedding party. Beginning and middle are thus not resolved in a fitting ending.

In holding that *The Graduate*'s plot betrayed the standards of great art and literature, its critics betrayed their own ignorance. Our secular age tends to define "classical" as exclusively Greek and Roman in origin and nature.[7] But Homer, Sophocles, Aristophanes, Vergil and Horace are not the only models for storytelling in our heritage. The story of Abraham, which begins in Genesis 12 and has yet to reach its end, is in many ways a far greater and more influential model than these. Greek drama typically gave us drama in three acts (beginning, middle, end), each quite finite in length. Abraham's story gives us drama in three *infinite* acts—a Jewish, a Christian, and an Islamic—and each portrays life as a pilgrimage with no obvious end in sight. The model for such a pilgrimage—such a straightening out of Aristotle's circle, if you will—is Abra(ha)m's leaving his father's house at the behest of Another, never to return. On the deepest level the great debate, and even the recently renewed conflict, between Western and Middle Eastern cultures has been and remains about which version of Abraham's continuing story provides the better formula for portraying and coping with life's tragicomedy. When the drama's last laugh will occur and who besides the Creator will be laughing remain mysteries, but thankfully its ongoing plot's demonstrations of creaturely foibles and creative grace continue to offer us many a lasting laugh.

Quick Wit to the Rescue
(Genesis 12:10-13, 26:6-7)

There was famine in the land; so Abram went down to Egypt. . . . When he was about to enter Egypt, he said to his wife Sarai: "I know that you are a beautiful woman. When the Egyptians see you, they will say, 'She is his wife'; then they will kill me, but let you live. Please say, therefore, that you are my sister. . . ."   12:10–13

So Isaac settled in Gerar. When the men of the place asked questions about his wife, he answered, "She is my sister." He was afraid that, if he called her his wife, the men of the place would kill him on account of Rebekah, since she was beautiful. . . .   26:6–7

What kind of misters
call their wives sisters
to keep from irking patrons
in friendly host nations?

The Abe who showed such care
in the face of the Demand Outrageous[8]
sadly couldn't spare
son Ike from a Sin Contagious.

It's unflattering,
indeed image-shattering,
when exalted heroes
get caught in evil's throes.

Yet so it goes:
such tidbits in Holy Writ
show us how its heroes
saved their hides by tricks of wit.

No Kiddin'
(Genesis 19:14-15, 30-32)

So Lot went out and spoke to his sons-in-law, who had contracted marriage with his daughters. "Get up and leave this place," he told them; "the LORD is about to destroy the city." But his sons-in-law thought he was joking. As dawn was breaking, the angels urged Lot on, saying, "On your way! Take with you your wife and your two daughters who are here, or you will be swept away in the punishment of the city." . . . Since Lot was afraid to stay in Zoar, he and his two daughters went up from Zoar and settled in the hill country, where he lived with his two daughters in a cave. The older one said to the younger: "Our father is getting old, and there is not a man on earth to unite with us as was the custom everywhere. Come, let us ply our father with wine and then lie with him, that we may have offspring by our father."

The girls' fiancés
went their merry ways,
with youthful disregard
for one they considered an aged retard.

Confusing his warning with joking
leads to their deaths by choking,
and their asphyxiation
to their fiancées' frustration.

So the boyfriends' failure to do Lot's bidding
and his, to make clear he wasn't kidding,
leaves the girls facing
a future of "no kids"ing.

When Knowing Little Led to Knowing Lot
(Genesis 19:6-8, 30-38)

". . . we will lie with him, that we might preserve seed of our father."

32 (NJB)

Genetics they didn't know
but they loved their father so
they were very eager
his seed to oversow.

> What he'd have let happen to them
> on behalf of strangers in need[9]
> they now did to him
> to preserve his seed.
>
> Were they aware that one way
> to hasten a family's closure
> is through incestuous play
> that leads to double exposure?

The Wrestler I: The Prelim
(Genesis 25:21-26a)

Isaac entreated the LORD on behalf of his wife, since she was sterile. The LORD heard his entreaty, and his wife Rebekah became pregnant. But the children jostled each other in the womb so much that she exclaimed, "If it is like this, why go on living!" She went to consult the LORD, and the LORD answered her: "Two nations are in your womb, two peoples are separating while still within you; but one will be stronger than the other, and the older will serve the younger." When the time of her delivery came, there were twins in her womb. The first to emerge was reddish, and his whole body was like a hairy mantle; so they named him Esau. Next his brother came out, gripping Esau's heel; so he was named Jacob.

> Twice he wrestled, first while still nestled
> in his mother's womb;
> did he even then,
> in that shared den,
> feel his Match with Destiny loom?
>
> Before either could see,
> Esau and he
> tested each other's tenacity.
> Neither's will to fight depended on light
> but each drew, it seemed, on the dark's intensity.
>
> Without the power of sight,
> reduced to using only the power to feel,

each struggled to grasp the firstborn's right,
leaving the loser grasping
only the winner's heel.

The Trade
(Genesis 25:29-34)

Once, when Jacob was cooking a stew, Esau came in from the open, famished. He said to Jacob, "Let me gulp down some of that red stuff; I'm starving." (That is why he was called Edom.) But Jacob replied, "First give me your birthright in exchange for it." "Look," said Esau, "I'm on the point of dying. What good will any birthright do me?" But Jacob insisted, "Swear to me first!" So he sold Jacob his birthright under oath. Jacob then gave him some bread and the lentil stew; and Esau ate, drank, got up, and went his way. Esau cared little for his birthright.

Hot was the hunt;
the hunter, exhausted,
spotted his brother the runt
and quickly him accosted.

The brother was stirring a pot,
its contents steaming hot,
while its aroma, redolent of spice,
reached out to entice.

The outspoken hunter,
of the two ever the blunter,
said to his twin, "Can I have some?,"
hoping as he did that Mom hadn't forgot the rum.

"You owe me if you do,"
said brother number two;
"Would you be willing to trade me
the birthright you're due?"

"What's a birthright to me," said Esau,
"but an abstraction?
When a man's about to starve,
it's a trifle, a whit's fraction."

So for some red pottage
the Hunter traded future financial freedom,
surrendering his begottage
for the nickname "Red" or "Edom."

A "Dreadful" Place
(Genesis 28:13-19)

And Jacob awaked out of his sleep, and he said, Surely the LORD is in this place; and I knew it not. And he was afraid, and said, How dreadful is this place! this is none other but the house of God, and this is the gate of heaven.
16–17 (KJV)

Imagine the look on Jacob's face
as he looks upon and names
this "dreadful" place.

"Dreadful" is hardly the word we'd expect
from one who beholds
heaven in prospect.

A vista frightful and austere
may seem particularly queer
as the foregate of wonders the devout anticipate.

No pearls loom into sight—
only stones for a pillar and one for a pillow
to lift his head that night.

But because his restless night
bears a dream's light
Jake learns a pact with Heaven is his birthright.

The Ladder
(Genesis 28:10-13)

Jacob departed from Beer-sheba and proceeded toward Haran. When he came upon a certain shrine, as the sun had already set, he stopped there for the night. Taking one of the stones at the shrine, he put it under his head and lay down to sleep at that spot. Then he had a dream: a stairway rested on the ground, with its top reaching to the heavens; and God's messengers were going up and down on it. And there was the LORD standing beside him and saying: "I, the LORD, am the God of your forefather Abraham and the God of Isaac; the land on which you are lying I will give to you and your descendants."

Why does it matter
that Jacob saw a ladder?
'Twas but a dream
beside a backwoods stream . . .

Most key scriptural decisions result not from seeing visions
but from hearing the Word;
those who see may hold their visions dear
but unless there's an interpreting word to hear
they can hardly know whether to cry or cheer.

The Word that reached Jacob via *his* dream
told him he'd been drafted
for a major league team,
founded by Avram, coached by Itzak,
while promising him as well his dad's playing field back.

And how about the ladder?
It really *does* matter:
As he sleeps on ground and stone,
recovering from fatigue,
it tells Jake he can play in a much higher league.

Coping
(Genesis 29:16-28)

"It is not the custom in our country," Laban replied, "to marry off a younger daughter before an older one. Finish the bridal week for this one, and then I will give you the other too, in return for another seven years of service with me." Jacob agreed. He finished the bridal week for Leah, and then Laban gave him his daughter Rachel in marriage.   26–28

Jacob was remarkably plucky
but given his personal history
even an optimist big as he
could hardly have thought
the number seven lucky.

He worked seven long years for Rachel's hand,
often a victim of the tricky Laban,
only, after much sweat and many a tear,
to awake on his honeymoon
with the weak-eyed Leah.

Though his uncle's awful cruelty joke
gave th'impression he'd be assuming
another seven-year yoke,
going along with the joke
had him, a week later, once more "grooming."

The Wrestler II: The Headliner
(Genesis 32:11-29)

Jacob was left there alone. Then a man wrestled with him until the break of dawn.   25

There was no arena
nor even a ring—
no publicist to tout it
as "world-class rassel-ing."

But the world's seen nothing like it
in all the centuries since

for it began a divine-human wrestling match
that's perpetual and intense.

We aren't told the holds
either grappler employed
but as the match unfolds
Jake's foe becomes annoyed.

"Let me go," the Stranger cries;
but, made increasingly bold
by the effect of his hold,
Jake refuses to let him rise.

"I will not let you go
unless you bless me,
and I'd also like to know
who's tried to arrest me."

"You first," said the Foe,
"what is *your* name?,"
then, soon as He'd got Jake to tell,
renamed him "Israel."[10]

"You are one who's wrestled with God
and held Him to a draw;
for your pains you've won a new name
and a conscience that'll always gnaw."

Reuben, Reuben, You Weren't Thinkin' (Genesis 35:22; 49:2-4)

While Israel was encamped in that region, Reuben went and lay with Bilhah, his father's concubine. When Israel heard of it, he was greatly offended. The sons of Jacob were now twelve. 35:22

"Assemble and listen, sons of Jacob, listen to Israel, your father. 'You, Reuben, my first-born, my strength and the first fruit of my manhood, excelling in rank and excelling in power! Unruly as water, you shall no longer excel, for you climbed into your father's bed and defiled my couch to my sorrow.'"
49:2–4

Reuben had failed to use his head
and been caught, red-faced,
in his father's bed.

Though he's the firstborn,
once his dad's caught 'im
this son on top sinks to the bottom.

The Pit from Joseph's Angle
(Genesis 37:12-24)

So when Joseph came up to his brothers, they stripped him of his tunic, the long ornamented tunic he had on; then they took him and threw him into the cistern (NRSV: pit) 23–24a

I was a surprise,
a product of the hope in Mama's eyes:
a hope destined to fall and rise,
rise and fall, 'til the Lord finally heard
her importunate cries.

It looked like I'd be Pa's last,
and in his eyes I grew up too fast,
so self-consciously precocious
my manners became atrocious,
whetting in my brothers an anger ferocious.

So great was my precocity that I couldn't contain it.
If my arrogance had been rain it
would have sloshed over the barrel's rim,
and I flaunted it in my brothers' faces
on the slightest whim.

Sent by Pa to take my brothers a meal,
I couldn't resist going into my spiel,
my sense of superiority so firm and sure
it soon proved more than my bros could endure.

Though I wound up in a pit,
as I look back and observe it,
it's hard to imagine anyone
could've done more to deserve it.

A Colorful Career
(Genesis 37:1-36; 39:1—50:26, esp. 37:3, KJV)

Now Israel loved Joseph more than all his children, because he was the son of his old age: and he made him a coat of many colors.   **37:3**

Joseph's many-colored life
bore the hues of languor, glamour, power, and strife:
the green of his brothers' envy, the beige of desert sand,
the blue of the Nile stretching across Egypt's land;
the pink of a mistress's boudoir
and a cell with gray shadows rife,
the silver of a vice-regent's throne
and the bronze of an Egyptian wife.

The dreams that bore him up were colorful too,
featuring stars' yellow glow and sheaves' gold hue,
the baker's brown bread, foretelling the loss of his head,
the butler's purple cup, that he was on his way back up;
at last (for real) his brothers' cheeks, the color of catsup—
redemption's requisite red,
saying it was time to patch things up.

Not Your Average Joe
(Genesis 41:38-40)

"Could we find another like him," Pharaoh asked his officials, "a man so endowed with the spirit of God?" So Pharaoh said to Joseph: "Since God has made all this known to you, no one can be as wise and discerning as you are. You shall be in charge of my palace, and all my people shall dart at your command. Only in respect to the throne shall I outrank you."

It seems very real, no mere show,
that the divinely charmed clan of Joe
has a special knack for making things go.

As many a pundit has noticed,
in the making and retaining of sacred lucre
things are seldom trusted to the average palooka.

It seems, then, a savvy measure
when a *goy* presidential Yankee,
seeking a guardian for the nation's treasure,
turns to a Rubin, a Geithner, or a Bernanke.

An Obituary for Jacob
(Genesis 47:7-10)

Jacob said to Pharaoh, "The years of my stay on earth add up to one hundred and thirty years. Few and unhappy my years have been, falling short of my ancestors' years in their stay on earth."   9

Though you entered life at your brother's heel
your mother-tutored capacity to wheel and deal
had you leap-frogging Esau even as a youth
and learning sundry ways to be clever with the truth.

As the most distinguished grad of Uncle Laban's school
you mastered his perversion of the Golden Rule:
"Do unto others *before* they do to you
and, however sleazy it becomes, to your Self be true."

Though lucky in love
you remained a victim of
your uncle's conniving
as he snatched away the prize
for your seven years of striving.

Though he promised to share his sheep,
he made the price too steep,
and because he cheated you
you decided to cheat too.

Having finally had enough
of the old man's guff,
you stole away in the dead of night,
taking wives, children, and much of Laban's stuff.

You weren't necessarily complicit in
Rachel's decision to steal her father's gods
but saw nothing illicit in
keeping them or the lambs striped by the mandrake rods.

You took the shortest route
back to Isaacland,
hoping to elude the hot pursuit
of the posse raised by a furious Laban.

With Laban behind and Esau ahead
you doubtless were filled with mounting dread,
with no time for quandaries about identity
like which was the devil, which the sea.

Overtaken by your wives' dad
on the crest of proud Mount Gilead
you managed to educe from that wily unk a truce
which left neither totally happy, neither totally sad.

That left only Esau to face
in a tête-a-tête you were loath to embrace.
But, reassured by an angel you managed to pin,
you managed to become his beloved brother again.

Twelve sons and two grands later,
ready for prime time in the divine-human theater,
you co-starred with your favorite son,
who was destined to become greater
than any of his bros, though (bar one) he was born later.

You and your kin were to survive hardship and famine
through the good offices of this gifted gamin
whose remarkable ability to understand dreams
saved him and you from foes' devious schemes.

Though you might like to rewrite your story's script
to match the new start you're given in Egypt,
all you can remember is a trail of tears:
*"Few and unhappy my years have been,
falling short of my ancestors' years."*

For sixty-two more reflections on humor and wit in *Genesis*, see the first volume of *Funny Things Can Happen on Your Way through the Bible*, pp. 3–52.

Exodus

A Pharaoh Foiled
(Exodus 1:15-17)

The king of Egypt told the Hebrew midwives . . . , "When you act as midwives for the Hebrew women, look on the birthstool: if it is a boy, kill him; but if it is a girl, she may live." The midwives, however, feared God; they did not do as the king of Egypt had ordered them, but let the boys live.

How can the Pharaoh limit
the Hebrew population?
Not, we may be sure,
by banning copulation . . .

We soon find that it won't work either
to have Egypt's monarch be the
one who humors his bile
by drowning babies in the Nile.

Powerful though he is,
and clever as a whiz,
the power of Pharaoh's imperial rod
proves no match for the fear of God.

Fast Women
(Exodus 1:19)

The midwives said to Pharaoh, "Because the Hebrew women are not like the Egyptian women, for they are vigorous and are delivered before the midwife comes to them."

Mothers whose parturition
doesn't last,
provide a new definition
of women who are fast.

Irony of Ironies
(Exodus 2:5-10)

Pharaoh's daughter came down to the river to bathe, while her maids walked along the river bank. Noticing the basket among the reeds, she sent her handmaid to fetch it. On opening it, she looked, and lo, there was a baby boy, crying! She was moved with pity for him and said, "It is one of the Hebrews' children." Then his sister asked Pharaoh's daughter, "Shall I go and call one of the Hebrew women to nurse the child for you?" "Yes, do so," she answered. So the maiden went and called the child's own mother. Pharaoh's daughter said to her, "Take this child and nurse it for me, and I will repay you." The woman therefore took the child and nursed it. When the child grew, she brought him to Pharaoh's daughter, who adopted him as her son and called him Moses; for she said, "I drew him out of the water."

How long and hard did the baby cry
before drawing a tear to the royal eye?
And what transpired in the royal heart
to produce the grit to take the baby's part
and her Dad's royal decree defy?

What a remarkable fortuity
that three women of ingenuity
could conspire
to frustrate the desire
of the Lord of the Great Empire!

What resolve, what intensity,
to pull off a deed of such immensity!
And what splendid, extended irony
that the tyrant's very own treasury
be used to subvert his tyranny!

The Name Game
(Exodus 3:13)

"But," said Moses to God, "when I go to the Israelites and say to them, 'The God of your fathers has sent me to you,' if they ask me, 'What is his name?' what am I to tell them?"

'Twas a favorite North African game
to disarm a god by invoking its name,
so round and round the burning bush
Moses danced like a son of Cush;
perhaps, using Cush bush magic,
he could make this meeting's result
copacetic instead of tragic.

To parlay this strange god's power
against certain future shame
maybe he could redeem the hour
by using a controlling name.

But the Lord beyond the constraints
of every heathen name
refused too to accept any
His chosen might want to claim.

"If you want to know who I AM
go to and come back from Egypt's land!
In the course of that Great Trip
you'll begin to understand:

"'Tis not in the pages of a dictionary
but in events expeditionary
that you'll learn who I AM;
'til then you may tell your people,
'It's only through our Trip's effects on us
that we'll know the God behind our Exodus.'"

Beating around the Bush
(Reflections of a Strawless Brick Maker)
(Exodus 3:1-22; 5:5-14)

We're up to our ankles in Egyptian mud,
likely to drown in the Nile's next flood,
and making bricks of quality or size
seems an impossible exercise.

Though skilled in the brick-baking enterprise
we're reduced to making baked mud pies;
lacking straw for our bricks, we're at a total loss
and the less straw we see, the more straw boss.

So will you Two puh-leeze get to the point,
hurry up, and get us out of this joint?
Enough already with the *introductions*!
Please, Lord! Give Moses our marching instructions!

Amazing Facility
(Exodus 5:1)

Afterward Moses and Aaron went to Pharaoh and said, "Let my people go . . ."

Where's the bureaucracy and the red tape?
How could Egypt's autocracy let Moses escape
from the complex folderol
needed to enter a pharaonic Taj Mahal?

Moses' trip through the Red Sea,
though done with seeming facility,
mightn't make moderns gape
as much as his ability to cut through red tape.

Futility
(Exodus 5:1-22)

Then the Israelite foremen came and cried out to Pharaoh: "Why do you treat your servants in this manner? No straw is supplied to your servants, and still we are told, 'Make bricks!' Look how your servants are beaten! It is you who are at fault." He answered, "Lazy! You are lazy! That is why you keep saying, 'Let us go and offer sacrifice to the LORD.' Now off to work! No straw will be supplied to you, but you must supply your quota of bricks."

15–18

One of the more intriguing ironies of political life in modern democracies is the persistent habit of voters and whole voting blocs to vote against what, from a rational perspective, seems to be their own self-interest. Ancient Egyptian economic policy appears to have provided a precedent for such behavior.

> An unenlightened employer
> is like a crime-committing lawyer.
> Both abandon the light for the shade
> by destroying the essential tools of their trade.
>
> As the lawyer can't work without law
> so the brick maker has to have straw.
> The maker of strawless brick
> is as off track as the doctor who makes people sick.

The Sacrificial Son
(Exodus 7:1–12:32)

Sacrifices of and by firstborn sons and heirs are an oft-sounded theme in Scripture. From Moriah's flank to Calvary's and from Esau to the Prodigal's elder brother, the firstborn suffer various degrees of loss in the advancement of the later-born. The gambit that clinches God's fateful chess match with the Pharaoh of Egypt is another riff on this theme.

> The Ten Plagues paved the way
> for the Ten Laws,
> serving as their necessary
> but not their sufficient cause.
>
> The bloodied Nile's unpotable water
> didn't force Pharaoh to do what he oughta
> while the next imperious eight
> worked not to persuade but to irritate.
>
> Though thwarted at turn after turn
> the Great Experimenter pushed on like Edison,
> using trial-and-error 'til at last (S)He'd won—
> finding the key to persuasion,
> as often happens in Scripture, in the sacrificial son.

The Shadow of Freud
(Exodus 7:8-13)

Aaron threw his staff down before Pharaoh and his servants, and it turned into a serpent. Pharaoh, in turn, summoned the wise men and the sorcerers, and they also, the magicians of Egypt, did the same thing by their magic arts. Each one threw down his staff, and they turned into serpents. But Aaron's staff swallowed their staffs.   10b–12

Though all that's implied in the yarns about snakes turned to sticks and vice versa in Pharaoh's court is not clear, it seems feasible that such tales had something to do with the ancient reverence for snakes as potent, fertility-conferring beings, suggesting that

> Even beyond the circle of trollops and rakes,
> when snakes turn to sticks and sticks turn to snakes
> it's hard to avoid
> the shadow of Freud.
>
> With the glee of boisterous, overgrown boys,
> Aaron and the magicians show off their toys
> 'til Aaron shakes the magi at their cores
> by proving "Mine's bigger than yours!"

Foundations Sought, Wrought, and Found
(Exodus 14:5-16; cp. Genesis 1:9)

"The LORD himself will fight for you; you have only to keep still." Then the LORD said to Moses, "Why are you crying out to me? Tell the Israelites to go forward. And you, lift up your staff and, with hand outstretched over the sea, split the sea in two, that the Israelites may pass through it on dry land."   15–16

> Israel's mad dash to the Sea
> alerted Pharaoh's cavalry
> who, determined to settle the score,
> joined the race for the nearer shore.
>
> As soon as their pursuers were spied
> the Israelites were terrified,

leading them, with snarlings snide,
t'accuse Moses of exposing them to genocide.

The people cried: "Let's go back!";
Moses, watching them squirm: "Stand firm!";
and the Lord, seeing their resolve crack:
"Forward! Don't look back!"

Moses then lifted his hand
and watched the Sea turn to land.
Not since the Third Day
had waters behaved in such a way.

On that Day, Earth at the Voice arose!
This day such a strong wind blows
that the mud-red waters recede
in response to Israel's critical need.

What epoch-making occasions!
In both, the Lord provides foundations:
in the earlier, for animate creation,
in the later, for the birth of a nation.

The Summit of Summits
(Exodus 18:1-6a)

"Among the old stories of Israel there is one telling that when it became known that God was about to make the revelation of the law (torah) to the people of Israel from a mountaintop, then all the mountains appeared before God to plead, each one, that it might be chosen for the great honor. 'God of all, choose me,' said Mount Hermon, 'I am the highest of the mountains. It was my summit which, alone of all, towered above the waters of the flood, even as thy torah stands as a great rock above all the sins of the world.' 'Choose me,' said Mount Carmel, 'for I am lovely as a garden. Plant upon me the tree of thy torah as thou didst plant the tree of life in the Garden of Eden.' 'Choose me, choose me,' said Mount Lebanon, 'for the voice of my cedars sings of thy greatness, as thy torah turns all the storms of the world into music, hymning thy praise.' But God said to Mount Sinai, 'From thy

summit shall my torah go forth to my people, for thou art set alone in the desert, even as Israel is alone among the peoples, even as I, Yahweh, am alone in the desert of the universe." [11]

A summit of the summits could only produce confusion
when each peak among them reached the same conclusion:
that, when it came to receiving Torah, the unique de unique,
it alone was suited to serve as the proper peak.

"You're right," said God to Hermon:
'I made you the point of a wonderful sermon,
using your peak above the raging water
to symbolize my everlasting order.

"And you too, Carmel:
Your garden's charm'll
remind my people forever of what they lost
when access to my Life-Tree became sin's cost.

"And you're right too, Lebanon:
Your demeanor reverend
provides the ideal venue
to let your cedars continue
to raise medleys of praise
through ceaseless nights and days.

"But though you all agree in calling on me
to act with all due speed
to sow on one of you my precious Torah's seed,
in my mind's eye 'tis only Sinai,
that isolated, deserted peak,
that's suited to bespeak a God as unique as I.

"Separated as it is
from your mountain community
it fitly represents
my solitary Unity."

Retailing the Law
(Exodus 18:13-27)

Moses listened to his father-in-law and did all that he had said. He picked out able men from all Israel and put them in charge of the people as commanders of thousands, of hundreds, of fifties, and of tens. They rendered decisions for the people in all routine cases. The more difficult cases they referred to Moses. . . .   24–26

Moses' bride-in-law,
a.k.a. his squaw,
had made sure Moses
stayed square with the Law.[12]

Her Dad, Jethro,
finding Moses slow,
traced his deficiency
to a lack of efficiency.

As a long-time resident of the Sinai,
forced by his environment to stay on the alert
spying out foes in the far flung desert,
Jethro developed the practiced eye
of the efficiency expert.

As he watched Moses administer the Law
he spotted a vital flaw
in
the magistrate's habit
of spreading himself too thin.

"Moses," said he,
"it's not all about you.
The Lord has other channels
to send His Word through.

"Though you're an insider
you're not the sole decider,
and you'll need many retail outlets
to be an adequate wholesale provider."

No Chiselers Allowed
(Exodus 20:23-26)

If you make me an altar of stone, do not build it of dressed stones; for if you use a chisel on it, you will profane it. 23 (*NJB*)

> Once the crowd's
> sufficiently cowed,
> the word comes down:
> "No chiselers allowed."

> Thus the Lord makes clear how
> the altar before which Israel's to bow
> is to be TL's creation and TL's alone;
> any human touch or tool would defile the stone!

> Any sacrifice or chant from a psalter
> depends for its effect on a kosher altar,
> not one whose corners have been cut
> by a chisel, an awl, or an if, and, or but.

Weighing the Lord's Works
(Exodus 20:1-17)

"Rabbi Hija ben Abba.... [said], 'Look how much greater is the Torah than the world: to give the world to the world, God needed but seven days. He needed full forty days to give to it the Torah.'" [13]

> Best listen to the rabbis
> to learn what Torah signifies:
> "Look always to the Lord's ways.
> Even count the number of days
> Adonai[14] invests
> before putting a project to rest.

> "God completes the world's every detail
> on a calendar of fairly small scale
> compared to that of the Torahic investment,
> not to mention the work of interpreting it
> in the book of the Original Test'ment."

If someone insists we find a lesson in this,
perhaps this one's not far amiss:
It's easier to fill space's every chink
than train people to act
only *after* they think.

The Commandment that's not There...
(Exodus 20:12)

"In the decalogue we are commanded to honour our fathers and mothers. No mention is made of the love of our children. Nature has sufficiently prepared us for the performance of this latter duty."
—Adam Smith, *The Theory of Moral Sentiments*, p. 164[15]

The law "Honor thy father and mother"
makes us wonder about another:
Why not an "Honor thy son and daughter"
or just a "Treat your kids as you oughta"?

The answer's likely, as Prof Smith suggests,
that parent-love happens without behest;
for while care for parents is prudential,
for helpless offspring it's existential.

We can only hope that this
doesn't cause excessive sorrowin'
among folks who think Holy Writ
leaves no room for Darwin.

Unwanted Exposure
(Exodus 20:26)

"You must not go up to my altar by steps, in case you expose your nakedness on them."

This prohibition is so curt
curious readers might blurt,
"What's it really mean?"
But an imagination keen

can easily envision a scene
featuring an altar pilgrim
wearing only a mini-skirt.

Saving Wisely
(Exodus 21:2)

When you purchase a Hebrew slave, he is to serve you for six years, but in the seventh year he shall be given his freedom without cost.

In commenting on this and similar biblical texts, John Calvin wrote: "In as much as God had given them [Israel] the use of the franchise, the best way to preserve their liberty was by maintaining a condition of rough equality, lest a few persons of immense wealth oppress the general body. Since, therefore, the rich if they had been permitted constantly to increase their wealth . . . would have tyrannized over the rest, God put a restraint on immoderate power by means of this law."

If you're determined to save,
choose another unit of currency
than the Hebrew slave.

Instead of a long-term dividend
your investment in a slave will meet a bad end—
unless, over the six years, you've made him or her a friend.

As Different as Night and Day
(Exodus 22:2)

(If a thief is caught in the act of housebreaking and beaten to death, there is no bloodguilt involved. But if after sunrise he is thus beaten, there is bloodguilt.)

If you catch a thief
you may cause his or her family grief
provided it happens at night.
But you'll be remiss
if you do this
when (s)he's stealing in broad daylight.

What's the difference, you say?
Isn't it the same crime, night or day?
In substance yes, perhaps,
but nighttime's for taking naps;
it appears you may make the thief's family weep
only if (s)he's disturbed your family's sleep.

The View from Behind
(Exodus 33:12-33)

"*. . . you may see my back; but my face may not be seen.*" The Lord   23b

Why should Moses expect
a view that would reflect
the full glory of God?
What if it's not that the Lord's by nature
unfriendly or unkind . . .
but that, once history's passed,
the One Who moved it ahead
can only be seen from behind?

Saving One's Ass
(Exodus 34:20a)

The firstling of an ass you shall redeem with one of the flock; if you do not redeem it, you must break its neck.

Then: The asinine
had no place in the shrine,
but to save the donkey's neck
its owner could make the trek
to present in its stead an off'ring ovine.

Now: In the book of the great I AM
the ass may remain as unkosher as ham—
but, if it's unworthy to serve as a sacrifice,
is it simply at the mercy of a roll of the dice,
or can it too count on the given-for-all Lamb?

A For all Time Exception?
(Exodus 36:2-6)

Moses then called Bezalel and Oholiab and all the other experts whom the LORD had endowed with skill, men whose hearts moved them to come and take part in the work. They received from Moses all the contributions which the Israelites had brought for establishing the service of the sanctuary. Still, morning after morning the people continued to bring their voluntary offerings to Moses. Thereupon the experts who were executing the various kinds of work for the sanctuary, all left the work they were doing, and told Moses, "The people are bringing much more than is needed to carry out the work which the LORD has commanded us to do." Moses, therefore, ordered a proclamation to be made throughout the camp: "Let neither man nor woman make any more contributions . . ."

> Among history's exceptions
> the least likely to recur
> is a decision by a raiser of funds
> to halt, midcourse, a fund raiser.
>
> Perhaps nothing's rarer,
> including "man bites dog,"
> than this peculiar episode
> in history's log.

For eleven more reflections on humor and wit in Exodus, see *Funny Things*, volume one, pp. 52–59.

Retrospective

The Garden and the Desert
(Genesis 3; Exodus 19-20; Numbers 21:4-9)

> Adam lived in the Garden of Innocence,
> with slight need for the arts of penitence,
> but Moses, residing in the Wilderness of Sin,
> needed thorough instruction therein.
>
> In Eden the animals were for naming
> and were candidates for Adam's mate;

in the desert of Sin they needed taming
and weren't considerable even for a date.

The innocent shepherd, Abel,
brought a lamb, in thanks, to the Lord's table
but Aaron, as a descendant of Cain,
must offer his to remove guilt's stain.

Eve found in a serpent
the source of her downfall;
Moses found in one
an amazing cure-all.[16]

As the jewel in creation's crown
Eve had no direction to go but down;
as shepherd of the thoroughly corrupt
it was Moses' job to lead them up.

Leviticus

Perspective

The Priest's Handbook
(Leviticus 1:1-27:34; cf. Exodus 19:6)

If you're looking for an ombudsman's omnibus,
look no further than Leviticus.
Before learning refined manners from Emily Post
you can here find the basics from the Holy Ghost.

What shall the pious eat?
Why shouldn't they mix milk and meat?
Where should we look for justice's seat?

Who's in charge of the tabernacle,
authorized th'atoning rites to tackle,
averting disorder and debacle?

What are the rules for ritual sacrifice?
Why are these rules so precise?
How be sure what's offered will suffice?

Fun reading it's not,
but, at the very least,
Leviticus is *must* reading for priests:

One or more of them wrote it
and in large part chose to devote it
to ways to conduct ceremonial feasts.

Yet ordinary things too fall under the priests' purview:
From quarantining lepers to controlling household mold,
they're called to be caring shepherds whose duties are manifold.

So, if you're seeking
a jack of all trades,
in a Levitical priest you'll find one in spades.

The Lord's Tithe
(Leviticus 3:16b)

All the fat belongs to the LORD.

Remembering all fat is the Lord's
can help keep us svelte and lithe,
but when enjoying the marbling
of a good prime steak
we may still thank TL for the tithe.

The Untouchables
(Leviticus 5:2-3; 6:11, 20; 11:8, 24-27, 31, 36-39; 12:4; 15:5-12, 19-23, 27; 22:4-6; 1 Chronicles 13:9-10)

. . . . if someone . . . touches any unclean thing . . . [(s)he] becomes unclean and guilty. . . .   Leviticus 5:2

As they reached the threshing floor of Chidon, Uzzah stretched out his hand to steady the ark, for the oxen were upsetting it. Then the LORD became angry with Uzzah and struck him; he died there in God's presence, because he had laid his hand on the ark.   1 Chronicles 13:9–10

> Whether you're dealing
> with the bad or the ultra-good
> there are strict rules
> about "shan't" and "should."
>
> Such rules prescribe the ultimate
> in holiness and hygiene
> lest by intent or accident
> the sacred be demeaned.
>
> Sacred things and places
> can't mix at all with crud,
> from beds of affliction, corpses,
> or even menstrual blood.
>
> And lest some think the Law's strictness
> shouldn't matter so much,
> Uzzah's case shows it extends
> even to a well-meaning touch.

Priestly Priorities
(Leviticus 10:1-2, 6-7)

Aaron's sons Nadab and Abihu took their censers and, putting incense on the fire they had set in them, they offered before the LORD unauthorized fire, such as he had not commanded. Fire therefore came forth from the LORD's presence and consumed them, so that they died in the LORD's presence . . . Moses said to Aaron and his sons Eleazar and Ithamar, "Do not dishevel your hair or tear your garments, lest you die and bring God's wrath also on the whole community. While your kindred, the rest of the house of Israel, may mourn for those whom the LORD's fire has burned up, you shall not go beyond the entrance of the tent of meeting, else you shall die; for the anointing oil of the LORD is upon you." So they did as Moses told them.

Put on your poker face;
as priests you must run the race
on the strength of pure devotion,
unfazed by emotion.

Sudden deaths in the family
are sure to test your serenity,
but beware lest the faithful see
any loss of devotion to Me.

Somehow you must learn what it means to be holy:
most importantly, that you belong to Me solely,
then, that you revere the Word given by Moses,
fulfilling each discipline and duty it imposes.

At worship you must bring Me no unauthorized fire,
lest My holy blaze devour you and all you desire;
and, whenever events conspire to make you take sides,
make sure devotion to Me all else overrides.

For eleven more reflections on humor and wit in the book of *Leviticus*, see the first volume of *Funny Things*, pp. 59–64.

Numbers

Perspective

The Boredom Quotient
(Numbers 1:1–36:13)

How much should we expect from a book named Numbers?
There're just ten basic ones, after all,
which constitutes a considerable fall
from the characters, twenty-two to thirty-six,
authors in most other "languages" have to make their picks.

Since most readers seek satiety
in an orthography of greater variety,

the author of Numbers starts far behind
in the quest to please tastes, crude to refined.

Thus readers of Numbers
may succumb to slumbers,
unless helped by a special docent
to avoid a new high in the Boredom Quotient.

Playing the Race Card
(Numbers 12:1-14)

While they were in Hazeroth, Miriam and Aaron spoke against Moses on the pretext of the marriage he had contracted with a Cushite woman. They complained, "Is it through Moses alone that the LORD speaks? Does he not speak through us also?" And the LORD heard this . . . So angry was the LORD against them that when he departed, and the cloud withdrew from the tent, there was Miriam, a snow-white leper! When Aaron turned and saw her a leper, "Ah, my lord!" he said to Moses, "please do not charge us with the sin that we have foolishly committed! Let her not thus be like the stillborn babe that comes forth from its mother's womb with its flesh half consumed." 1-2, 9-12

To oppression's victims
social progress must seem glacial,
especially when it comes to matters racial,
so Moses' choice of a Cushite wife
regrettably leads to sibling strife.

Aaron and Miriam invoke the canard
about the curse of Ham
to support a charge awkward and odd,
disparaging both Moses' marital life
and his standing with God.

Instead of asking the siblings
if their prejudice is right
the Lord strikes back,
justifying Moses' choice of a black
by turning Miriam blindingly white.

Humble Maybe, but Bold Too
(Numbers 12:3, 14:3-19)

Now the man Moses was very humble, more than anyone else on earth.
12:3

If now you slay this people all at once, the nations who have heard such reports of you will say, 'The LORD was not able to bring this people into the land he swore to give them; that is why he slaughtered them in the wilderness.' Now then, may my Lord's forbearance be great, even as you have said, 'The LORD is slow to anger and abounding in kindness, forgiving iniquity and rebellion . . ."
14:15–18a

Moses here seems to call God's bluff,
asking if Yahweh is God enough
to see the divine promise through
even when Israel proves untrue.

Does making his meaning so plain
amount to treating God's word with disdain?
Will the Lord not take it as an insult
when challenged to deliver on a promised result?

What's it say about the character
of Moses and his theology
that he can talk thus to God
without apology?

Head of the Class
(Numbers 22:21-30)

And Balaam rose up in the morning, and saddled his ass, and went with the princes of Moab. And God's anger was kindled because he went: and the angel of the LORD stood in the way for an adversary against him. Now he was riding upon his ass, and his two servants were with him.

And the ass saw the angel of the LORD standing in the way, and his sword drawn in his hand: and the ass turned aside out of the way, and went into the field: and Balaam smote the ass, to turn her into the way. But the angel of the LORD stood in a path of the vineyards, a wall being on this side, and a wall on that side. And when the ass saw the angel of the LORD, she thrust herself unto the wall, and crushed Balaam's foot against the wall: and he smote her again. And the angel of the LORD went further, and stood in a narrow place, where was no way to turn either to the right hand or to the left. And when the ass saw the angel of the LORD, she fell down under Balaam: and Balaam's anger was kindled, and he smote the ass with a staff. And the LORD opened the mouth of the ass, and she said unto Balaam, What have I done unto thee, that thou hast smitten me these three times? And Balaam said unto the ass, Because thou hast mocked me: I would there were a sword in mine hand, for now would I kill thee. And the ass said unto Balaam, Am not I thine ass, upon which thou hast ridden ever since I was thine unto this day? was I ever wont to do so unto thee? And he [Balaam] said, Nay. (KJV)

> The way King James's scribes
> translated the diatribes
> between Balaam and his articulate ass
> surely pushed those scribes to the head
> of the court's jester class.
>
> After the prophet's patient beast
> had successfully sued for peace,
> asking if he had good reason her to slay,
> all the scribes' Balaam could say
> was a He-brayic "Nay."

Getting the Point the Hard Way
(Numbers 25:6-8)

At this a certain Israelite came and brought in a Midianite woman to his kindred in the view of Moses and of the whole Israelite community, while they were weeping at the entrance of the tent of meeting. When Phinehas, son of Eleazar, son of Aaron the priest, saw this, he rose up from the assembly, and taking a spear in his hand, followed the Israelite into the tent where he pierced the two of them, the Israelite and the woman. 6–8a

> It once came to pass
> that an Israelite named Phinehas
> caught a son of Israel with a Midianite maid, mid-trespass.

The tales of Jethro and Gideon
(neither totally a pretty 'un)
illustrate Israel's mixed history with Midian.

Here, the gist of that history plays out
amid a gathering of the devout
when a sinful distraction prompts a violent reaction.

In a single scene we see
how messin' 'round with Midian can be
a mix of hanky-panky and ferocity.

For fifteen more reflections on humor and wit in Numbers, see *Funny Things*, volume one, pp. 64–72.

Deuteronomy

Sauce for the Goose, but no Sass from the Gander
(Deuteronomy 16:18-19)

"You shall appoint judges and officials throughout your tribes to administer true justice for the people in all the communities which the LORD, your God, is giving you. You shall not distort justice; you must be impartial. You shall not take a bribe; for a bribe blinds the eyes even of the wise and twists the words even of the just."

Those on both sides of the bar
bear stains as black as tar.
Both know the sensation,
the sweet allure, of temptation.

The sins of the one on the bench,
seasoned by a grain of salt,
raise less of a stench
and a slighter assumption of fault.

The sins of those in the dock
possess greater power to shock

and they enjoy less benefit of the doubt,
for they're outside looking in, not inside looking out.

The accused may also run the risk
of prejudice against their tribe
and may think their only way out
is a judge who loves a bribe.

The Word is Near You
(Deuteronomy 30:11-14)

. . . this command which I enjoin on you today is not too mysterious and remote for you.
    It is not up in the sky, that you should say, 'Who will go up in the sky to get it for us and tell us of it, that we may carry it out?' Nor is it across the sea, that you should say, 'Who will cross the sea to get it for us and tell us of it, that we may carry it out?' No, it is something very near to you, already in your mouths and in your hearts; you have only to carry it out.

How easy it is to say,
"If a challenge would only come my way
that's worthy of me
I'm sure I'd carry the day
and join the meritocracy.

"I'm stuck in this morass of mediocrity
because worthy challenges are far, far away,
on Himalayan peaks that brush against Heaven
or on the farther shores of the Oceans Seven."

Still, there gnaws inside me
an elemental honesty,
whispering, "It's not a challenge you lack,
but a good stiff bone in your back."

Two Views
(Deuteronomy 34:1-9; Joshua 1:1-8; compare Numbers 13:1-33)

Then Moses went up from the plains of Moab to Mount Nebo the peak of Pisgah which faces Jericho, and the LORD showed him all the land. . . .
                                                                    Deuteronomy 34:1

What Moses saw
from the flank of Mount Nebo
Joshua had seen earlier
from down below.

The view from the eagle's aerie
and that from the mole's hill
were as different as they could be:
Moses saw the sweep of the land from his mountain to the sea
while Joshua focused, closer up, on positions of the enemy.

Moses the eagle,
charismatic, regal,
was master of the long view
while, like that of the mole,
Josh's myopia obscured the whole.

Yet, with the enemy in his sights
from his slight hill,
Josh was better positioned
to close in for the kill.

Conditions for both were right:
the eagle poised up high to take flight,
the mole positioned below
for the coming fight.

For nineteen more reflections on humor and wit in *Deuteronomy*, see the first volume of *Funny Things*, pp. 73–83.

2—History

Joshua

The Choice
(Joshua 24:1-16)

"If it does not please you to serve the LORD, decide today whom you will serve, the gods your fathers served beyond the River or the gods of the Amorites in whose country you are dwelling. As for me and my household, we will serve the LORD."   15

As the one who'd spearheaded Israel's fights
against the dug-in Amorites,
Joshua began to wonder what they'd fought for—
whether they'd won many battles only to lose the war.

Shepherds against farmers had been arrayed
and the shepherds had enjoyed the victory parade,
but as they put down roots in Canaan's land
it seemed all they'd won was a great wasteland.

In an environment hostile to the keeping of sheep,
they were drawn into the Canaanite culture of farming
but ran into a learning curve so steep
that their many crop failures proved alarming.

The fault of course couldn't be theirs!
They were praying to a god who couldn't answer their prayers!
At crop-raising, Canaan's gods were old, old hands,
way ahead of the Shepherd who'd led them through arid lands.

When it came to farming,
the Baalim were lords of the dance;
worshipping them gave Israel's crops
a far, far better chance!

> So it appears the Israel-Baal alliance
> was not so much a religious romance
> as a play for the gods' influence
> as a form of crop insurance.

> 'Tis against this backdrop that we hear Joshua's voice
> posing for Israel a very clear choice:
> to stick to farmer-gods at the risk of great harm
> or to win the reassurance of the Shepherd's strong arm.

For sixteen more reflections on humor and wit in *Joshua*, see *Funny Things*, volume one, pp. 84–93.

Judges

Jael and Sisera
(Judges 5:24-26)

Most blessed of women is Jael, the wife of Heber the Kenite, blessed among tent-dwelling women! He asked for water, she gave him milk, in a princely bowl she brought him curds. With her hand she reached for the peg, with her right hand, the workman's hammer. She hammered Sisera, crushed his head; she smashed, pierced his temple.

> Beneath her tent's fold
> she buttered him up
> with curds in a bowl
> and milk in a cup.

> This show of hospitality
> disguised well her treachery,
> and during his subsequent nap
> she gave him a bloody nightcap.

Wigging Out
(Judges 16:13-22)

She put him to sleep on her lap, and called for a man who shaved off the seven locks of his hair. He immediately became helpless, for his strength had left him.   19

There's surely no truth to the rumor
that, facing the rage her haircut unleashed,
Delilah attempted to humor
hubby Sam with a hairpiece.

I suppose it's just as well:
When facing the tides of Hell,
peace would be a very hard sell
even if the chosen way
were a ward-off-Hell toupee.

More Brides for Benjamin
(Judges 21:13-23)

The people were still disconsolate over Benjamin because the LORD had made a breach among the tribes of Israel. And the elders of the community said, "What shall we do for wives for the survivors? For every woman in Benjamin has been put to death." They said, "Those of Benjamin who survive must have heirs, else one of the Israelite tribes will be wiped out. Yet we cannot give them any of our daughters in marriage, because the Israelites have sworn, 'Cursed be he who gives a woman to Benjamin!'" Then they thought of the yearly feast of the LORD at Shiloh, north of Bethel, east of the highway that goes up from Bethel to Shechem, and south of Lebonah.

And they instructed the Benjaminites, "Go and lie in wait in the vineyards. When you see the girls of Shiloh come out to do their dancing, leave the vineyards and each of you seize one of the girls of Shiloh for a wife, and go to the land of Benjamin. When their fathers or their brothers come to complain to us, we shall say to them, 'Release them to us as a kindness, since we did not take a woman apiece in the war. . . ."   15–22

> For Benjaminites whose luck had been bad
> in the crapshoot for wives at Jabesh-Gilead
> Israel's elders devised another chance
> to roll the dice in the name of romance.
>
> The lovelorn bachelors were told to lie low,
> then each grab for a bride a maid of Shiloh.
> While hiding among vines ripe with fruit,
> each was to seize a maiden to whom to pay suit.
>
> Should the maids' fathers or brothers come later to protest,
> they were to be told, in a spirit firm but modest:
> "*Be generous and allow us to have them,*[17]
> for we took them in desperation, not on a whim."

For fifteen additional reflections on humor and wit in the book of *Judges*, see the first volume of *Funny Things*, pp. 93–102.

Ruth

Getting Her (Their!) Man
(Ruth 3:1-13)

So she went down to the threshing floor and did just as her mother-in-law had instructed her. Boaz ate and drank to his heart's content. Then when he went and lay down at the edge of the sheaves, she stole up, uncovered a place at his feet, and lay down. In the middle of the night, however, the man gave a start and turned around to find a woman lying at his feet. He asked, "Who are you?" And she replied, "I am your servant Ruth. Spread the corner of your cloak over me, for you are my next of kin." He said, "May the LORD bless you, my daughter! You have been even more loyal now than before in not going after the young men, whether poor or rich. So be assured, daughter, I will do for you whatever you say; all my townspeople know you for a worthy woman. Now, though indeed I am closely related to you, you have another relative still closer. Stay as you are for tonight, and tomorrow, if he wishes to claim you, good! let him do so. But if he does not wish to claim you, as the LORD lives, I will claim you myself. Lie there until morning."

6-13

Life was desperately hard in antiquity
for a widow who had no son;
maybe that's why Naomi gave Ruth
instructions to find her one.

In a manner humble but not effete,
Ruth was to lie at Boaz's "feet"
and, as unblushingly as possible,
appeal to his male conceit.

If he weren't by her action flattered,
the women's hopes could be shattered,
but, as they were pleased to learn,
he had a nose for what mattered.

Was he being entirely chivalrous
when he asked her to stay the night?
Though the story's teasingly ambiguous,
before it ends he does what's right.

For three more reflections on humor and wit in *Ruth*, see the first volume of *Funny Things*, pp. 102–105.

1 and 2 Samuel

Hanky Panky on the Threshold
(1 Samuel 2:22–25a)

When Eli was very old, he heard repeatedly how his sons were treating all Israel (and that they were having relations with the women serving at the entry of the meeting tent). So he said to them: "Why are you doing such things? No, my sons, you must not do these things! It is not a good report that I hear the people of the LORD spreading about you. If a man sins against another man, one can intercede for him with the LORD; but if a man sins against the LORD, who can intercede for him?" But they disregarded their father's warning . . .

They don't appear to be innocent greeters,
more, instead, like trick-turning treaters,
these women who "serve" at the door of the tent.

Are they offering sex for sale
or perhaps, like the brides of Baal,
a last shot at kids for a forlorn childless male?

In theory their task is more innocent, less crass—
to help Eli's sons, Hophni and Phinehas,
judge who's qualified to pass.

Alas, our hopes are dashed: the doorkeepers of the shrine
seem to have something else in mind
than the task to which they're assigned.

For such brazen sinners who can intercede?
For to defile the aisle to the House of El
is blasphemy indeed!

Saul in the Hands of Spirits
(1 Samuel 19:9-24)

Then an evil spirit from the LORD came upon Saul as he was sitting in his house with spear in hand and David was playing the harp nearby. Saul tried to nail David to the wall with the spear, but David eluded Saul, so that the spear struck only the wall, and David got away safe. The same night, Saul sent messengers to David's house to guard it, that he might kill him in the morning. David's wife Michal informed him, Then Michal let David down through a window, and he made his escape in safety. Michal took the household idol and laid it in the bed, putting a net of goat's hair at its head and covering it with a spread. When Saul sent messengers to arrest David, she said, "He is sick." Saul, however, sent the messengers back to see David and commanded them, "Bring him up to me in the bed, that I may kill him." But when the messengers entered, they found the household idol in the bed, with the net of goat's hair at its head. Saul therefore asked Michal: "Why did you play this trick on me? You have helped my enemy to get away!" Michal answered Saul: "He threatened me, 'Let me go or I will kill you.'" Thus David got safely away; he went to Samuel in Ramah, informing him of all that

Saul had done to him. Then he and Samuel went to stay in the sheds. When Saul was told that David was in the sheds near Ramah, he sent messengers to arrest David. But when they saw the band of prophets, presided over by Samuel, in a prophetic frenzy, they too fell into the prophetic state. Informed of this, Saul sent other messengers, who also fell into the prophetic state. For the third time Saul sent messengers, but they too fell into the prophetic state. Saul then went to Ramah himself. Arriving at the cistern of the threshing floor on the bare hilltop, he inquired, "Where are Samuel and David?," and was told, "At the sheds near Ramah." As he set out from the hilltop toward the sheds, the spirit of God came upon him also, and he continued on in a prophetic condition until he reached the spot. At the sheds near Ramah he, too, stripped himself of his garments and he, too, remained in the prophetic state in the presence of Samuel; all that day and night he lay naked. That is why they say, "Is Saul also among the prophets?"

King Saul, it appears, became the virtual toy of various spirits. In this curious story, for example, an "evil spirit from the Lord" fell on him, driving him into an insane rage and an attempt to kill David. Before the story's end, abetted by a Samuel-led band of prophets, God's own spirit (v. 23) overcomes the king, diverting him from his murderous mission. Apparently, a totalitarian monotheism lies behind the story, its one God jerking Saul first toward evil, then changing direction to achieve a nobler aim.

> The first king of Israel
> succumbed to spell after spell
> and today's medics would likely conclude
> he was not mentally well.
>
> After his spear barely missed
> David (son-in-law, music therapist,
> and dauntless nemesis)
> Saul set his chin doggedly to persist.
>
> Lurching from high to low
> he groped for a clear path
> and even a beloved daughter
> couldn't escape his wrath.

After posse after posse
had gone all wishy-washy,
he himself hit the trail,
only to fall, like them,
under Samuel's prophets' spell.

As such evidence amassed
and enough time had passed,
Saul's climbs to the top and repeated falls off it
made even his best friends ask
if he was less king than crazed prophet.

Changes of Fortune
(2 Samuel 6:6-15)

The ark of the LORD remained in the house of Obed-edom the Gittite for three months, and the LORD blessed Obed-edom and his whole house. When it was reported to King David that the LORD had blessed the family of Obed-edom and all that belonged to him, David went to bring up the ark of God from the house of Obed-edom into the City of David amid festivities. As soon as the bearers of the ark of the LORD had advanced six steps, he sacrificed an ox and a fatling. 11–13

The Ark's awesome power
made even bold David cower;
filled with anger and fear
he blurted "Get it out of here!"

Thus, rather than being borne ahead
of the chosen people to lead 'em,
the Ark wound up instead
in the house of Obed-edom.

When David got the word
of O-E-'s improving fortunes
he realized how absurd
were his self-torturin's.

> So he led the posse himself
> to recover the Holy Box,
> then celebrated his restored fortune
> via the *misfortune of an ox.*

A Crestfallen Queen
(2 Samuel 6:16-22)

As the ark of the LORD was entering the City of David, Saul's daughter Michal looked down through the window and saw King David leaping and dancing before the LORD, and she despised him in her heart. The ark of the LORD was brought in and set in its place within the tent David had pitched for it. Then David offered holocausts and peace offerings before the LORD. When he finished making these offerings, he blessed the people in the name of the LORD of hosts. He then distributed among all the people, to each man and each woman in the entire multitude of Israel, a loaf of bread, a cut of roast meat, and a raisin cake. With this, all the people left for their homes. When David returned to bless his own family, Saul's daughter Michal came out to meet him and said, "How the king of Israel has honored himself today, exposing himself to the view of the slave girls of his followers, as a commoner might do!" But David replied to Michal: "I was dancing before the LORD. As the LORD lives, who preferred me to your father and his whole family when he appointed me commander of the LORD'S people, Israel, not only will I make merry before the LORD, but I will demean myself even more. I will be lowly in your esteem, but in the esteem of the slave girls you spoke of I will be honored."

> The death knell for their romance
> chimed when he lowered himself to dance.
> If she'd known she'd be marrying a go-go guy
> she would've almost certainly taken a bye.

> A hero to his people he'd be,
> achieving new highs in popularity
> as, going beyond a chicken in every pot,
> he gave bread, meat, and fruitcakes to the lot.

> "Who cares for your esteem?"
> he asked his queen;

"It seems impossible to make you proud,
so I'll seek instead the cheers of the crowd."

Thus the proud house of Saul,
long since under a pall,
was humiliated again
as Queen Michal was left to stew in her gall.

Changing Targets
(2 Samuel 11:1-17)

At the turn of the year, the time when kings go to war, David sent out Joab along with his officers and all Israel, and they laid waste the Ammonites and besieged Rabbah. David himself remained in Jerusalem. One evening David rose from his bed and strolled about on the roof of the king's house. From the roof he saw a woman bathing; she was very beautiful. 1–2

In the Spring, when kings go to battle
wearing war mail and making sabers rattle,
King David decides to fight by proxy
and find a different use for his Spring-sprung moxie.

A Study in Contrasts
(2 Samuel 16:1-14)

As King David was approaching Bahurim, there was a man coming out; he was of the same clan as the house of Saul, and his name was Shimei, son of Gera. He kept cursing as he came out and throwing stones at David and at all King David's officers, . . . Abishai, son of Zeruiah, said to the king: "Why should this dead dog curse my lord the king? Let me go over and take off his head." But the king replied: "What business is it of mine or of yours, sons [sic] of Zeruiah, that he curses? Suppose the LORD has told him to curse David; who then will dare to say, 'Why are you doing this?'" 5–6a, 9–10

A dynasty goes down hard,
losing both the crown and the crowd's regard.
It was certainly so with the House of Saul
when it suffered its ignominious fall.

History bears few scenes as pathetic
as this of Shimei, peripatetic,
slouching along the roadside, stones in hand,
determined to avenge his woebegone clan.

What's David think as he beholds Shimei?
Why is he so ready to grant him leeway,
bearing with his curse and his shower of rocks and dust
and reconciling it all with a notion of God as just?

Here again our author's David's man,
eager to portray him in the best light (s)he can—
the real David, warts and all, but always
a happy counter to Saul's embittered clan.

It all goes to show, doesn't it,
that there's more than one way to gild a lily,
one of which is clearly
to depict what's around it as ugly or silly.

The High Cost of Ignorance
(2 Samuel 16:15-23)

So a tent was pitched on the roof for Absalom, and he visited his father's concubines in view of all Israel.   22

He was a victim of bad advice,
a gullible lad, easy to entice—
one whose head was naturally inclined to swell,
especially under the sway of the suave Ahitophel.

Though many would-be Gordian knots
can with wit be undone,
the very cruelest is tied
when you're cuckolded by your son.

If he'd recalled Father Jacob's stewin'
when so treated by his rude son Reuben,
Ab would have looked for another way
to tweak his father's nose that day.

> Scriptural lore that's unread or untold
> does naught to spare us ills manifold;
> Ab might have lived but was killed instead,
> in part 'cuz he wasn't adequately well-read.

For twenty more reflections on humor and wit in the *Samuels*, see *Funny Things*, volume one, pp. 105–120.

1 and 2 Kings

Bending an Ear
(1 Kings 1:5–31)

So Bathsheba visited the king in his room. The king was very old, and Abishag the Shunamite was caring for the king. Bathsheba bowed in homage to the king. The king said to her, "What do you wish?" 15–16

> Though their fidelity over the years remains unclear
> Bathsheba to David apparently remained dear;
> related more by nostalgic affection
> than by intimate interaction,
> they still had a knack for bringing each other cheer.

> Besides their love they shared a son,
> the precociously wise Prince Solomon,
> for whom Bathsheba was so ambitious
> that she cast eyes jaundiced and suspicious
> toward his fellow, rival princes.

> On his deathbed it isn't at all clear
> how well David can see and hear
> but the one who'd captured his heart
> by way of his eye
> proves here still able to bend his ear.

A Special Royal Visit
(1 Kings 10:1–13)

The queen of Sheba, having heard of Solomon's fame, came to test him with subtle questions. She arrived in Jerusalem with a very numerous retinue, and with camels bearing spices, a large amount of gold, and precious stones. She came to Solomon and questioned him on every subject in which she was interested. King Solomon explained everything she asked about, and there remained nothing hidden from him that he could not explain to her. When the queen of Sheba witnessed Solomon's great wisdom, the palace he had built, the food at his table, the seating of his ministers, the attendance and garb of his waiters, his banquet service, and the holocausts he offered in the temple of the LORD, she was breathless. 1–5

Was she Arabic, or was she Negro,
this queen on whom Solomon was to bestow
wisdom and other gifts resplendent
in venues both public and intimate?

Whittier gave her an ebony hue[18]
while Yeats wrote of a tone ecru,[19]
but neither tells us of the glass or lens
he happens to be viewing her through.

In either case she'd given Sheba a name
which now on its own received wide acclaim
and her visit to the wise and heralded king
could only have enhanced his resplendent fame.

Was she the love object of the Song of Songs,[20]
the one to whom the poet-king's heart belongs,
whose éclat sets the standard for *haut couture* fashion
and whose charms inspire fiery passion?

Sol's interest in her was likely just for show
for of wives and lovers he had enow;
the main thing was, her visits of state
could make the court historian crow.

This Was Wise?
(1 Kings 11:1a, 2)

King Solomon loved many foreign women . . . from nations with which the LORD had forbidden the Israelites to intermarry, "because," he said, "they will turn your hearts to their gods." But Solomon fell in love with them.

> The influence of his head
> was apparently quickly shed
> when Solomon caught a glimpse
> of neighboring kingdoms' nymphs.
>
> Though he was known for being wise
> he let shapely busts and thighs
> almost cause his ship of state
> to founder and capsize.

The 700 Club
(1 Kings 11:1-4)

King Solomon loved many foreign women besides the daughter of Pharaoh (Moabites, Ammonites, Edomites, Sidonians, and Hittites), from nations with which the LORD had forbidden the Israelites to intermarry, "because," he said, "they will turn your hearts to their gods." But Solomon fell in love with them. He had seven hundred wives of princely rank and three hundred concubines, and his wives turned his heart. When Solomon was old his wives had turned his heart to strange gods, and his heart was not entirely with the LORD, his God, as the heart of his father David had been.

> The closest thing in antiquity
> to worldwide communion
> must have been King Solomon's family reunion:
> virtually every court in the ancient Middle East
> contributed to his harem one wife at least.
>
> Seven hundred kings,
> seven hundred queens,
> each an in-law,
> could make even Guinness's Record keeper
> drop a jaw.

Sol must indeed
have hewn wisdom to an art
to find a caterer able
to design a seating chart
with only head seats at each table.

Do you suppose Sol's invocations
before family convocations
for pagan revelry and eating
ever managed to persuade the Lord
to join them for the meeting?

The Other 300
(1 Kings 11:3)

He had as wives seven hundred princesses and three hundred concubines, and they turned his heart. . . .

They didn't fight at Thermopylae
nor even enjoy a monopoly
on Solomon's affections,
but they remain one of history's
intriguing souvenir collections.

At the family reunion
the king likely practiced closed communion,
excluding from the table
the concubines in his stable.

Looking closer, we may ask,
of these ladies' role at court,
Did they have other tasks?
Or were they just draftees
for Sol's favorite sport?

From a more negative angle
the apt question might be this:
If we were to meet King Solomon,
would we be meeting a masochist?

A High Stakes Game
(1 Kings 19:1-3; 21:1-26; 2 Kings 9:30-37)

Ahab told Jezebel all that Elijah had done—that he had put all the prophets to the sword. Jezebel then sent a messenger to Elijah and said, "May the gods do thus and so to me if by this time tomorrow I have not done with your life what was done to each of them."   1 Kings 19:1-2

Gamblers both,
they play for high stakes,
each willing to wager
whatever it takes.

Jezebel holds the cards
in most important ways
but can't win her foe's regard
however well she plays.

She's able, often, to win,
using her King and powers to deceive,
but she *must* lose in the end
'gainst the Ace up Elijah's sleeve.

Elisha's One-upmanship
(2 Kings 4:8-36; cp. 1 Kings 17:17-24)

When Elisha reached the house, he found the boy dead, lying on the bed. He went in, closed the door . . . , and prayed to the Lord. Then he lay upon the child in the bed, placing his mouth upon the mouth, his eyes upon the eyes, and his hands upon the hands. As Elisha stretched himself over the child, the boy's flesh became warm . . . .   2 Kings 4:32-34

The wealthy but childless Shunammite
was kind enough t'invite
Elisha to make her home his second,
prompting him to pray successfully
that the Lord should make her fecund.

The fruit of that feat, a lad,
made his mother terribly sad,
when one day, complaining of his head,
he collapsed and seemed quite, quite dead.

After taking him to the prophet's room and bed
she called Elisha in from afar
and watched in suspenseful dread
as he administered full-body CPR.

In this way did Elisha
give *two* lives to her son,
whereas Elijah'd given the scion
of *his* beneficiary just one.

Thus Elisha outshines Elijah
(again![21]) in relative worth
by giving *his* lad and ward
a *first* as well as a second birth.

Naaman's Lament
(2 Kings 5:1–19a)

"... .please let me, your servant, have two mule-loads of earth, for your servant will no longer make burnt offerings or sacrifices to any other god except the LORD." 17

On many a mission he'd been sent
but none before had brought on
so loud a lament.

His noble career's story he'd become reluctant to tell
as he writhed amid the horrors
of a leper's hell.

At last a slender straw tendered by a slave from Israel
gave him some hope
that things might yet end well.

Now, of the many rivers he'd faced fordin',
none so repulsed him
as the lowly Jordan.

The Abana-and-Pharpar syndrome[22]
tempted him to go home
in haughtiness, untreated,
till, praise be, his servants convinced him
to see the treatment completed.

Finally, setting his fame aside
and swallowing his besetting pride,
with the foe-prophet's word he fully complied.

Because one of Israel's daughters
and one of her prophets had led him to her waters,
healing was soon found!

Hark, hear his praises resound!
"Quick, load two mules with the sacred sod:
I must pay homage to Israel's God!

"Any god who can produce such ecstasy
I must be sure
to take home with me!"

Hell's Angel
(2 Kings 9:1-37)

"The driving is like that of Jehu, son of Nimshi, in its fury."   20b

Jehu the Israelite wasn't the sort to heed a red light;
the place he saw red was mainly in his head
and the consequence consistently filled his foes
with spine-chilling dread.

He was known as so relentless a charioteer
word of his pursuit filled his prey with fear,
and his dogged chasing down of Queen Jezebel
earned him the name "avenger from Hell."

Once he'd found her she hadn't a chance
and, after a brief exchange of rants,
what the dogs left
would have fed few plants.

A Well Earned Degree
(2 Kings 20:12-18)

At that time, when Merodachbaladan, son of Baladan, king of Babylon, heard that Hezekiah had been ill, he sent letters and gifts to him. Hezekiah was pleased at this, and therefore showed the messengers his whole treasury, his silver, gold, spices and fine oil, his armory, and all that was in his storerooms; there was nothing in his house or in all his realm that Hezekiah did not show them. Then Isaiah the prophet came to King Hezekiah and asked him: "What did these men say to you? Where did they come from?" "They came from a distant land, from Babylon," replied Hezekiah. "What did they see in your house?" the prophet asked. "They saw everything in my house," answered Hezekiah. "There is nothing in my storerooms that I did not show them." Then Isaiah said to Hezekiah: "Hear the word of the LORD: The time is coming when all that is in your house, and everything that your fathers have stored up until this day, shall be carried off to Babylon; nothing shall be left, says the LORD. Some of your own bodily descendants shall be taken and made servants in the palace of the king of Babylon."

When everything's been said, here's the rub:
King Hezekiah's become a burntout bulb.
Perhaps it's because he's been sick—
or maybe just become irreparably thick.

A monarch who shows a delegation
visiting from an imperial nation
the contents of his treasure hall
sets his country up for a fall
and earns, says Isaiah, an advanced degree
in the school of royal stupidity.

"I Got Mine, Jack"
(2 Kings 20:12-19)

Hezekiah replied to Isaiah, "The word of the LORD which you have spoken is favorable." For he thought, "There will be peace and security in my lifetime." 19

> In the gallery of heroes
> where King Hez is a fixture
> somebody's stuck
> another unflattering picture.
>
> 'Tis not for him to play with fire;
> he had the sort of
> aversion to pain
> that plagued Neville Chamberlain.
>
> Like politicians of 'most all stripes,
> Hez hated Cassandra-types
> who painted futures of gloom
> in which troubles would mushroom.
>
> When Isaiah said he would run out of luck,
> each of his sons become a eunuch,
> then refused to let him blink or from reality shrink,
> Hez responded with a shrug,
> his attitude cool and smug,
>
> How could a great king seem so indifferent
> to a heritage of sons made impotent?
> Yet Hezekiah finds the nerve t'invent
> the equivalent of the hackneyed crack,
> "To each his own! I got mine, Jack!"

For twenty-three more humorous reflections on characters and stories in the books of *Kings*, see the first volume of *Funny Things*, pp.120–40.

1 and 2 Chronicles

Perspective

The Books of Samuel and of Kings are devoted largely to the *political* fortunes of the Houses of Saul, David, and Solomon. The recasting of the same history in 1 and 2 Chronicles, on the other hand, focuses on the *religious* ventures and achievements of David's dynasty.

Writing about 400 B.C., the Chronicler has a clear and sober fix on the results of Israel's political history. Though the history (s)he records hangs onto the messianic hope for a renewal of David's kingdom, it is more concerned for a revival of Israel's religious vocation than her political hegemony. ". . . . [I]ts purpose was to disclose the action of the living God in the affairs of men. For this reason we speak of it as 'sacred history'; its writer's first concern was to bring out the divine or supernatural dimension in history. . . . If Judaism was to survive and prosper, it would have to heed the lessons of the past and devoutly serve Yahweh in the place where he had chosen to dwell, the temple of Jerusalem. From the Chronicler's point of view, David's reign was the ideal to which all subsequent rulers of Judah must aspire."[23]

Israel's Who's Who
(1 Chronicles 1:1–9:44 et al.)

Thus all Israel was listed in family lists, and these are recorded . . .   9:1a

No other writer of sacred scrolls
was such a recorder of rolls
as the Chronicler.

(S)He completely tames
a humongous ménagerie of names,
letting nothing deter him or her.

People put to shame
as well as achievers of fame
make up the resulting roster.

> Long before the Mayflower sailed
> pioneers and heroes are hailed,
> the virtue of courage to foster.
>
> But as for every Nathan Hale
> there's a Benedict Arnold whose courage failed
> so in the Torah there's a Korah[24]
> for each Noah who bravely sailed.
>
> So First and Second Chronicles, like Scripture as a whole,
> sees that various sides of the story are told.
> Even characters who stand noble and tall
> are portrayed without blinking, warts and all.
>
> Every genealogist risks having her pride pinched
> by an ancestor who'd been justly lynched,
> but that was a risk the Chronicler was willing to run
> to secure Israel's Who's Who a place in the sun.

For eight more humorous reflections on aspects of the books of *Chronicles*, see *Funny Things*, volume one, pp. 140–45.

1 Esdras (Ezra)

(Eastern Orthodox canon only)

Perspective

The Greek rendering (with some expansion) of the canonical book of Ezra, known in modern translations as 1 Esdras or 1 Ezra, is accepted as canonical by Orthodox churches but denied such status among the churches of the West. 1 Esdras adds about ninety-nine verses to the Hebrew version of Ezra's story found in Western canons.

Games History Plays
(1 Esdras 1:25–2:30)

"... this city from of old has fought against kings ... the people in it were given to rebellion and war, and ... mighty and cruel kings ruled ... and exacted tribute ...." From Emperor Cyrus's response to a letter from Jerusalem seeking relief from imperial repression,   2:26b, 27 (NRSV).

>Judah had gone so far wrong
>that she became the ball in a game of ping pong.
>Egypt to the south and Babylon to the north
>paddled her viciously back and forth,
>then into an exile fifty years long.

>Then Jerusalem became a yoyo
>spinning on a string
>as Cyrus's commission to go
>clashed with 'Xerxes' "No"
>in swings bewildering.

>'Twas ever so with tiny fiefdoms,
>always forced to take their briefs from
>powerful players of history's game
>who build their pride on others' shame.

The Guardsmen's Contest
(1 Esdras 3–4)

Then the three young men of the bodyguard, who kept guard over the person of the king, said to one another, "Let each of us state what one thing is strongest; and to him whose statement seems wisest, Darius the king will give rich gifts and great honors of victory. He shall be clothed in purple, and drink from gold cups, and sleep on a gold bed, and have a chariot with gold bridles, and a turban of fine linen, and a necklace about his neck; and because of his wisdom he shall sit next to Darius and shall be called kinsman of Darius." Then each wrote his own statement, and they sealed them and put them under the pillow of Darius the king ...   3:4–8 (RSV)

> The three designed the contest
> with shrewdness and zest;
> th' inventor of the thesis most wise
> was supposed to take the prize.
>
> Though determining who was wisest was their aim
> describing who was strongest was their theme
> as each guardsman put mind and pen to the task
> of anticipating in his essay whatever the king might ask.
>
> As the three reckon what finally holds sway,
> wine and women have their usual say,
> but, appealing though they are, the songs people sing
> are replaced in the traditional triad by the office of king.
>
> The first guard praises wine,
> enticing and fine,
> with power first to sharpen,
> then cloud, its drinker's mind.
>
> The second, with cunning disguised as loyalty,
> lavishes superlatives on the powers of royalty,
> hoping no doubt that such flattering of the king
> will make his play for the prize a sure thing.
>
> Next the third guard (good Jew Zerubbabel)
> pours lavish praise on women
> for their power to keep men's heads swimmin'—
> to use beauty and charm stunning
> to o'erpower mere males with feminine cunning.
>
> It's this third opinion that makes the rafters ring
> and later wins plaudits from the people and the king,
> for it closes by insisting
> that neither wine, king, or ladies can win the day
> without hearing and following what God's truth has to say.

2 Esdras
(Eastern Orthodox canon: 2 Esdras, Part 1)

Perspective

The Second Book of Esdras, a.k.a. Latin Esdras, is an apocalyptic book found in many English translations of the Bible. Its authorship is ascribed to Ezra. Although it exists in its complete form only in Latin, the book was originally written in Hebrew. Nonetheless, like many other works dating from the period of the Second Temple, it did not make it into the Hebrew canon.

As with 1 Esdras, there is some confusion about the numbering of this book. Some early Latin manuscripts call it *3 Esdras*, while Jerome and the medieval Latin manuscripts denoted it *4 Esdras*, which to this day is the name used for it in modern critical (typically Latin) editions. Once Jerome's 1 and 2 Esdras were denoted Ezra and Nehemiah in more recent times, the designation *2 Esdras* became common in English Bibles. It appears in the Appendix to the Old Testament in the Slavonic Bible, where it is called *3 Esdras*, and the Georgian (Eastern Orthodox) Bible dubs it *3 Ezra*. This text is known in some circles as the *Apocalypse of Ezra*.

The Undertaker's Advantage
(2 Esdras 2:23; compare Tobit 1:18-20; 2:3-8; 4:3-4; 6:15; 14:10-13; Ezekiel 39:14,16b)

Wheresoever thou findest the dead, take them and bury them, and I will give thee the first place in my resurrection.   2 Esdras 2:23 (*KJV*)

> It's not common to cut much slack
> for the people in black
> but Ezra says the buriers of the dead
> will go straight to the Final Line's head.
>
> While modern morticians seem to work mainly for profit,
> and their profession's much disdained because of it,
> their ancient counterparts would have practiced the burial arts
> neither for profit nor from the modern fear of germs—
> much less from concerns about the diet of worms.

> No. Ancient Hebrew practitioners
> of the funerary profession
> acted mainly to sate a kosher obsession:
> 'Twas their sacred duty, as their neighbors' keeper,
> to harvest the grisly crop of the sinister reaper.
>
> Isn't it fitting, then,
> that, as the most caring of women and men,
> these harvesters should be the first harvested
> when the Lord of Harvests gathers His own in?

Nehemiah
(Eastern Orthodox canon: 2 Esdras, Part 2)

How Rumors Get Started
(Nehemiah 2:6)

Then the king, and the queen seated beside him, *asked me how long my journey would take and when I would return. I set a date that was acceptable to him, and the king agreed that I might go.*

A footnote in the New American Bible annotates this text thus: "*Because Nehemiah could appear in the queen's presence* (Nehemiah 2:6), *it is commonly presumed that he was a eunuch . . .*" Assuming such a presumption had some basis in ancient custom, we can imagine that

> Few men would be keen
> to keep company with the queen
> if accepting the invitation
> meant so demanning an operation.
>
> Even if such a requirement weren't imposed,
> a man might fret over what people supposed;
> for, even absent such an operation,
> many might be concerned for their reputation.

For four additional reflections on humor and wit in *Nehemiah* and *Ezra*, see pages 145 through 148 of *Funny Things*, volume one.

Tobit

The Blind Man and the Black Widow
(Tobit 1:1-14:15, esp. 2:9-10, 3:1-17)

So Raphael was sent to heal them both: to remove the white scales from Tobit's eyes, so that he might again see with his own eyes God's light; and to give Sarah, the daughter of Raguel, as a wife to Tobiah, the son of Tobit, and to rid her of the wicked demon Asmodeus. For it fell to Tobiah's lot to claim her before any others who might wish to marry her.   3:17

Tobit's eyes weren't on the sparrows,
nor were they even on his mind,
until they administered eye drops
of a disastrously caustic kind.

In his daughter-in-law's case it was hard to ignore
that she was a bride, then widow, seven times o'er,
but one thing Tobit may have been proud to tell
was how still-virginal Sarah, daughter of Raguel,
had rallied each time, answering the bell.

Victims between them of much tragic loss,
these two sad souls' paths eventually crossed.
The sparrows had ruined his eyes
and she must have asked herself,
"Why marry again, when every husband dies?"

Driven by injury and the Reaper
deep, then deeper,
into despair,
there seemed nothing either could do
except launch a prayer.

"Spare me, Lord," Tobit prayed,
"I've fought life's battles, though often afraid,
but is it not enough that I can't see?

Must I bear endless insult
after grievous injury?"

Sarah, meanwhile, on her separate way,
was led by events thus to pray:
"I would hang myself if I could,
but that might blight my father's fatherhood;
so, if I can't be a wife, please, Lord, take my life,
and may You be praised for all things good."

Before God *the prayer of each . . . found favor*
and Rafael saw to it they could respectively savor
the gift to him of sight
and to her, a true bridal night.

Judith

The Beast-beheading Beauty
(Judith 1:1–16:25)

During the lifetime of Judith and for a long time after her death, no one ever again spread terror among the Israelites.   16:25 (*NRSV*)

As bad as a Trojan horse,
the Assyrians learned to their remorse,
is a widow mysterious, alluring, erotic—
in sum, irresistibly exotic.

Exploiting foibles common in men,
Judith sank the hook deep,
and, after reeling her big catch in,
beheaded him as he lay asleep.

Thus did the fate that befell
Holofernes, bane of Israel,
make of Judith's name
an object of immortal acclaim.

Esther

Because they're based on the Septuagint (Greek) instead of the older Hebrew texts, the Catholic and Orthodox versions of Esther include 103 verses not found in the Protestant version.

Esther, the Greek Version
(11:2-12:5, 1:1-3:13, 13:1-7, 3:14-4:17; 13:8-15:16; 5:3-8:12; 16:1-24; 8:13-11:1)[25]

With or without original publishers' permissions
Esther's Greek editors make significant additions.
Noting with apparent horror God's name's omission
they drop it more than fifty times in the Greek edition.

As in the Hebrew, conspiring eunuchs hatch a devious plot,
but Mordecai acts *sans* Esther to get the king off the spot.
Vashti's dismissed from the court *before* she becomes queen,
as a warning to wives and courtesans not to become too mean.

A eunuch named Gai, in charge of the king's harem,
is more inclined to pamper the girls than he is to scare 'em.
And because in harem etiquette class she's extremely keen
Esther becomes his favorite in the sweepstakes for queen.

That Esther's something special
where larger issues are at stake
becomes clear when the king, on marrying her,
gives his people a tax break.[26]

Meantime Haman, also elevated,
becomes fatefully aggravated
when Mordecai the Jew
refuses his line to hew.

So began the first pogrom
aimed at killing the Jews,
a precedent for efforts so frequent
they've become old news.

Following Haman's ideas about making his empire better
the king dictates and dispatches a cynical cyclical letter;
each of Persia's provinces, six score and seven in all,
learns the Jews are to be eradicated— totally, wall to wall.

On a future date certain the governors were to draw the curtain,
ushering the Jewish race off this mortal orb,
leading Mordecai and his fellow Jews to don sackcloth
as they find in such news more than they can absorb.

To Esther and to the Lord Mordecai makes repair,
to the former through her eunuch, to the latter through prayer.
And Esther too turns to the Lord, imploring Him to care
as she dresses as a mourner and makes a mess of her hair.

The Lord of the Jews and Heaven,
moved by Mordecai and the Queen,
takes note of their predicament
and acts to intervene.

Robbing the king of sleep,[27]
(S)He sends a disturbing dream,
leading him through his kingdom's annals
to learn things aren't what they seem.

Providentially guided, Esther sees that the storm's soon subsided,
intervening with his royal majesty to expose Haman's travesty
and hounding the scoundrel hard
till he's hoist on his own petard.

The Hateful Haman and the Hardy Race
(Book of Esther, Catholic canon, passim)

"... we Jews are as the dew on every blade of grass,
trodden under foot today and here tomorrow morning..."
—Charles Reznikoff, "Babylon: 539 B.C.E."

By heritage an Amalekite
and by hardened habit quite uptight,
Haman the Agagite, without hint of grace,
took umbrage at the slightest slight
from any of the hated race.

Small wonder then that, when the insolent Mordecai
all but spat in his eye,
Haman erected a gallows
for the Jew's quick despatch
to dwell among the hallows.

The sound of gallows-building hammers kept the king awake,
ironically and providentially, for Mordecai's sake;
for 'twas while reading from court annals before going back down
that his majesty learned of the old Jew's actions
to save his crown.

Thus Haman joined the ranks of enemies of the Jews
whose efforts to tread on them like grass
lead anon to the unlikely pass
that the Chosen's fortunes rise again
like the morning dews.

For two more reflections on humor and wit in *Esther*, see volume one of *Funny Things*, pp. 148–49.

1 and 2 Maccabees

The Latin Vulgate, Douay-Rheims, and Revised Standard Version Catholic Edition place First and Second Maccabees after Malachi; other Catholic translations place them after Esther. We here follow the order of the New American Bible.

An Abomination Enrages a Nation
(1 Maccabees 1:1-3:9)

The king [Antiochus Epiphanes] sent messengers with letters to Jerusalem and to the cities of Judah, ordering them to follow customs foreign to their land; to prohibit holocausts, sacrifices, and libations in the sanctuary, to profane the sabbaths and feast day, to desecrate the sanctuary and the sacred ministers, to build pagan altars and temples and shrines, to sacrifice swine and unclean animals, to leave their sons uncircumcised, and to let themselves be defiled with every kind of impurity and abomination, so that they might forget the law and change all their observances. . . . On the fifteenth day of the month Chislev, in the year one hundred and forty-five, the king erected the horrible abomination upon the altar of holocausts, and in the surrounding cities of Judah they built pagan altars. 1:44–49, 54

Then his son Judas, who was called Maccabeus, took his [Mattathias's] place. All his brothers and all who had joined his father supported him, and they carried on Israel's war joyfully. He spread abroad the glory of his people, and put on his breastplate like a giant. He armed himself with weapons of war; he planned battles and protected the camp with his sword. In his actions he was like a lion, like a young lion roaring for prey. He pursued the wicked, hunting them out, and those who troubled his people he destroyed by fire. The lawbreakers were cowed by fear of him, and all evildoers were dismayed. By his hand redemption was happily achieved, and he afflicted many kings; He made Jacob glad by his deeds, and his memory is blessed forever. He went about the cities of Judah destroying the impious there. He turned away wrath from Israel and was renowned to the ends of the earth . . . 3:1–9a

Antiochus Epiphanes,
vilest of the Jews' enemies,
earned that distinction
by his attempts at extinction
of their pious sensibilities.

Believing himself an epiphany of God
Anti felt entitled to run roughshod
over all the Chosen's anxieties
about their faith's corruption
by pagan pieties.

The Jews swore to hate him to their last generation
for insulting the holy mission of their holy nation,
most of all by his atrocious violation
of the Temple's precincts
through the "abomination."

Some say it was a statue or off'ring
of a pig on the altar,
others, an act of wholesale human slaughter.
Whatever: it was enough to offend and alienate
every Israelite—man, wife, son, daughter.

The Jew who led the counterattack
was a Hammer[28] named not Mike but Mac.
Inspired by the pluck of his father Matt,
who'd dissed Anti's attempts to pass the hat,
Mac matched his every angry tit with an angry tat.

Who Wields the Hammer?
(1 Maccabees 4:6-11)

. . . at daybreak Judas appeared in the plain with three thousand men, who lacked such armor and swords as they would have wished. They saw the army of the Gentiles, strong and breastplated, flanked with cavalry, and made up of expert soldiers. Judas said to the men with him: "Do not be afraid of their numbers or dread their attack. Remember how our fathers

were saved in the Red Sea, when Pharaoh pursued them with an army. So now let us cry to Heaven in the hope that he will favor us, remember his covenant with our fathers, and destroy this army before us today. All the Gentiles shall know that there is One who redeems and delivers Israel."

The conflict had ignited a conflagration
that threatened the very being of the Hebrew nation.
The clash of imperial 'gainst Jewish ire
generated heat like a smithy's fire.

Wielding the Hammer in this clash
and determining whether His blows would leave more than ash
was not Vulcan, Greek god of the smith,
but Yahweh, the God Israel had long lived with.

Leaving It All on the Field . . .
(1 Maccabees 6:42-46)

Judas with his army advanced to fight, and six hundred men of the king's army fell. Eleazar, called Avaran, saw one of the beasts bigger than any of the others and covered with royal armor, and he thought the king must be on it. So he gave up his life to save his people and win an everlasting name for himself. He dashed up to it in the middle of the phalanx, killing men right and left, so that they fell back from him on both sides. He ran right under the elephant and stabbed it in the belly, killing it. The beast fell to the ground on top of him, and he died there.

Eleazar, as befits all heroes,
evoked much praise and chatter;
remarkably, in Eleazar's case, much of the latter
was because, on the list of heroes,
none became flatter.

The Enemy of my Enemy . . .
(I Maccabees 8:17-23, 24a, 25-27)

Judas chose Eupolemus . . . and Jason, son of Eleazar, and sent them to Rome to establish an alliance of friendship with them. He did this to get rid of the yoke, for it was obvious that the kingdom of the Greeks was subjecting Israel to slavery. After making a very long journey to Rome, the envoys entered the senate and spoke as follows: "Judas, called Maccabeus, and his brothers, with the Jewish people, have sent us to you to make a peaceful alliance with you, and to enroll ourselves among your allies and friends." The proposal pleased the Romans, and this is a copy of the reply they inscribed on bronze tablets and sent to Jerusalem, to remain there with the Jews as a record of peace and alliance: May it be well with the Romans and the Jewish nation at sea and on land forever. . . . But if war is first made on Rome . . . , the Jewish nation will help them wholeheartedly, as the occasion shall demand; and to those who wage war they shall not give nor provide grain, arms, money, or ships; this is Rome's decision. They shall fulfill their obligations without receiving any recompense. In the same way, if war is made first on the Jewish nation, the Romans will help them willingly. . . .

> The people of the Covenant were no good at blending in,
> for their Law declared doing so to be a grievous sin.
> (Where interfaith marriages had been allowed to start
> Ezra the repatriate had even forced spouses apart.[29])
>
> Though the people now bear an irksome yoke
> imposed by unkosher neighbor folk,
> they decide shrewdly neither to submit nor cower
> but to seek with Rome's aid a new balance of power.

The Worm Turns ... and Turns and Turns
(1 Maccabees 9:1-72)

The battle became intense, and many on both sides fell wounded. Then Judas fell. . . . Jonathan and Simon took their brother Judas and buried him in the tomb of their fathers at Modein. All Israel bewailed him in great grief. They mourned for him many days, and they said, "How the mighty one has fallen, the savior of Israel!" . . . Then all the friends of Judas came together and said to Jonathan: "Since your brother Judas died, there has been no one like him to oppose our enemies . . . Now therefore we have chosen you today to be our ruler and leader in his place, and to fight our battle." From that moment Jonathan accepted the leadership, and took the place of Judas his brother. 17–21, 28–31

The Hammer had sadly fallen from Judah's hand,
and, with him, many others in his doughty band;
when morale fails to rise as Jonathan takes command
a pall of gloom descends across the land.

Judas had hammered to their knees
the unity-imposing armies of Epiphanes,
making it Jonathan's fate
to face down threats from many a liberated city state.

In this effort Jon's fortunes wax and wane
not just once but again and again.
Like a ball in a pool game they carom back and forth,
but their course seems as determined as a compass's fix on north.

Though his name is Jonathan he fights more like a David,
his enemies oblivious to him 'til after they've been raided.
Against Bacchides and company he wages a guerrilla campaign
and, routing the tyrants, ends King Terror's reign.

Promise 'em Anything
(1 Maccabees 10:1-47)

Jonathan put on the sacred vestments in the seventh month of the year one hundred and sixty at the feast of Booths, and he gathered an army and procured many arms. When Demetrius heard of these things, he was distressed and said: "Why have we allowed Alexander to get ahead of us by gaining the friendship of the Jews and thus strengthening himself? I too will write them conciliatory words and offer dignities and gifts, so that they may be an aid to me." So he sent them this message: "King Demetrius sends greetings to the Jewish nation. We have heard how you have kept the treaty with us and continued in our friendship and not gone over to our enemies, and we are glad. Continue, therefore, to keep faith with us, and we will reward you with favors in return for what you do in our behalf. We will grant you many exemptions and will bestow gifts on you. "I now free you, as I also exempt all the Jews, from the tribute, the salt tax, and the crown levies. Instead of collecting the third of the grain and the half of the fruit of the trees that should be my share, I renounce the right from this day forward: Neither now nor in the future will I collect them from the land of Judah or from the three districts annexed from Samaria. Let Jerusalem and her territory, her tithes and her tolls, be sacred and free from tax. I also yield my authority over the citadel in Jerusalem, and I transfer it to the high priest, that he may put in it such men as he shall choose to guard it. Every one of the Jews who has been carried into captivity from the land of Judah into any part of my kingdom I set at liberty without ransom; and let all their taxes, even those on their cattle, be canceled." . . . When Jonathan and the people heard these words, they neither believed nor accepted them, for they remembered the great evil that Demetrius had done in Israel, and how sorely he had afflicted them. They therefore decided in favor of Alexander, for he had been the first to address them peaceably, and they remained his allies for the rest of his life.

10:21–33, 46–47

Demetrius was a wily king
whose strategy of hedging his bets
led him to promise the Jews anything
if they'd help him counter his enemies' threats.

We don't know what the Jews knew
about Trojan history

> but it appears that from somewhere they drew
> the lesson that vict'ry in international rifts
> requires wariness toward enemies who come bearing gifts.

Surprise!
(2 Maccabees 1:14-16; 9:1-29; cp. 1 Maccabees 6:1-16)

On the pretext of marrying the goddess, Antiochus with his friends had come to the place to get its great treasures by way of dowry. When the priests of the Nanaeon had displayed the treasures, Antiochus with a few attendants came to the temple precincts. As soon as he entered the temple, the priests locked the doors. Then they opened a hidden trapdoor in the ceiling, hurled stones at the leader and his companions and struck them down. They dismembered the bodies, cut off their heads and tossed them to the people outside. 2 Maccabees 1:14–15

The body of this impious man [Antiochus] swarmed with worms, and while he was still alive in hideous torments, his flesh rotted off, so that the entire army was sickened by the stench of his corruption. Shortly before, he had thought that he could reach the stars of heaven, and now, no one could endure to transport the man because of this intolerable stench. At last, broken in spirit, he began to give up his excessive arrogance, and to gain some understanding, under the scourge of God, for he was racked with pain unceasingly. When he could no longer bear his own stench, he said, "It is right to be subject to God, and not to think one's mortal self divine." Then this vile man vowed to the Lord, who would no longer have mercy on him, that he would set free the holy city, toward which he had been hurrying with the intention of leveling it to the ground and making it a common graveyard; he would put on perfect equality with the Athenians all the Jews, whom he had judged not even worthy of burial, but fit only to be thrown out with their children to be eaten by vultures and wild animals; he would adorn with the finest offerings the holy temple which he had previously despoiled; he would restore all the sacred vessels many times over; and would provide from his own revenues the expenses required for the sacrifices. Besides all this, he would become a Jew himself and visit every inhabited place to proclaim there the power of God. 2 Maccabees 9:9–17

Scripture makes a surprising amount of fuss
over the death of the tyrant Antiochus,
recounting not one story but three
that differ in describing his destiny.

Each of the accounts is brief,
the first saying he died from grief,
the second, of priestly treachery,
and the third— surprise to the nth degree!—
as a moribund penitent, frantic'ly seeking relief.

In his own eyes Antiochus was a star,
but in Judah's, their *bête noir,*
so it may strike us as a surprise
that any Jew gave a hoot
about the details of his demise.

Oil Strike?
(2 Maccabees 1:19-36)

When our fathers were being exiled to Persia, devout priests of the time took some of the fire from the altar and hid it secretly in the hollow of a dry cistern ... Many years later, when it so pleased God, Nehemiah, commissioned by the king of Persia, sent the descendants of the priests who had hidden the fire to look for it. When they informed us that they could not find any fire, but only muddy water, he ordered them to scoop some out and bring it. After the material for the sacrifices had been prepared, Nehemiah ordered the priests to sprinkle with the water the wood and what lay on it. When this was done and in time the sun, which had been clouded over, began to shine, a great fire blazed up, so that everyone marveled. ... After the sacrifice was burned, Nehemiah ordered the rest of the liquid to be poured upon large stones. As soon as this was done, a flame blazed up, but its light was lost in the brilliance cast from a light on the altar. When the event became known and the king of the Persians was told that, in the very place where the exiled priests had hidden the fire, a liquid was found with which Nehemiah and his people had burned the sacrifices, the king, after verifying the fact, fenced the place off and declared it sacred. To those on whom the king wished to bestow favors he distributed the large revenues he received there. Nehemiah and his companions called the liquid nephthar, meaning purification, but most people named it naphtha.   1:19–22, 32–36

> As one soul's solution
> is another's pollution
> so what priests take as a miracle
> scientists often describe in terms less lyrical.
>
> With just a slight alteration
> in a word's pronunciation
> *nephtar* becomes *naphtha*
> and assumes a new meaning thereafter.
>
> 'Tis a short logical step from there
> 'til we arrive at a situation where
> people look to "muddy water" not for purification
> but in hopes of lavish remuneration.
>
> It seems an awful shame, though,
> that, because it makes them so much dough,
> it doesn't turn its peddlers' faces red
> when they seek to restore oil to a status sacred.

A Glimpse Inside a Mystery
(2 Maccabees 2:1–32)

These same things are also told in the records and in Nehemiah's memoirs, as well as how he founded a library and collected the books about the kings and the prophets, the books of David, and the royal letters about votive offerings. In like manner Judas also collected for us all the books that had been scattered because of the war, and we now have them in our possession. . . . All this, which Jason of Cyrene set forth in detail in five volumes, we will try to condense into a single book. In view of the flood of statistics, and the difficulties encountered by those who wish to plunge into historical narratives where the material is abundant, we have aimed to please those who prefer simple reading, as well as to make it easy for the studious who wish to commit things to memory, and to be helpful to all. For us who have taken upon ourselves the labor of making this digest, the task, far from being easy, is one of sweat and of sleepless nights, just as the preparation of a festive banquet is no light matter for one who thus seeks to give enjoyment to others. Similarly, to win the gratitude of many we will gladly endure these inconveniences, while we leave the responsibility for exact details to the original author, and confine our efforts to giving only a summary outline.

> *As the architect of a new house must give his attention to the whole structure, while the man who undertakes the decoration and the frescoes has only to concern himself with what is needed for ornamentation, so I think it is with us. To enter into questions and examine them thoroughly from all sides is the task of the professional historian; but the man who is making an adaptation should be allowed to aim at brevity of expression and to omit detailed treatment of the matter. Here, then, we shall begin our account without further ado; it would be nonsense to write a long preface to a story and then abbreviate the story itself.* 1:13–14, 23–32

Biblical scribes offer us prefaces few,
notably just this one and St. Luke's two.
From this one among the things we learn
is that the writer sees himself, indeed i.d.'s himself,
as a meticulous, conscientious historian.

As it reveals the author's reasons for writing,
the preface shows us too
a scholar's care in citing
sources unheard of before
and the chronicling exploits of scribes of yore.

3—Wisdom and Poetry

Job

The Wizard of Uz, Part One
(Job 1:1–42:17)

In the land of Uz there was a blameless and upright man named Job. . . . 1:1

Can we assume that the wizard of Uz
lived in a land that actually wuz
or should we assume instead that Uz is a land of the mind,
as present and ahead as it is behind?

Does Uz, from beginning to brink,
exist only in the land of words,
or is it a land, as some think,
where today's Arabs vie for space with Kurds?

Whatever the answer may be,
our minds should remain worry free—
until, with God,
we're in a position to see.

The Wizard of Uz, Part Two

A wizard by definition should be wise
and Job's rep for wisdom was supersize;
Satan's reports to the Boss above
cast doubts instead on the Uzzite's *love*.

The answer to doubts about this man of Uz
lies not in some ethereal wisdom
nor in what, pre- or mid-ordeal, is his'n,
but in what, in loving loyalty, he does.

A Knowledge More Telling
(Job 2, 42)

"Job . . . sat among the ashes"—Job 2:8; compare 42:5–6: *"Before I knew you only by hearsay but now, having seen you with my own eyes, I retract what I have said, and repent in dust and ashes."* (NJB)

Knowledge based on hearsay
eventually gave way
in Job's heart and mind
to acquaintance of a personal kind.

Though he refused to forgo having his say
Job remained faithful to his Lord's way,
remaining one with Yahweh in heart
if not always in mind.

Thus, to the surprise of his soul's analysts,
his quarrels with God worked as catalysts,
unleashing in him the gumption
to jettison all pious presumption.

Unlike many other kin of Adam and his Madam,
Job was made by these quarrels to see
that without God dust and ashes
is all people can ever be.

Pleading Parity, not Purity
(Job 7:17–10:22)

Why do you not pardon my offense, or take away my guilt? For soon I shall lie down in the dust; and should you seek me I shall be gone. 7:21

It's time to put to rest
the myth of Job's spotlessness:
he never makes such a claim
despite his concern to save his good name.

To his friends he's not loath to confess
a typical human sinfulness
but this doesn't diminish his defiance
gainst the dominidiabolic alliance.

In all, his aim appears to be
to claim human solidarity
not by proving personal purity
but by pleading parity.

Job's Answer
(Job 9:30-31)

"If I wash myself in melted snow, clean my hands with soda, you will only plunge me into the dung, till my clothes themselves recoil from me!" (NJB)

"You're right, of course, Bildad,
my record as God sees it must seem bad,
and no words of mine can ever serve
to prove my fate worse than I deserve.

"In my case it's not true that clothes make the man;
mine will unmake me if they can.
In their hatred for me, it seems quite plain,
they're reality's allies in giving me pain.

"In its 'comic extremity of . . . self-alienation,'
my story defies all explanation
and the phenomenon of 'clothes rejecting the person wearing them'[30]
becomes a sad theme of my enduring hymn."

++++

Job's clothes, like Luther's crackling twig,
prove creation's not prone to renege
on the conscience's pledge never to hedge
but instead to remain the Lord's ally
in hanging the sinner out to dry.

The King of Pride
(Job 40:25-26; 41:17-26)

The Lord answered Job:

"Can you lead about Leviathan with a hook, or curb his tongue with a bit? Can you put a rope into his nose, or pierce through his cheek with a gaff? ... When he rises up, the mighty are afraid; the waves of the sea fall back. Should the sword reach him, it will not avail; nor will the spear, nor the dart, nor the javelin. He regards iron as straw, and bronze as rotten wood. The arrow will not put him to flight; sling stones used against him are but straws. Clubs he esteems as splinters; he laughs at the crash of the spear. His belly is sharp as pottery fragments; he spreads like a threshing sledge upon the mire. He makes the depths boil like a pot; the sea he churns like perfume in a kettle. Behind him he leaves a shining path; you would think the deep had the hoary head of age. Upon the earth there is not his like, intrepid he was made. All, however lofty, fear him; he is king over all proud beasts."

"Meet Leviathan,
antipode of the sun:
lord of all ocean premises,
Jonah's cavernous nemesis,
source of Job's consternation
and muse of Hobbes' imagination.

"Meet Leviathan,
free the seas to run:
master of the deep
and haunter of sailors' sleep,
who frustrates and renders farcical
every weapon in their arsenal.

"Meet Leviathan,
monster Mediterranean,
whose rule of middle-earth,
reflected in his girth,
leaves every child of pride
chastened and terrified.

"Meet Leviathan, My multi-gifted scion:
on meeting this king of the sea
and pondering its immensity,
you need only know it's made by Me
to abandon all hope of fathoming
the depths of My mystery."

The Daughters of Job
(Job 42:12-15)

Thus the LORD blessed the latter days of Job more than his earlier ones. For he had fourteen thousand sheep, six thousand camels, a thousand yoke of oxen, and a thousand she-asses. And he had seven sons and three daughters, of whom he called the first Jemimah, the second Keziah, and the third Keren-happuch. In all the land no other women were as beautiful as the daughters of Job; and their father gave them an inheritance among their brothers.

We assume conferring names was no sin
in the house of Job and his kin,
but 'til the story's end no one in his family proper
(not even the wife who with him came a cropper[31])
is assigned a name by the dramatist's pen.

But when at last 'tis the will of the Lord
that Job's estate be restored
and three daughters be born to him,
the scribe provides marquee names for them,
before whom other maidens' charms grow dim.

Could this signify that, after his season of shame
and the restoration of the Lord's favor,
the dominion reflected
in the power to name
is a gift Job can once again savor?[32]

Yet a second distinction Job's daughters had
reminds us of the daughters of Zelophehad:
in sharing *an inheritance*
with *their brethren*
they too broke new ground in estate-severin'.[33]

For six more reflections on humor and wit in *Job*, see volume one of *Funny Things*, pp. 150–153.

Psalms

Adam or Atoms? Which Defines Reality?
(Psalms 8)

When I see your heavens, the work of your fingers, the moon and stars that you set in place— What are humans that you are mindful of them, mere mortals that you care for them? Yet you have made them little less than a god, crowned them with glory and honor. You have given them rule over the works of your hands, put all things at their feet . . . 4–7

We run across a clear instance of the psalmist's use of ironic humor in Psalms 8:3–9. As (s)he looked out at the immensity of the creation and measured the minute physical stature of human beings against it, the writer must have been strongly tempted to laugh. Any claim that the God who fashioned such a universe takes note of, let alone cares about, humble human creatures must be somebody's idea of a joke. Yet the powers humans can exercise over creatures who lack their mental and spiritual endowments make it clear that God has crowned them "with glory and honor" and has "put all things under . . . [their] feet."

This irony can hardly escape the eye of anyone with a sense of scale. Albert Einstein is said to have remarked that, as far as scientists can determine, human beings could be "mere atoms in somebody else's shirt." Yet from his personal as opposed to his scientific perspective, he saw a kinship between the human mind and the intelligence reflected in nature's laws and realized that evidence of intelligence in the larger world is discernible by earth-bound beings only through the medium of the human mind. Similarly, much earlier, the Catholic philosopher and mathematician Blaise Pascal captured both the experience behind and the meaning within the psalmist's awe-filled remark when he wrote:

> If the universe were to crush him, man would still be more noble than that which killed him, because he knows that he dies and the

advantage which the universe has over him; the universe knows nothing of this . . . By space the universe swallows and encompasses me; by thought I comprehend the world.[34]

As we reflect further on Psalm 8, it may dawn on us that it contains the peculiar paradox that made sparks of brilliance fly from the insights, first of Pascal, then later of Einstein, as their religious contemplation and scientific passions introduced each of them to God in two guises:

> God as Person/God as Order,
> is it Your will that fellow persons beget disorder?
> Or do You prefer an iron conformity
> to a cosmic harmony
> You as Order have determined must be?

> Nature's laws work with dignity and finesse
> but personality inevitably produces a mess.
> Can Ought and Is, Ethics and Science
> ever get beyond mutual defiance?

> If everything's a "Must,"
> whence comes our sense of Ought?
> If conscience is a meaningless, illusory "plus,"
> why should we care whether criminals get caught?

> Are the Law Natural
> and the Law Moral
> predestined to engage
> in an infinite quarrel?

> "*Que sera, sera,*" says one,
> "You can, so you ought," the other,
> so should I simply bow to Nature's way,
> or treat it like a caring and cared-for mother?

Out of the Mouths of Babes
(Psalms 8:2-3; Matthew 21:16; Luke 10:21; 1 Peter 2:2)

O LORD, our Lord, how awesome is your name through all the earth! You have set your majesty above the heavens! Out of the mouths of babes and infants you have drawn a defense against your foes, to silence enemy and avenger.   Psalms 8:2–3a

. . . like newborn infants, long for pure spiritual milk so that through it you may grow into salvation . . . .   1 Peter 2:2

As the unaccustomed visitor
often makes the best inquisitor,
so a child's inquiring
may be insight-inspiring.

What parent has not often wished
a conversation to die,
only to be thwarted again and again
by an insistent "Why?"

When we think we have it sealed
or at least have that hope,
here comes that "Why?" again
to push our envelope.

How many light bulbs have gone on
or insights been stumbled on
because a child pushes through the dark
'til there comes a dawn?

Moral Apples and Factual Oranges
(Psalms 14:1, 53:1)

Fools say in their hearts, "There is no God." Their deeds are loathsome and corrupt; not one does what is right.

In a September 7, 2010 New York Times review of Stephen Hawking's book "The Grand Design," Dwight Garner wrote, "The arguments in 'The Grand Design'—especially those about why God isn't necessary to imagine the beginning of the universe—put me in mind of something Mr. [Timothy] Ferris said in his excellent book "The Whole Shebang" (1997).

"'Religious systems are inherently conservative, science inherently progressive,' Mr. Ferris wrote. Religion and science don't have to be hostile to each other, but we can stop setting them up on blind dates. 'This may be an instance,' Mr. Ferris writes, 'where good walls make good neighbors.'"

> It may be a bit much
> to view atheists as so out of touch
> that they aren't able to do
> what's right in the clutch,
> but woe to the soul
> who's discovered God ain't
> and thinks the discovery's
> made her or him a saint.
>
> In the final analysis
> atheism may lead to moral paralysis,
> at best reducing ethics to a sport—
> for what's the weight of a Law
> that can never bring Hitler to court?
> Still, a purely faith-based science
> we can't depend on,
> for a faith-proved fact is an oxymoron.

The Shepherd's Angle
(Reflections on God's flock, the Church)
(Psalms 23; Matt 25:31-46)

> Bleaters are many,
> bleeders very rare,
> but not one of them lives
> beyond the reach of My care.

The former offer only wool,
the latter their very lives
but all drink from My Cup Full
from which all life derives.

Those standing meekly to be sheared
scarcely seem to compare
with those of vocation weird—
recumbent on an altar, off'ring their lives there.

But that lamb on My altar and the one who can only bleat—
and, yes, even that black one who seems able only to cheat—
may make it through the Valley
walking humbly by My feet.

Can Thinking of God as a Holy Terror Amount to Anything More than an Error? (Psalms 47:1-2)

Clap your hands, all peoples! Shout to God with loud songs of joy! For the LORD, the Most High, is terrible, a great king over all the earth.... (RSV)

Can a God who's "terrible" be a God of grace?
Must we see such a God as a fierce bloodhound
giving rabid, terrifying chase?
It may be hard for the overly cerebral
to bear thinking of God as "terrible."

A mind convinced the word defines the thing
confines itself to a tiny evidentiary ring,
but letting the thing define the word
unleashes the mind
to soar like a bird.

If "terrible" a la the dictionary
alarms us like a mineshaft canary,
the "terrible" we meet in an I-Thou encounter
may make our cerebral certainty founder,
but the freedom it confers is salutary.

No wonder, then, the psalmist here
finds in holy terror an occasion to cheer,
to clap her hands and shout songs of joy
as (s)he learns that, though (s)he tremble in God's hands,
(s)he's not a worthless toy.

Counting Your Tossings
(Psalms 56:8)

"You have kept count of my tossings..." (NRSV)

Getting to sleep
by counting sheep
doesn't work anymore,
so you find yourself lying awake
wond'ring what's at stake
and whether you'll ever learn the score.

Finally, as you near your wits' end
and doubt whether slumber will ever set in,
you thumb through Holy Writ
seeking in it
a calming word from its Author-Spirit.

The text remains dumb
'til finally your thumb
finds the needed fix
in Psalm Fifty-six.

"When a sheep census
won't lower sleep's defenses
don't despair,
for when you're totally at a loss,
I'm there,
counting your every turn and toss."

The Most Subtle Creature
(Psalms 58:4-5)

They [the wicked] are poisonous as any snake, deaf as an adder that blocks its ears so as not to hear the magician's music, however skilful his spells.
(NJB)

Could anything possibly make you madder
than the guile of folks resembling a wanton deaf adder?
Invulnerable to the most gifted charmer
and beyond the reach of the wiliest disarmer,
they slither beneath our consciousness,
planting seeds of future distress.

Unlike Eve's subtle tempter,
whose clever conversation
served to preempt her
efforts to please her Maker,
these tempters preempt instead
all efforts at communication.

Thus varied and subtle
are the ways of the Devil,
employing many a device
on many a level,
sometimes convincing us to march to his drum,
sometimes simply rendering us mum.

Consuming Passions
(Psalms 69:10; Matthew 23:15)

. . . zeal for your house consumes me . . .	69:10

"Woe to you, scribes and Pharisees, you hypocrites. You traverse sea and land to make one convert, and when that happens you make him a child of Gehenna twice as much as yourselves."   23:15

"There have been some who were so occupied in spreading Christianity that they never gave a thought to Christ." —C. S. Lewis[35]

In two forms consumption can be a deadly disease—
the form that attacks the organs with which we breathe
and the passionate grasping after pleasure and ease.

The latter form today is very much in fashion
and many are consumed
by consuming passion.

But perhaps the form of the disease that's most perfidious
and hides under pretenses thoroughly insidious
is the use of Christ's mission to serve personal ambition.

Can "coming to know Christ"
be accomplished in a trice
and restless hearts find rest in acts of self-saving selfishness?

Even the most passionate pilgrim
should be warned of the danger
of reaching Bethlehem and finding only the manger.

David Signs Off
(Psalms 72:18-20)

Blessed be the LORD, the God of Israel, who alone does wonderful deeds. Blessed be his glorious name forever; may all the earth be filled with the LORD'S glory. Amen and amen.

The end of the psalms of David, son of Jesse.

What's Psalm 72:20 mean?
Is there no more Davidic wisdom to glean?
Has David quit offering our poor souls alms
in the form of passionate, soul-stirring psalms?

They're "psalms of David," we say,
but it appears, mid-hymnbook, he's pulling away,
taking himself out of the game
and hereafter only lending his name
by something like the arts of franchise
to hymnody's premier enterprise.

Breaking Out of the Box
(Psalms 113; 1 Kings 8:27)

Who is like Yahweh our God? His throne is set on high, but he stoops to look down on heaven and earth.   Psalms 113 (*NJB*)

"Why, the heavens, the highest of the heavens, cannot contain you. How much less this temple built by me!"   1 Kings (*NJB*)

"On *heaven*" too?
Does that surprise you?
It's hard to break our race
out of the box of time and space.

Thinking outside this box
entails so much paradox,
rendering useless every map, every clock,
that theology leaves many scientists in shock.

"God's in his heaven!"
Whether heaven nine or heaven seven,
our physics-formed attitude
wants t'assign God a longi- and a lati-tude.

We catch even the great Dante
in delicto flagrante,
hoping his sublime muse's work'll
show us the Trinity in a Perfect Circle.

Perhaps, in our theological despair,
we can only pray Solomon's prayer:
*"Why, the heavens, the highest of heavens, cannot contain Thee.
How much less this temple built by me!"*

Precious Death
(Psalms 116:15; Luke 15:7)

"*Precious to the Lord is the death of his saints*"   Psalms 116 (*KJV*)

I tell you, there will be more rejoicing in heaven over one sinner repenting than over ninety-nine upright people who have no need of repentance.
                                                                Luke 15 (*NJB*)

> We ordinary folks
> may need God to refresh us
> as to why (S)He considers
> each saint's death precious.
>
> Is God simply delighted that,
> in the strength of divine grace,
> another of His devotees
> has completed the race?
>
> Does "precious" imply
> a cry of delight
> when an embattled warrior
> wins a long, hard fight?
>
> Or, more likely yet,
> does it involve winning a bet
> when Heaven gains a soul
> the odds said it shouldn't get?

A Dream beyond the Nightmare
(Psalms 137:1-4, 7-8)

By the rivers of Babylon we sat mourning and weeping when we remembered Zion. On the poplars of that land we hung up our harps. There our captors asked us for the words of a song; Our tormentors, for a joyful song: "Sing for us a song of Zion!" But how could we sing a song of the LORD in a foreign land? ... Remember, LORD, against Edom that day at Jerusalem. They said: "Level it, level it down to its foundations!" Fair Babylon, you destroyer, happy those who pay you back the evil you have done us!

> Beside these waters nothing's funny,
> much less joyous, to behold;
> all our prospects seem unsunny,
> all trails to a worthwhile future, cold.
>
> Our lives have now been reduced
> to a meaningless, tone-deaf charade,
> for we've been forced to leave behind
> our faith's musical hit parade.
>
> Yet to so sad a fate we refuse to surrender,
> nor long will we brood over wounds sore and tender;
> instead, of Edom's and Babylon's doom we'll dream,
> hoping our vengeful tears pollute their history's stream.

No Vacancy
(Psalms 139:1-13)

O LORD, you have probed me, you know me: you know when I sit and stand; you understand my thoughts from afar. My travels and my rest you mark; with all my ways you are familiar. Even before a word is on my tongue, LORD, you know it all. Behind and before you encircle me and rest your hand upon me. Such knowledge is beyond me, far too lofty for me to reach. Where can I hide from your spirit? From your presence, where can I flee? If I ascend to the heavens, you are there; if I lie down in Sheol, you are there too. If I fly with the wings of dawn and alight beyond the sea, Even there your hand will guide me, your right hand hold me fast. If I say, "Surely darkness shall hide me, and night shall be my light" — Darkness is not dark for you, and night shines as the day. Darkness and light are but one. You formed my inmost being; you knit me in my mother's womb.

An atheist may be described as a person with a strong sense of vacation. The writer of Psalm 139, on the other hand, is overwhelmed by a sense of divine occupation. All of space (from the depths of Sheol to "the farthest limits of the sea") and all of time (the whole way back by and beyond memory lane to pre-natality, "when I was being made in secret") convey an overpowering sense of the divine presence.

Are the atheist's and the theist's diametrically opposite reactions to life just matters of perception? What led a Thales to conclude, "All things are full of gods," while an equally observant Lucretius could see in the same data only the working of lifeless and godless atoms?

Reflection suggests that habits of observation, while equal in intensity and perceptiveness, may be different in the questions they put to the perceived world and may thus draw sharply different conclusions about that world. Perhaps the final determinant may lie with the percipient's need or lack of need for Company, a Comforting Presence, a Coach in his or her corner as life throws its punches. In Psalm 139 the hymnist seems intent on describing God as Someone who does something like that:

> Whether we're just a day old
> or have wandered at life's end into Sheol—
> indeed, even when we've yet to be born—
> the Maker of our DNA finds a way
> to see to it we're never forlorn.

Divine Versatility
(Psalms 147:2,4; Matthew 10:29-31)

The LORD ... numbers all the stars, calls each of them by name.
Psalm 147

Are not two sparrows sold for a small coin? Yet not one of them falls to the ground without your Father's knowledge. Even all the hairs of your head are counted. So do not be afraid; you are worth more than many sparrows.
Matthew 10

> God's an Artist, not a mere statistician,
> a fact made plain in His declared mission.
> After making each Adam or Dick or Harry,
> (S)He makes an Eve, a Jane or Carrie, for each of them to marry.

> God knows all creatures, Scripture says,
> by name not just by number,
> with no hint that doing so
> the divine memory might encumber.

For twelve more reflections on wit and humor in the *Psalms,* see the first volume of *Funny Things,* pp. 153–163.

The Prayer of Manasses King of Judah, when he was held captive in Babylon
(Found in the Eastern Orthodox canon only, sometimes under the title The Book of Odes)

Stretching Belief
(The Prayer of Manasses, verses 13b-14)

> . . . *you, O Lord, are the God of those who repent,*
> *and in me you will manifest your goodness;*
> *for, unworthy as I am, you will save me according to your great mercy.* . . .

According to the unedited full text of the 1906 edition of the Jewish Encyclopedia, reproduced at JewishEncyclopedia.com, "There appears to be no trace of the Prayer of Manasseh in Jewish tradition. The Jerusalem Talmud (Sanh. x. 2) relates that [Manasseh] was put into an iron mule, beneath which a fire was kindled. In his torture he prayed in vain to the idols he had formerly worshiped. At last he besought the God of his fathers, and was delivered . . . ."

> Manasses is with sin obsessed,
> reckoning he's been dispossessed
> because of his infidelity.
> Greater than *the sands of the sea*
> are the number of his sins, yet he
> (deceived by his own duplicity?)
> counts on the Lord's charity.

Proverbs

The Simple and the Wise
(Proverbs 1:1-6)

The Proverbs of Solomon, the son of David, king of Israel: That men may appreciate wisdom and discipline, may understand words of intelligence; may receive training in wise conduct, in what is right, just and honest; that resourcefulness may be imparted to the simple, to the young man knowledge and discretion. A wise man by hearing them will advance in learning, an intelligent man will gain sound guidance, that he may comprehend proverb and parable, the words of the wise and their riddles.

Proverbs differ from parables
as wise words from riddles,
for proverbs go straight to the point
while parables lack logical middles.

If understanding proverbs
is like falling off a log
understanding parables
entails mental leap frog.

Most proverbs are thus for the simple soul,
to make him or her resourceful or clever,
but parables have a higher goal—
preparedness for noble endeavor.

The simple soul may ride history's waves
but the wiser something greater craves—
to harness the power of history's tides
and mine from its mysteries trustworthy guides.

The Theological Jail[36]
(Proverbs 12:15; Sirach 33:5; Isaiah 55:8)

The way of the fool seems right in his own eyes, but he who listens to advice is wise.   Proverbs

Like the wheel of a cart is the mind of a fool; his thoughts revolve in circles.   Sirach

. . . my thoughts are not your thoughts and your ways are not my ways, declares Yahweh.   Isaiah (*NJB*)

Luther called it a jail,
this human effort God's truth to impale
and pull it aboard Pete's Bark like a fish
and scale or skin it to suit the helmsman's wish.

'Tis self-deception as well as pride
to think you have a track inside
God's mind and creative design,
enjoying a theology that leaves error behind.

The Best Use of the Rod
(Proverbs 13:34)

He who spares his rod hates his son, but he who loves him takes care to chastise him.

It seems ironically odd
that some who claim to share the heart of a loving God
often, quickly and harshly,
wield the punishing rod.

To the ancient proverb
such folk are devoutly true,
taking it now and then to points absurd
and leaving plenty of evidence black and blue.

If God too doesn't spare the rod,
on whom is (S)He likeliest to come down hard?

Those who innocently or inadvertently blunder?
Or those who come on soon after,
fierce as lightning, loud as thunder?

Since the effects of wielding the rod
aren't precisely known
perhaps the rod's most effectively used
when it's only shown.

Odes to Wise L'il Critters
(Proverbs 30:24-28)

Four things are among the smallest on the earth, and yet are exceedingly wise:
- *Ants—a species not strong, yet they store up their food in the summer;*
- *Rock-badgers—a species not mighty, yet they make their home in the crags;*
- *Locusts—they have no king, yet they migrate all in array;*
- *Lizards—you can catch them with your hands, yet they find their way into king's palaces.*

An Ode to Ants . . .

My hunch is
Your bunch is
Where lunch is.

. . . to Rock-Badgers

As a species you're no heart-melter
but, though nature doesn't cuddle you to her heart,
you're wise enough to do your part
and, instead of acting helter-skelter,
between rock and hard place find adequate shelter.

. . . to Locusts

If any critter's likely to lose focus
you'd think it might be the locust.

Governed totally by its appetite
its mind's always on its next bite.
Yet some guiding instinct in the group
makes each locust part of an orderly troupe.

. . . to Lizards

Lizards seem lazy and mentally slow,
but is there a place in the world lizards can't go?
So, before granting ideas "matter of fact" clearances,
we'd be wise to distinguish real things from appearances.

For six more reflections on humor and wit in *Proverbs*, see volume one of *Funny Things*, pp. 164–168.

Ecclesiastes

Solomon's Work?
(Ecclesiastes 1:1–3)

The words of David's son, Qoheleth [the Preacher], *king in Jerusalem: Vanity of vanities, says Qoheleth, vanity of vanities! All things are vanity!*
1:1–2

Is Ecclesiastes an addendum
to the great proverbist's agendum
and its view of *everything under the sun*
properly attributable to Solomon?

Though not usually known as The Preacher—
rather as creation's wisest creature[37]—
Solomon's here represented to be
the famed Qoheleth, soul of sermonic sagacity.

Still, with his penchant for pomposity,
his court's well known grandiosity,
and his preening for feminine humanity,
Sol might be Exhibit A that *All is vanity*.

Who Knows?
(Ecclesiastes 3:21-22)

Who knows if the life-breath of the children of men goes upward and the life-breath of beasts goes earthward? And I saw that there is nothing better for a man than to rejoice in his work; for this is his lot. Who will let him see what is to come after him?

> We dance around in a circle and suppose,
> while the secret sits in the middle and knows.
> —Robert Frost

Whether we're lay or cler'cal
we each stand mid-circle—
cruelly stuck *in medias res*.

It's our lot to bear the stigma,
as ciphers amid an enigma,
of Idiocy staring Mystery in the face.

Whither goes the breath that departs us—
to the hole to which the Black Car carts us?
or back to the Spirit who starts us?

Knowing Your Limits
(Ecclesiastes 7:16)

Be not righteous over much; neither make thyself over wise; why shouldest thou destroy thyself? (KJV)

What's the proper amount of "good,"
and how much "wise"
should we try on for size?
How much should we listen to the whispered "should,"
how much IQ try to realize?

The Preacher's a cautious type,
warning us against all hype,
lest a market run by presumed smart Alecs

send us scavenging
for sparkling but worthless relics.

Justice is a valuable prize,
but one who shines it
in the public's eyes
may gain by a censorious righteousness
a name for inglorious spitefulness.

It's easy too to make folly seem wise,
still easier to let it
change your head's size,
eventually becoming counted
among "those foolish wise guys."

The Game Changer
(Ecclesiastes 9:4-7)

... for any among the living there is hope; a live dog is better off than a dead lion. For the living know that they are to die, but the dead no longer know anything. There is no further recompense for them, because all memory of them is lost. For them, love and hatred and rivalry have long since perished. They will never again have part in anything that is done under the sun.

As a mother readies her child for the rays of the raw sun
so The Preacher counsels his flock to proceed with caution.
Life is exciting, though full of problems and strife,
but could anything be more boring
than the absence of life?

Though the dead may hold, funereally, a distinguished position,
their earthly prospect thence is only decomposition;
live dog may never match the roar of live lion,
but if Leo is dead it's live Fido instead
who can walk the sacred flanks of Zion.

For six additional reflections on humor and wit in *Ecclesiastes*, see the first volume of *Funny Things*, pp.168-72.

Song of Songs

In the prequel I declared the Song of Songs to be, in intention at least, as humorless as a high school crush. On the read-through for this sequel I discovered an account of a lover's reverie that's as funny as anything in Scripture— perhaps, indeed, in the whole of world literature.

Finding and Keeping Mr. Goodbar
(Song of Songs 3:1-5)

On my bed at night I sought him whom my heart loves—I sought him but I did not find him. I will rise then and go about the city; in the streets and crossings I will seek him whom my heart loves. I sought him but I did not find him.

The watchmen came upon me as they made their rounds of the city: Have you seen him whom my heart loves? I had hardly left them when I found him whom my heart loves. I took hold of him and would not let him go till I should bring him to the home of my mother, to the room of my parent.

I adjure you, daughters of Jerusalem, by the gazelles and hinds of the field, Do not arouse, do not stir up love before its own time.

You reside all aglow in my mind
but in the flesh you're terribly hard to find.
My heart cries its siren song
but it comes back void, no matter how I long.

Though I seek the watchmen's aid
success is further delayed;
but finally, proving it pays to persist,
I find the very one who tops my list.

Pardon my drama,
but I must get him home, quick, to Mama,
secure her aid in assigning him a grade,
and, to help romance bloom,
take him out of circulation, into my trophy room.

> But to every other pining maiden
> I say relax, leave to me the gradin'—
> if you do as I say, not as I do,
> love may eventually reach you too.

> (And, if in following my advice you'll perdure
> that will almost certainly insure
> that you, like my beloved, remain out of circulation,
> leaving me, worry-free, to continue my celebration!)

For two reflections on the generally *un*humorous character of the *Song of Songs*, see *Funny Things*, volume one, pp. 173–175.

Wisdom of Solomon

Why Death?
(Wisdom of Solomon 1:13-15, 2:23-24)

For God did not make death; he takes no pleasure in destroying the living. To exist—for this he created all things; the creatures of the world have health in them, in them is no fatal potion, and Hades has no power over the world; for uprightness is immortal.   1:13–15 (*NJB*)

> Was death a divine intention
> when God made the world begin?
> Or is it a human invention—
> a consequence of sin?

> When Lucifer thought it possible
> to fight the Lord and win,
> did the fruit of death lie dormant
> in seed sown by that Sin?

> Borne to earth in the bright star's fall
> did sin's possibility cast that slight pall
> over Eden's blindingly bright horizon
> that brought into focus the Tree
> Eve was first to lay eyes on?

> That tree could teach partakers
> evil as well as good,
> so posed a clear danger
> to Eve's neighborhood.
>
> But to the Landlord's warning
> Eve turned a deaf ear,
> perhaps fearing the Lord was horning
> in, lest she become His peer.
>
> But why should the Creator
> permit the possibility of sin,
> the Inventor of breath
> the invention of death?
>
> Is death something creatures
> can't remain ignorant of
> if they're to learn the meaning
> of Grace as *infinite* love?

Fates
(Wisdom of Solomon 3:14-16)

So also the eunuch whose hand wrought no misdeed, who held no wicked thoughts against the LORD—For he shall be given fidelity's choice reward and a more gratifying heritage in the LORD'S temple. For the fruit of noble struggles is a glorious one; and unfailing is the root of understanding. But the children of adulterers will remain without issue, and the progeny of an unlawful bed will disappear.

> Better to have no seed to plant
> than to strew seed ambulant.
> The eunuch's loss on earthly terrain
> will prove his gain when the Lord comes to reign,
> but seed that's been scattered in the wrong bed
> can look for rough sledding ahead.

Fates, Part Two
(Wisdom of Solomon 4:12-16)

For the witchery of paltry things obscures what is right and the whirl of desire transforms the innocent mind. Having become perfect in a short while, he reached the fullness of a long career; for his soul was pleasing to the LORD, therefore he sped him out of the midst of wickedness. But the people saw and did not understand, nor did they take this into account. Yes, the just man [who is] dead condemns the sinful who live, and youth swiftly completed condemns the many years of the wicked man grown old.

> The good die young, or so they say,
> hustled from evil's enticements away,
> while those who stick around, making hay,
> may rue having done so, come settle-up day.

> So length of years is not everything;
> quality of life's a better brass ring;
> better to die pure as masters and missies
> than be the long-lived soul who a righteous God disses.

Like the Chaff that the Wind Drives Away . . .
(Wisdom of Solomon 5:12-14)

Or as, when an arrow has been shot at a mark, the parted air straightway flows together again so that none discerns the way it went through— Even so we, once born, abruptly came to nought and held no sign of virtue to display, but were consumed in our wickedness. Yes, the hope of the wicked is like thistledown borne on the wind, and like fine, tempest-driven foam; like smoke scattered by the wind, and like the passing memory of the nomad camping for a single day.

> The wicked leave no mark:
> their future is stark,
> for they try to write on air,
> capture no one's heart,
> and leave no friends to care
> after they depart.

In Praise and Pursuit of Wisdom
(Wisdom of Solomon 7:21b-27)

... Wisdom, the artificer of all, taught me. For in her is a spirit intelligent, holy, unique, manifold, subtle, agile, clear, unstained, certain, not baneful, loving the good, keen, unhampered, beneficent, kindly, firm, secure, tranquil, all-powerful, all-seeing, and pervading all spirits, though they be intelligent, pure and very subtle. For Wisdom is mobile beyond all motion. ...

22–24a

Wisdom's a paradox,
solid as the hardest of rocks,
yet almost as evanescent
as the moods of an adolescent.

Though it enjoys the allure of a brilliant shine, it
seems to slip away when we try to define it,
for it *"is mobile beyond all motion,"*
eluding each and every fully fixed notion.

Though easy, then, to praise,
wisdom's hard to state or paraphrase;
and, while worthy of every lauding salute,
it much prefers fervent pursuit.

A Worthy and Hard-to-Get Companion
(Wisdom of Solomon 8:16)

When I go home I shall take my ease with...[Wisdom], for nothing is bitter in her company; when life is shared with her, there is no pain, nothing but pleasure and joy. (NJB)

When it comes to an ideal mate
there's none to whom I'd rather relate
than wisdom—pleasing, elegant, sedate.

But I've learned I can't win her hand
simply through gestures grand...
nor is she fair game for a one-night stand.

Somewhere between unreachable goddess
and accessible courtesan,
wisdom requires efforts earnest and modest
to win and hold her hand.

A History with Just One Hero
(Wisdom of Solomon 10:1–12:27)

How could a thing remain, unless you willed it; or be preserved, had it not been called forth by you? But you spare all things, because they are yours, O Ruler and Lover of souls. . . .   11:25–26

Through humanity's history of accomplishment and shame
Wisdom honors only one Name,
yet honors it not by a saying of it
which would amount to a betraying of it
but by a recounting of its deeds.

From the bush that burned,
the Hero spoke true:
"The only way you'll know Me is through
what I enable you to see
in critical turns of history."

Thus Wisdom speaks even yet:
"The only knowledge of me you're going to get
won't reach you through abstract propositions
but through life's offerings—especially its oppositions—
that you'll need to take pains to vet."

Sirach, or Ecclesiasticus

With All Your Getting, Get Wisdom
(Sirach 1:1-7)

All wisdom comes from the LORD and with him it remains forever. The sand of the seashore, the drops of rain, the days of eternity: who can number these? Heaven's height, earth's breadth, the depths of the abyss: who can explore these? Before all things else wisdom was created; and prudent understanding, from eternity. To whom has wisdom's root been revealed? Who knows her subtleties? There is but one, wise and truly awe-inspiring, seated upon his throne: It is the LORD; he created her, has seen her and taken note of her. He has poured her forth upon all his works, upon every living thing according to his bounty; he has lavished her upon his friends.

>Wisdom's a unique commodity,
>maybe the very oddest oddity.
>Her root no mind can find
>by looking before or behind,
>nor grasp by either end—
>unless that mind's God's friend.
>
>Yet Wisdom's everywhere,
>a thing God's eager to share.
>She's the Word's first creation,
>used in the world's formation
>and serving still and always
>as its true foundation.
>
>Though she has much to teach us
>Wisdom finds it hard to reach us
>because so attuned to time's noise are we
>that we're deaf to the whispers of Eternity.

Fear and Joy
(Sirach 1:11-19)

The fear of the Lord maketh a merry heart, and giveth joy, and gladness, and a long life.   12 *(KJV)*

> Rare are those who'd deem fear
> to be an associate of good cheer.
> But Sirach, not at all shy,
> looks his reader in the eye
> and names fear joy's surprising ally.

> If fearing the Lord means going around scared
> it could hardly account for those who've dared
> to go with Daniel into a den of lions
> or, with him and others, face kings in defiance.

> Anyone who's studied the Holy History's record
> from Nathan the court chaplain to Amos the shepherd
> knows that pious respect for the true King
> is a pretty good remedy for knee-knocking.

> Though the joyful fear they knew
> didn't make them court jesters,
> it did make these faithful few
> courageous and ardent protesters,
> in many a critical hour,
> against abuses of court power

Social Security
(Sirach 3:8-16; cf. Mark 7:9-13)

In word and deed honor your father that his blessing may come upon you; For a father's blessing gives a family firm roots, but a mother's curse uproots the growing plant. Glory not in your father's shame, for his shame is no glory to you! His father's honor is a man's glory; disgrace for her children, a mother's shame. My son, take care of your father when he is old; grieve him not as long as he lives. Even if his mind fail, be considerate with him;

revile him not in the fullness of your strength. For kindness to a father will not be forgotten, it will serve as a sin offering—it will take lasting root. In time of tribulation it will be recalled to your advantage, like warmth upon frost it will melt away your sins. A blasphemer is he who despises his father; accursed of his Creator, he who angers his mother.

    As they approach advanced maturity
    in a world without Social Security,
    what can parental elders look for
    to keep rav'nous wolves from the door?

   They'll be wise to look to their major investment,
   one great consequence of their shared test'ment
   with the Planter and Grower of their family tree,
   in Whom rests their future's sole guarantee.

   With neither taxation nor privatization
   to help them maintain their fiscal station
and with children they can count on through better but not worse,
  they may need to resort to the threat of a curse.

   So, as Sirach reminds reluctant offspring,
  failing to shield Ma and Pa from a harsh fate's sting
or cheating and depriving them through some clever scheme[38]
  will put them in the same niche as those who blaspheme.

    Those children are smart
    who act from the heart,
    and those families abide
    where filial duty is known to preside.

A Good Word for the Tongue
(Sirach 4:23-24)

Do not refrain from speaking at the proper time, and do not hide your wisdom; For wisdom becomes known through speech, and knowledge through the tongue's response.

> Experience doesn't lack for champions
> and tongues have many detractors,
> but at times statement and response
> are learners' truest benefactors.

Going Nowhere Fast
(Sirach 5:11b)

> . . . *start not off in every direction.*

The political gridlock we've seen among national governments lately illustrates the dilemma of those who want to keep their cake while eating it. We all know the condition: both satisfying (and/or gratifying) our needs and keeping our books balanced are desirable. Some politicians insist on the first as more important, others on the second. The gridlocked congress that results is reminiscent of 14th century philosopher Jean Buridan's famous donkey who, placed between equally appealing bales of hay, was paralyzed by the equal and opposite attractions on either side of him.

A wise Jesus ben Sirach warns us against such asinine impasses. The following crhyme tries to express what I take to be his point.

> Can there be hope of correction
> for those who'd go every direction,
> or must they reach the sorry pass
> that confronted Buridan's ass?

> Stuck equal distances away
> between equally appealing bales of hay
> the ass was able only to bray,
> his hunger held completely at bay.

We've all met the kind:
with nothing to help make up their mind,
they remain stuck in neutral:
all efforts to move prove futile.

Thus those who'd at once go every which way
are bound to hear Buridan's critter's "Neigh,"
while blessed are they who, choosing a way,
find a healthful path on which to stay.

Ignoble Warming
(Sirach 8:16)

Provoke no quarrel with a quick-tempered man, nor ride with him through the desert.

When temper and temperature conspire
to start and stoke a simmering fire
the consequences can't be good
for the immediate neighborhood.

So stay away from the intemperate soul
who can't keep his emotions under control.
And it's extra important, if you don't want to be hurt,
not to *ride with* a hothead *through* a *desert*.

The Wrong Kind of Compound Interest
(Sirach 9:4)

With a singing girl be not familiar, lest you be caught in her wiles.

Wine, women, and song
all can entice a man to go wrong.
Any one or two of these three
can test one's honor and sanity.

When combined any two
can mean extra trouble

for, paired up, their effect
may more than double.

What Ulysses knew is especially true:
an enchanting siren
can have strange effects
on the strongest man's wirin'.

So lash yourself to the mast
and give chorines a wide berth,
for a clear lesson from the past
is that misery can follow prurient mirth.

Both Cash and No Cash Bring Change
(Sirach 12:8)

In our prosperity we cannot know our friends; in adversity an enemy will not remain concealed.

Riches multiply "friends,"
impoverishment, enemies;
the people we attract change
with changing economies.

Another Ultra-Ironic Irony
(Sirach 15:14)

God in the beginning created human beings and made them subject to their own free choice.

Subject or free?
Which are we?

In a most delicious irony,
God's making me free
makes me subject to me.

The I of today
can hardly outlive the sway
of that of yesterday.

When Deciding Whom to Trust . . .
(Sirach 19:26)

A man's attire, his hearty laughter and his gait, proclaim him for what he is.

> Of all the body parts you might judge among
> the least trustworthy is probably the tongue.
> Better to put what it says aside
> and check for a hearty laugh, poise,
> good grooming, and merited pride.

The Epitome of Ineffectiveness, or Speaking of Frustration
(Sirach 20:4)

Like a eunuch lusting to violate a young woman is the one who does right under compulsion.

> When you're out of steam the impossible dream
> may still haunt you, day and night.
> But t' expect to inspire love using force from above
> is like shooting at a target that's not even in sight.

A Lot of Knowledge Can Be a Boring Thing
(Sirach 23:20)

The one who knows all things before they exist still knows them all after they are made.

> Of omnisciency our Maker has a sufficiency.
> From the creation's drawing board
> to everything in the cosmic cupboard,
> there's in God's knowing no deficiency.
>
> But if all we found in God's story
> was a comprehensive inventory,
> we'd have as much right to be bored

> as the reader of any story
> re a miser reciting the ledger
> listing all (s)he's managed to hoard.

Two-edged Words
(Sirach 28:12-18)

If you blow upon a spark, it quickens into flame, if you spit on it, it dies out; yet both you do with your mouth! Cursed be gossips and the double-tongued, for they destroy the peace of man. A meddlesome tongue subverts many, and makes them refugees among the peoples; It destroys walled cities, and overthrows powerful dynasties. A meddlesome tongue can drive virtuous women from their homes and rob them of the fruit of their toil; Whoever heeds it has no rest, nor can he dwell in peace. A blow from a whip raises a welt, but a blow from the tongue smashes bones; many have fallen by the edge of the sword, but not as many as by the tongue.

> The mouth's a marvelous thing,
> useful for damping down *and* igniting;
> like a powerful two-edged sword
> its good or ill effects can't be ignored.

> Since its effect on the spark of life can ignite or reduce strife,
> be careful what you let your mouth say,
> for what you let it say has a definite way
> of affecting the quality of many a life.

On Not Ruining Good Times with Talk
(Sirach 32:1-13)

You who are older, it is your right to speak, but temper your knowledge and do not interrupt the singing. Where there is entertainment, do not pour out discourse, and do not display your wisdom at the wrong time. 3–4 (NAB)

If someone is singing, do not ramble on and do not play the sage at the wrong moment. 4 (NJB)

> Why's the saga of God's creation
> say so little about recreation?
> What's it betoken that Scripture's always jokin'
> but ignores other avocations, like hikin' and smokin'?
>
> Surely Scripture's failure to mention these
> doesn't mean there weren't such activities:
> Sirach reminds us that things like a refreshing walk
> may be spoiled by rambling, idle talk.
> And who can stand it when a gorgeous solo
> is spoiled by some loquacious igmo?

The Gift that Keeps on Testing
(Sirach 42:9-11a)

A daughter is a treasure that keeps her father wakeful, and worry over her drives away rest: Lest she pass her prime unmarried, or when she is married, lest she be disliked; While unmarried, lest she be seduced, or, as a wife, lest she prove unfaithful; Lest she conceive in her father's home, or be sterile in that of her husband. Keep a close watch on your daughter, lest she make you the sport of your enemies.

> A daughter is a precious gift;
> just having one around can give parents a lift.
> But if from the right path she happens to drift,
> say goodbye to comfort and rest
> and hello to your fortitude's severest test.
>
> Almost as bad as having her drift
> is watching as she drops out of the draft.
> When no suitors knock on your door,
> prepare to spend time pacing the floor.
> It can become a parent's greatest distraction
> when your lass's social life becomes a fatal or a futile attraction.
>
> Even if you've walked her down the aisle and given her away
> she remains your child in every conceivable way.
> And if she doesn't conceive she'll remain so too—
> in spades should her husband choose
> to give her back to you.

4—The Prophets

Isaiah

A Call to Futility?
(Isaiah 6:8-10)

Then I heard the voice of the Lord saying, "Whom shall I send? Who will go for us?" "Here I am," I said; "send me!" And he replied: "Go and say to this people: Listen carefully, but you shall not understand! Look intently, but you shall know nothing! You are to make the heart of this people sluggish, to dull their ears and close their eyes; Else their eyes will see, their ears hear, their heart understand, and they will turn and be healed."

Is the Lord out for blood?
If not, why this flood
of contempt for a people whose name
appears to TL to be mud?

Might some—any—be exempt?
Is none of them worth an attempt
to break through the crusty indifference
that dulls their every sense?

Isaiah seems called to give it a shot
to see if any is . . . or not.

But wait! There's another way
to read what the Lord tells Isaiah to say.
Failing to read the Lord's advice
as filled with sarcastic spice
may be why what some preachers preach
suggests that what *they* hear TL here teach
is that they're to let no subject rest
'til every hearer's lulled into sluggishness.

Lucifer
(Isaiah 14:12-15)

How art thou fallen from heaven, O Lucifer, son of the morning! how art thou cut down to the ground, which didst weaken the nations! For thou hast said in thine heart, I will ascend into heaven, I will exalt my throne above the stars of God: I will sit also upon the mount of the congregation, in the sides of the north: I will ascend above the heights of the clouds; I will be like the most High. Yet thou shalt be brought down to hell, to the sides of the pit.
(KJV)

His name means Prince of Light,
    but he sought to trade
      his light for power,
his ability to light up the night
for a shot at a triumphal hour.

Thus, withdrawing his light from the night
where it had stood regally in contrast stark,
    Luci attacked the Domain of Light,
    only to fall, repelled, into the dark
and watch it absorb his every spark.

Is he, then, still King of the Dark,
    Inventor and Lord of Hell,
  glad broker for any with a soul to sell—
one so unhappy with being judged second-rank
he's traded his created grandeur for eternity in the tank?

Or is he, instead, an innocent like Eve,
    uncertain who or what to believe,
one who's earned the title Prince of Confusion
    by playing victim as well as creator
      of self-delusion?

Is Lucifer really, in short,
    Milton's brave anti-hero
    or actually, ultimately,
      a cosmic zero?

Between, yet Beyond, the Cherubim
(Isaiah 37:15-16)

And Hezekiah prayed unto the LORD, saying, O LORD of hosts, God of Israel, that dwellest between the cherubim, *thou art the God, even thou alone, of all the kingdoms of the earth:* thou hast made heaven and earth.

(KJV)

        Hezekiah's emphatically vocal
    in asserting God's at once ubiquitous and local;
  The Lord's rule of all nations can't and won't falter
though (S)He sits meekly 'twixt cherubs on a local altar.

      Should it surprise us that One so involved
        in a small nation's course from birth
    encompasses and governs the whole globe's girth
when we know it was (S)He Who made heaven and earth?

For eleven more reflections on humor, wit, and irony in *Isaiah*, see the first volume of *Funny Things*, pp. 177–184.

Jeremiah

The Last Yoke's on Hananiah
(Jeremiah 28:10-17)

. . . *the prophet Hananiah took the yoke from the neck of the prophet Jeremiah, broke it, and said in the presence of all the people: "Thus says the LORD: 'Even so, within two years I will break the yoke of Nebuchadnezzar, king of Babylon, from off the neck of all the nations.'" At that, the prophet Jeremiah went away. Some time after the prophet Hananiah had broken the yoke from off the neck of the prophet Jeremiah, the word of the LORD came to Jeremiah: Go tell Hananiah this: Thus says the LORD: By breaking a wooden yoke, you forge an iron yoke! For thus says the LORD of hosts, the God of Israel: A yoke of iron I will place on the necks of all these nations serving Nebuchadnezzar, king of Babylon, and they shall serve him; even the beasts of the field I give him. To the prophet Hananiah the prophet Jeremiah said: Hear this, Hananiah! The LORD has not sent you, and you have raised false confidence in this people. For this, says the LORD, I will dispatch you from the face of the earth; this very year you shall die, because you have preached rebellion against the LORD. That same year, in the seventh month, Hananiah the prophet died.*

It was no joke
when Jeremiah donned a yoke
signaling Judah's impending submission
to Babylon's imperious disposition.

Having stood all he could of it,
Hananiah, a prophet-counterfeit,
broke the yoke, chided his rival,
and predicted Judah's liberation's arrival.

"Less than two years is all it'll take
Nebuchadnezzar's bonds to shake!"
So said Hananiah,
then heard in retort from Jeremiah:

"You've done all you could,
but a yoke of iron will replace the wood;
and soon you'll see that fighting Yahweh
leads ineluctably to a reckoning day."

'Twasn't long 'til Jerry's threat came true
and the ills Hanni's advice helped brew
came down on his head,
leaving him irreversibly dead.

The Loose End
(Jeremiah 51:20)

"You are my hammer, my weapon for war; with you I shatter nations, with you I destroy kingdoms." The Lord to Judah through Jeremiah

Who'd picture little Judah
as the Lord's barracuda—
the object of so much derision
as a source of global division?

> And who would contemplate
> that the modern Israeli state
> would on her neighbors'
> nerves so grate?

> Yet the fabric of civilization is so loosely woven
> that pulling a single, tiny loose end,
> especially that of the self-conscious Chosen,
> might very well the whole thing rend.

For nine more reflections on humor and wit in *Jeremiah*, see volume one of *Funny Things*, pp. 184–190.

Lamentations

It's Always Darkest before . . .
(Lamentations 1:1–5:21)

How solitary sits the city, once filled with people. She who was great among the nations is now like a widow. Once a princess among the provinces, now a toiling slave. She weeps incessantly in the night, her cheeks damp with tears. She has no one to comfort her from all her lovers; Her friends have all betrayed her, and become her enemies. Judah has gone into exile, after oppression and harsh labor; She dwells among the nations, yet finds no rest: All her pursuers overtake her in the narrow straits. The roads to Zion mourn, empty of pilgrims to her feasts. All her gateways are desolate, her priests groan, Her young women grieve; her lot is bitter.   1:1–4

> From the glory of a queen
> to conditions vile and mean,
> the Judean lion and the pride of Zion
> have become laughing stocks
> on the global scene.

> *"All her gateways are deserted,"*
> and she is so disconcerted
> that *"her priests groan."*

> With no hope of relief
> *"her virgins sigh; she is in bitter grief."*[39]
>
> *"Her princes, like rams
> that find no pasture,
> have gone off without strength
> before their captors."*
>
> Grown accustomed before their Lord
> to living the life of a cheat
> they've become a shepherdless flock
> with little left beyond their bleat.
>
> Their Protector's become their Predator,
> their grace-impelled Mentor their *Tor*mentor,
> their Shepherd a Wolf among the fold,
> bringing on them terrors manifold.
>
> *Even when I cry out for help, he stops my prayer;*
> Why pray at all, if God will not hear?
> *A lurking bear he has been to me, a lion in ambush!*
> Can I count on such a Lord to stand by me
> when shove comes to push?
>
> Yet *the favors of the LORD are not exhausted,
> his mercies are not spent;*
> I may repose my hope in God yet
> if, fulfilling *His* hopes, I repent.
>
> *My portion is the LORD, says my soul;*
> to do God's will my goal;
> *therefore will I hope in Him*
> to rescue me from fortunes grim.

For another humorous reflection on *Lamentations*, see the first volume of *Funny Things*, p. 190.

Baruch

(In Catholic Bibles, Baruch includes a sixth chapter called the Letter of Jeremiah. Baruch is not in the Hebrew and Protestant Bibles. The Orthodox canon contains Baruch and the Letter of Jeremiah as separate writings.)

Light from Afar
(Baruch 1:1—6:72)

Jerusalem, take off your robe of mourning and misery; put on the splendor of glory from God forever: Wrapped in the cloak of justice from God, bear on your head the mitre that displays the glory of the eternal name. For God will show all the earth your splendor: you will be named by God forever the peace of justice, the glory of God's worship.   5:1–4

    Here's Jeremiah's presumed amanuensis
    begging mourning Zionists to make full use of their senses.
    He hadn't gone with the exiles; nor had his master;
    but both sought to provide, across great distances,
    a transforming perspective on the Disaster.

    Jerry and Barry too would go into exile,
    not in Babylon's land but Egypt's,
    both sure that neither Tigris nor Nile
    could God's light eclipse.

In foreign lands the Chosen have perforce become denizens
    and Jerry and Barry urge them
    to become exemplary citizens,
letting their devout witness be a light to the Gentiles
though separated from Zion's beacon by many, many miles.

The Letter of Jeremiah

Broken Tools and Utter Fools
(Baruch 6:8-15, 39-41)

People bring gold, as to a maiden in love with ornament, and furnish crowns for the heads of their gods. Then sometimes the priests take the silver and gold from their gods and spend it on themselves, or give part of it to the harlots on the terrace. They trick them out in garments like men, these gods of silver and gold and wood; but though they are wrapped in purple clothing, they are not safe from corrosion or insects. They wipe their faces clean of the house dust which is thick upon them. Each has a scepter, like the human ruler of a district; but none does away with those that offend against it. Each has in its right hand an axe or dagger, but it cannot save itself from war or pillage. Thus it is known they are not gods; do not fear them. As useless as one's broken tools. . . . How then can it be thought or claimed that they are gods? Even the Chaldeans themselves have no respect for them; for when they see a deaf mute, incapable of speech, they bring forward Bel and ask the god to make noise, as though the man could understand; and they are themselves unable to reflect and abandon these gods, for they have no sense.

> Gods who are mere tools
> are the inventions of fools
> and even when unbroken
> can barely betoken
> mysteries their inventors
> can't understand.

> Born of human superstition
> and fear of sinning by omission,
> they're weak as thin tissue
> in confronting the issue
> of shielding their makers from forces
> they can't command.

Ezekiel

A Strange New Kind of Prophet
(Ezekiel 1:1-28; Psalm 137:1,4)

In the thirtieth year, on the fifth day of the fourth month, while I was among the exiles by the river Chebar, the heavens opened, and I saw divine visions. On the fifth day of the month, the fifth year, that is, of King Jehoiachin's exile, the word of the LORD came to the priest Ezekiel, the son of Buzi, in the land of the Chaldeans by the river Chebar.—There the hand of the LORD came upon me.
Ezekiel 1:1–3

By the rivers of Babylon we sat mourning and weeping when we remembered Zion. . . . how could we sing a song of the LORD in a foreign land?
Psalm 137:1, 4

Ezekiel was a pioneer,
the first Hebrew prophet to hear
his Call from the Lord
not at home but abroad.

He was thus first to see how things had changed:
that in this new situation of trial and pain
it would henceforth be necessary
for the prophet to be a missionary.

The call to Abram to be a light to the nations
had fallen prey to patriots' aspirations,
and theology had assumed such a jingoist slant
that the Lord was commonly treated like a Palestinian plant.

As a portrait of a self-moving God,
unbound by any expanse of sod,
Ezekiel's vision of the Lord as a God on wheels
could have become the patented concept for future automobiles.

Though Zeke longs as much as any for Jerusalem's restoration
he radically changes the notion of the Holy Nation

> by declaring it's considerably more
> than a matter of location.

For six more humorous reflections on *Ezekiel,* see volume one of *Funny Things,* pp. 191–95.

Daniel

In Catholic and Orthodox Bibles, Daniel includes three sections not found in Protestant Bibles. The Prayer of Azariah and the Song of the Three Holy Children are recounted between Daniel 3:23 and 3:24. The Story of Suzanna is told in Daniel 13 while that of Bel and The Dragon is recounted in chapter 14.

Beauty, Bel, and the Beast
(Daniel 13:1—14:27)

> The Apocrypha presumes to append
> the tales of Susanna, Bel, and a Dragon
> to Daniel—virtually another book at that book's end.
>
> The first tale is that of a great beauty.
> the last that of a great beast
> and in-between lies the story
> of Bel, great god of the East.
>
> Susanna was the name of the beauty,
> a paragon of honor and duty
> whose charms bedazzled two corrupt judges
> and whose chaste refusals left them bearing grudges.
>
> Famous for his appetite
> Bel ate only beyond mortals' sight
> 'til Daniel brought his career to closure
> by arranging his clever priests' exposure.
>
> As a threat last but certainly not least
> comes that frightening specter, the dragon-beast.

> Killing it seemed out of the question
> 'til Daniel induced lethal indigestion.
>
> Thus with ingenious ingenuity
> apocryphal Dan spins exotic yarns three:
> of Susannah, with Dan's help a foiler of rakes;
> of Bel, whom Dan proves the greatest of fakes;
> and a Dragon, victim of the awf'lest of tummy aches.

For five more reflections on humor and wit in *Daniel*, see the first volume of *Funny Things*, pp. 195–200.

Hosea

Names that Break More than Bones. . . .
(Hosea 1:1–9)

When the LORD began to speak with Hosea, the LORD said to Hosea: Go, get for yourself a woman of prostitution and children of prostitution, for the land prostitutes itself, turning away from the LORD. So he went and took Gomer, daughter of Diblaim; and she conceived and bore him a son. Then the LORD said to him: Give him the name "Jezreel," for in a little while I will punish the house of Jehu for the bloodshed at Jezreel. . . . She conceived again and bore a daughter. The LORD said to him: Give her the name "Not-Pitied," for I will no longer feel pity for the house of Israel. . . . After she weaned Not-Pitied, she conceived and bore a son. Then the LORD said: Give him the name "Not-My-People," for you are not my people, and I am not "I am" for you.   2–4a, 6, 8–9

> What's the opposite of adoption?
> Whatever it is, the Lord here takes that option.
> Though Israel's long since been known as God's child
> and TL hates to consign her to a refuse pile,
> (S)He's tired of hearing her the Name defile.
>
> Lo-ruhamah—"not my people"
> and Lo-ammi—"not to be pitied"

makes you wonder how long Israel
must weep 'til
the price of her sins is remitted.

The Lord doesn't want
those to bear His Name
who bring on it only
discredit and shame.

The Remedy
(Hosea 2:1-23)

On that day—oracle of the LORD—You shall call me "My husband," and you shall never again call me "My baal." 18

In falling whole-soul into the arms of Baal
Gomer sold her favors and charms wholesale.
In this she'd just adopted the style of her day,
commonly known as Israel's way.

'Tis not enough just to marry a willing Hosea
nor for Israel to re-wed her faithful Yahweh;
nor is there any other panacea
for either of the errant brides.

Should either wife or nation long to see a
future of higher tides,
both will have to become and stay
joined at the hip to their husbands' sides.

For another reflection on *Hosea*, see *Funny Things*, volume one, pp. 200–201.

Joel

A God beyond Presumption and Prediction
(Joel 4:10-11; compare Isaiah 2:4, Micah 4:3)

Beat your plowshares into swords, and your pruning knives into spears; let the weakling boast, "I am a warrior!" Hurry and come, all you neighboring peoples, assemble there! Bring down, LORD, your warriors!

> The Lord keeps all options open
> and, when vigilance gives way to mopin,'
> (S)He's not averse to sounding alarms
> and issuing surprising calls to arms.
>
> Each of us is mightily inclined
> to reduce God to the size of our mind
> and limit the range of divine decisions
> to the terms of our slender human visions.
>
> Through Christ we know God's a God of Peace,
> but to defend the oppressed from tyrannical beasts
> mightn't (S)He keep or seek peace in a critical hour
> by a judicious and measured use of power?

For another reflection on wit in the prophecies of *Joel*, see the first volume of *Funny Things*, p. 201.

Amos

Another Paradox
(Amos 1:1; 2:6-13)

The words of Amos, who was one of the sheepbreeders from Tekoa, which he received in a vision concerning Israel in the days of Uzziah, king of Judah . . . Thus says the LORD: For three crimes of Israel, and now four, I will not revoke my word; Because they sell the just man for silver, and the poor man *for a pair of sandals. They trample the heads of the weak into the dust of the earth, and force the lowly out of the way. Son and father go to the same prostitute, profaning my holy name. Upon garments taken in pledge they recline beside any altar; And the wine of those who have been fined they drink in the house of their god. Yet it was I who destroyed the Amorites before them, who were as tall as the cedars, and as strong as the oak trees. I destroyed their fruit above, and their roots beneath. It was I who brought you up from the land of Egypt, and who led you through the desert for forty years, to occupy the land of the Amorites: I who raised up prophets among your sons, and nazirites among your young men. Is this not so, O men of Israel? says the LORD. But you gave the nazirites wine to drink, and commanded the prophets not to prophesy. Beware, I will crush you into the ground as a wagon crushes when laden with sheaves.*

> Who knew the bumpkin from Tekoa
> had the slightest knowledge of the score?
> And who was he to give such hell
> to the neighbor-nation, Israel?
>
> Still, in him we find a hillbilly who dares
> critique the state of international affairs.
> Resorting often to rustic metaphors,
> he raises all manner of holy what-fors.
>
> But then in Scripture it's no novel paradox
> for a humble tender and companion of flocks
> to be rendered by God's Call a leader
> whose oracles scare and transfix the reader.

For three more reflections on wit and irony in the oracles of *Amos*, see *Funny Things*, volume one, pp. 202–204.

Obadiah

Woe Awaits the Proud
(Obadiah 1-4)

The vision of Obadiah. (Thus says the Lord GOD:) Of Edom we have heard a message from the LORD, and a herald has been sent among the nations: "Up! let us go to war against him!" See, I make you small among the nations; you are held in dire contempt. The pride of your heart has deceived you: you who dwell in the clefts of the rock, whose abode is in the heights, who say in your heart, "Who will bring me down to earth?" Though you go as high as the eagle, and your nest be set among the stars, From there will I bring you down, says the LORD.

> Their pride was regal,
> their ascent like that of an eagle,
> yet the arrogance of Edom,
> its misuse of its power and freedom,
> God deems unjust even if legal.

> The precedent, to be sure, was set against Esau
> when Jacob broke both custom and law
> by stealing his older twin's blessing and birthright,
> initiating a bitter, centuries-old fight,
> reignitable in a nonce by the slightest slight.

> Why then are the cards stacked against Edom, né Esau?
> Why are they doomed, in- or outside the law?
> The answer given by the Lord of all living
> is that, in remaining aloof and unforgiving,
> they in their malice have drawn the short straw.

For another reflection on the use of irony in Obadiah, see the first volume of *Funny Things*, p. 204.

Jonah

Symbolic Sailors
(Jonah 1:1–4:11; cp. Genesis 6:5–8:19)

Not since Noah had the fate of so many
been put to sail on a boat;
but Jonah went farther than Noah,
taking Nineveh's fate into a fish's throat.

If Noah was a model sailor who followed his Admiral's orders
into the perils of raging waters,
Jonah, in launching a secret mutiny,
tried to dodge *his* Commander's scrutiny.

Thus Noah's now the symbol of divine compassion,
Jonah, of reluctant and rebellious preachers,
but each became, in his own fashion,
an instrument of God's love for unlovable creatures.

For two more reflections on humor in the story of *Jonah*, see the first volume of *Funny Things*, pp. 204–205.

Micah

Capital Punishment
(Micah 1:2–9)

Hear, O peoples, all of you, give heed, O earth, and all that fills you! Let the Lord GOD be witness against you, the Lord from his holy temple! For see, the LORD comes forth from his place, he descends and treads upon the heights of the earth. The mountains melt under him and the valleys split open, Like wax before the fire, like water poured down a slope. For the crime of Jacob all this comes to pass, and for the sins of the house of Israel. What is the crime of Jacob? Is it not Samaria? And what is the sin of the house of Judah? Is it not Jerusalem? I will make Samaria a stone heap in the field, a place to plant for vineyards; I will throw down into the valley her stones, and lay bare her foundations. All her idols shall be broken to pieces, all her wages shall be burned in the fire, and all her statues I will destroy. As the wages of a harlot they were gathered, and to the wages of a harlot shall they return. For this reason I lament and wail, I go barefoot and naked; I utter lamentation like the jackals, and mourning like the ostriches. There is no remedy for the blow she has been struck; rather, it has come even to Judah, It reaches to the gate of my people, even to Jerusalem.*

> Micah brings an indictment forth
> citing the crimes of the capitals, south and north.
> It was hard to imagine who'd been contrarier,
> Judah's Jerusalem or Ephraim's Samaria.

> The prophet warns that both of these cities
> are all but out of their allotted times
> as the Lord's just and ironic wit is
> devising punishments to fit their crimes.

For two more humorous reflections on the oracles of *Micah*, see *Funny Things*, volume one, pp. 205–206.

Nahum

Enemy Number One
(Nahum 1:11)

From you he came who devised evil against the LORD, the scoundrel planner.

> Nothing produces in juries more aggravation
> than proof of culpable premeditation.
> That's what proves a crime sufficiently worse
> to change its degree from second to first.

> The engagement of its head in such premeditation
> makes Nineveh head of the nastiest nation.
> Tormenting small nations is not just its hobby
> but a tactic for which its field generals lobby.
>
> So what makes Nineveh enemy number one,
> the most evil to see the light of the sun,
> is not its militant mood or vicious manner
> but its crimes as the pawn of *the scoundrel planner*.

For another reflection on *Nahum*, see the first volume of *Funny Things*, pp. 206–207.

Habakkuk

Learning to Give is Learning to Live
(Habakkuk 2:1-4)

I will stand at my guard post, and station myself upon the rampart, and keep watch to see what he will say to me, and what answer he will give to my complaint. Then the LORD answered me and said: Write down the vision clearly upon the tablets, so that one can read it readily. For the vision still has its time, presses on to fulfillment, and will not disappoint; If it delays, wait for it, it will surely come, it will not be late. The rash man has no integrity; but the just man, because of his faith, shall live.

> Habakkuk launches a new chapter in theology[40]
> when he raises the issues of theodicy.
> Can a God who tolerates pride, greed, and lust
> rightly be deemed a God who's just?
>
> Having levied his vigorous complaint,
> the prophet waits patiently, showing constraint,
> resorting neither to sorcerer nor necromancer,
> 'til he gets from the Lord a straightforward answer.
>
> In the form of a vision the answer comes,
> foretelling great joy and laughter

> when the faith of the just is justified
> in a hope-fulfilling Hereafter.
>
> Faithless, evil folk
> will then be the butt of a last-laugh joke
> as those whom faith teaches justice to give'll
> survive those who surrender the just way for th' evil.

For another reflection on *Habakkuk*, see *Funny Things*, volume one, p. 207.

Zephaniah

Bad Days Ahead for Stargazers
(Zephaniah 1:4-5a)

I will stretch out my hand against Judah, and against all the inhabitants of Jerusalem; I will destroy from this place the last vestige of Baal, the very names of his priests. And those who adore the host of heaven on the roof....

Zephaniah prophesied during the reign of young King Josiah (641–609 B.C.), who emulated his great grandfather Hezekiah by launching a campaign against foreign gods. Among such gods were the host of heaven, star deities imported from Assyria and Babylon (the same deities who inspired the construction of the tower of Babel, which was likely meant to serve as an observatory for astrologer-priests).

> The fiasco at Babel
> didn't conclusively disable
> the theory and practice of astrology.
>
> Demoted to gazing from a roof,
> its seers, still haughty, remained aloof,
> scorning Judah's simple, unitarian theology.
>
> Believing divine secrets lived in geometry and numbers,
> these sages eagerly forsook their slumbers
> to search heaven for omens of the future's course.

> Provoked by this and other idolatries, young Josiah
> assumed the mantle of Great Gramps Hezekiah
> to attack the star gods and Baal with main force.

> All of which goes to show
> that, when "adoring" star gods and seeking what they know,
> you'd best keep your rooftop profile low.

For another reflection on *Zephaniah*, see the first volume of *Funny Things*, p. 208.

Haggai

Comparisons
(Haggai 2:3, 5, 7, 9)

Who is left among you that saw this house in its former glory? And how do you see it now? Does it not seem like nothing in your eyes?. . . This is the pact that I made with you when you came out of Egypt, And my spirit continues in your midst; do not fear! . . . I will shake all the nations, and the treasures of all the nations will come in, And I will fill this house with glory, says the LORD of hosts. . . . Greater will be the future glory of this house than the former, says the LORD of hosts; and in this place I will give you peace, says the LORD of hosts.

> "Distance lends enchantment to the view"
> is a saying old and moldy but true.
> Haggai urges those still awed by the temple of Solomon
> to withhold judgment 'til the new temple's done.

> Time lends old things a certain glow
> and the new'll never make the Antique Road Show,
> but a faith reposing all value in a glorious past
> is one smart folk won't expect to last.

Zechariah (or Zacharias)

Hewing the Line
(Zechariah 1:14-16)

And the angel who spoke with me said to me, Proclaim: Thus says the LORD of hosts: I am deeply moved for the sake of Jerusalem and Zion, and I am exceedingly angry with the complacent nations; whereas I was but a little angry, they added to the harm. Therefore, says the LORD: I will turn to Jerusalem in mercy; my house shall be built in it, says the LORD of hosts, and a measuring line shall be stretched over Jerusalem.

If you're seeking evidence of God's design,
consider the line.
When we're lost
and seemingly without a prayer
a line will unfailingly lead us somewhere.

A line, then, is a useful thing
with a very generous capacity to bring
salvation from desperation
by saving us
from endless meandering.

You may, it's true, come to hate
a line that doesn't take you straight,
costing you your orientation
and keeping you from getting
directly from station to station.

Though a circle, for example, might appear
to make a way out of confusion clear,
it'll only take you from here to there
and eventually
back to here.

So, though God no doubt created the line,
it's a hapless thing without a mind,

and God has to have had to create that too
so people like I and you
can, by hewing the line,
conform to the terms of His design.

So when the Lord tells the people of Jerusalem
(S)He's providing a measuring line for them
(S)He re-minds them to see it as no mere surcee[41]
but instead to regard it as an act of mercy.

The Apple of God's Eye
(Zechariah 2:12; Genesis 3:5-7)

For thus said the LORD of hosts (after he had already sent me) concerning the nations that have plundered you: Whoever touches you touches the apple of my eye.   Zechariah

But the serpent said to the woman: "You certainly will not die! No, God knows well that the moment you eat of it your eyes will be opened and you will be like gods who know what is good and what is bad." The woman saw that the tree was good for food, pleasing to the eyes, and desirable for gaining wisdom. So she took some of its fruit and ate it; and she also gave some to her husband, who was with her, and he ate it.   Genesis

The story of Israel attests
that this apple of God's eye,
graciously favored in God's sight,
is for that very reason subject
to many an envious bite.

Eve, looking on Eden's special fruit,
found qualities that seemed to suit
the noblest of her desires:
food, beauty, and wisdom to fuel
the body's, the soul's, and the mind's fires.

So Israel, as God's low-hanging fruit,
seemed similarly to suit,
to the point of haunting,

other nations who, compared to her,
in their own eyes came up wanting.

Though being bitten again and again
brought sharp and lingering pain,
it fulfilled the vocation of the Chosen
to bring to the biters the news of God's reign
to which they needed exposin.'

Malachi

Crucial Conditions
(Malachi 1:14a)

Cursed is the deceiver, who has in his flock a male, but under his vow sacrifices to the LORD a gelding. . . .

As we offer ourselves
on the theater table
we want conditions sterile
as well as a surgeon able.

Not so the Lord, Who wants to see
from those who are able
no hint of sterility
on His sanctum's table.

On the surgeon's table a patient desires
perfection to the last suture;
on the Lord's table perfection requires
an animal *and* its future.

The Prosperity Gospel?
(Malachi 3:7-10)

Since the days of your fathers you have turned aside from my statutes, and have not kept them. Return to me, and I will return to you, says the LORD of hosts. Yet you say, "How must we return?" Dare a man rob God? Yet you are robbing me! And you say, "How do we rob you?" In tithes and in offerings! You are indeed accursed, for you, the whole nation, rob me. Bring the whole tithe into the storehouse, that there may be food in my house, and try me in this, says the LORD of hosts: Shall I not open for you the floodgates of heaven, to pour down blessing upon you without measure?

TV preachers have seen
in this marvelous text
something that's not there:
that, if we'll just respect
what the text suggests,
we can be free of financial care.

The Prosperity Gospel, it's called,
and millions have become enthralled
with the promises it offers;
but usually what's occurred
is that followers of their word
have filled only the promisers' coffers.

For three more reflections on *Haggai*, *Zechariah*, and *Malachi*, see the first volume of *Funny Things*, pp. 208–209.

Straddling the Testaments

Trees of Eden and Calvary
(Genesis 3:8-14; Luke 23:32-43)

Beneath Eden's trees
they could but cower
fearful their deed's seeds
would reach full flower.

From access to the Life-Tree
they were curtly banished;
as their hope for Life shrank,
their spirit languished.

Upon Calvary's trees
they hang suspended,
hoping the poison-fruit's effects
will soon be ended.

From among the trees' poisoned fruit
one pendant, penitent, brings suit,
and his cry through anguished throat
reaches the needed Antidote.

Part Two

The Book of The New Covenant

The Happy Exchange
(John 2:7–11a, 19:28–30)

He had served them
the best wine last,
but they thanked Him
with the spoils
of their ruinous past.

The sop was meant to slake the pain
but 'twas a gesture largely vain.
It was mostly a taunt,
its aroma lingering to haunt
and render his last hour even more sour.

The world for whom he'd saved
the best wine 'til last
now offered him for his final repast
the bitter dregs
of its befouled kegs.

Yet He'd once more hear
His mother's prayer
and bring forth,
from his blood and the surrounding air,
a wine that conveys for e'er His saving care.

5—The Gospels

Perspective

Numbers that Count

The book of Numbers is in the OT.
In the NT a few numbers are key.
Numbers that are key in the NT
are *twelve, seven, four,* and *three.*

Twelve, the product of three times four,
numbers the baskets of loaves and fish
filled to repletion at the end of the day
our Lord held the hunger of thousands at bay.

Twelve's also the number of men (just men!)
Christ names to help lead the fight against sin.
Presumably the women, by sin less encumbered,
were so numerous they're largely unnamed and unnumbered.

Seven, the *sum* of four and three,
is the number of signs, revealing God's glory,
John the evangel recounts
in telling the Christ's story.

As a symbol of perfection seven
also stands for Heaven
and Heaven's special day on earth,
the Sabbath giv'n us for rest and rebirth.

Matthew, Mark, Luke, and John
are writers believers have learned to count on.
They make us appreciate the number *four*
though they seem largely indiff'rent
to any numerical score.

Finally, *three* enumerates our Savior's days
in the realm of night
when against Death He took up our fight—
three too the women who went to the tomb
to learn that for Him it hadn't enough room.

Nativity and Childhood

The Author of Word and World
(Matthew 1–2; Luke 1–2; Genesis 1; John 1:14)

"The earth was without form and void when . . . [the] Spirit appeared; just so Mary's womb was a void until the Spirit of God filled it with a child who was His Son."   —Raymond Brown, *The Birth of the Messiah* [42]

Words biological bear truths theological
as both the creation's birth
and the incarnate Word's arrival on earth
evoke images of a womb serving as delivery room,
first, for the evolving creation, then, for the Author of its salvation.

Both *tohu*[43] and Mary's womb,
void and barren of form,
become media of *Spiritus Creator*
who's also holy writ's
Muse and Translator.

As Creator of the World and Speaker of the Word
the Spirit's the source of all good that's occurred.
Was the intention, first, to juxtapose this disparate pair,
then lead World to conform to Word,
getting the "I" out of there?

Turning Points
(Luke 1:30-32a)

Then the angel said to her, "Do not be afraid, Mary, for you have found favor with God. Behold, you will conceive in your womb and bear a son, and you shall name him Jesus. He will be great and will be called Son of the Most High...."

> Blake's painting of history's frontispiece[44]
> shows Eve and the serpent, mid-kiss,
> at the fateful moment of release
> when passed the fruit that led us amiss.
>
> Responding to God's angel in a later year
> and reversing our race's trajectory south,
> Mary conceives the bodied Word by ear,
> countering that sad exchange by mouth.
>
> The experiences of these mothers
> and those of sainted others
> show we must hear with Mary's ear
> the Word offering life in a higher gear.

"Can Anything Good...?"
(Matthew 1:18-25; John 1:46)

But Nathanael said to him, "Can anything good come from Nazareth?" Philip said to him, "Come and see." John

Now this is how the birth of Jesus Christ came about. When his mother Mary was betrothed to Joseph, but before they lived together, she was found with child through the holy Spirit. Matthew 1:18

Nature doth better work than art, yet Thine
Out vie both works of nature and of art ...
   —*Meditation Fifty-Six, Second Series*, Edward Taylor (1642–1729)

> His conception, though hardly conventional,
> was clearly divinely intentional—

beyond the bounds of natural law
but on a course the Lord oversaw.

The story says little else
relating to its how,
but we can be sure it raised
many a Nazarene brow.

Surprised Mothers
(Luke 1:26-45)

During those days Mary set out and traveled to the hill country in haste to a town of Judah, where she entered the house of Zechariah and greeted Elizabeth. When Elizabeth heard Mary's greeting, the infant leaped in her womb, and Elizabeth, filled with the holy Spirit, cried out in a loud voice and said, "Most blessed are you among women, and blessed is the fruit of your womb...." 39–42

Miracle meets miracle, virgin maid, barren frau,
astounded by the what, ignorant of the how:
pregnant with awe but unafraid,
exuberant in the stories they trade.

The word had reached Elizabeth third hand
delivered by an angel to and through her man;
she, the older of the two,
could scarcely wait for its promise to come true.

Mary the virgin, for her part,
first heard the Word in her heart,
then cradled Him in her womb,
totally elated despite portents of doom.

Were they aware,
this unlikely pair,
of the infinite gains
latent in their labor pains?

The Do-Plenty Dad
(Matthew 1:24)

When Joseph awoke, he did as the angel of the Lord had commanded him and took his wife into his home.

Though he seems just a bystander
Joseph hardly deserves the slander
of the epithet, "do-nothing dad."

True, like many a man he may have slept through the night
while his beloved labored, through pain and through fright,
to bear him an heir in truth and in right.

Yet of all such slumberers it is only this man
who helped launch the family Christian,
which on that night of nights began.

Through a love miraculously transcendent
he'd banished all doubt, all resentment,
taking Mary at her word.

Then, caught between Caesar's law and God's gospel,
he saw her through conditions hostile
to see that the Holy Birth occurred.

The No-Show
(Luke 2:1-7)

Where was Mary's mama
in the Nativity drama?

During Mary's conception
she'd been central to a miracle,
and, if she'd been there for Jesus' reception,
Mary surely would've been lyrical.

For some reason, though,
St. Anne was a no-show,
leaving the midwifing
to an average Joe.

Focus on the Gift, but Don't Ignore the Packaging
(Luke 1:26-31, 2:1-7)

She wrapped him in swaddling clothes and laid him in a manger....   2:7b

It's extremely hard to catch God's drift
when we see how (S)He packages the first Christmas Gift.
Couldn't (S)He have found a fitter Labor Room
than a peasant teenager's humble womb?

And couldn't God have provided, too, a more elegant wrap
for the Savior of the world's first out-of-the-womb nap?
With one sniff Social Services could have scented danger
as they found him swaddled meekly in an animal's manger.

Though what shepherds and Magi saw must have caused a sensation,
it probably won no prizes for style of presentation,
but before letting its tawdriness put our noses out of joint,
perhaps we should stop to ask: "Lord, what's Your point?"

When, later, we hear the Gift say, "You must be born of the Spirit,"
like Nicodemus we're inclined not to believe but to fear it.
But God's willing, says the Story, to be born of lowly flesh,
to give us reborn spirits, redeemed and refreshed.

Don't ignore the tawdry trimmings, then, but take in the sharp contrasts
in this scene of God born Human, framed by ox and ass,
and be grateful that the Story makes us all sort and sift
through ugly but telling packaging to find the glorious Gift.

In Simeon's Wake
(Luke 2:28)

Simeon took him in his arms and praised God ...   (NRSV)

The pastor's face bears a smile
as (s)he walks the east-facing aisle,
raising before the congregation
a new child of salvation.

In a window above
depicting a descending dove
centuries are shorn
and a vision reborn.

Just risen from the waters
with his holy orders
Jesus recalls from his mother's lore
a significant day of yore.

Then 'twas not the hands of John
but those of Simeon
that raised him for all to see
in a V for Victory.

Foreshadowings
(Luke 2:34-35)

... and Simeon blessed them and said to Mary his mother, "Behold, this child is destined for the fall and rise of many in Israel, and to be a sign that will be contradicted (and you yourself a sword will pierce) so that the thoughts of many hearts may be revealed."

In commenting on the event at hand
thus spoke the wise and wizened man:
"As thy riven womb
foreshadows the shattered tomb,
so thy child's cleft penis
portends a sword cleaving
the earthbound love of Venus."

Two Orphans
(Matthew 1:18-24; Luke 2:39-49; Genesis 2:18-23, 3:1-6)

Born without a mother,
could Eve have turned out other
than a babe in the wood,
fuzzy re the difference between evil and good?

Jesus came up a parent short too,
yet was surer-footed in getting through
the critical choices along his way
toward the Creation's most fateful day.

Though having no natural father
may have left him knowing less than he oughta,
the man whose feet led him to Bethlehem
helped give him the wisdom that lit up Jerusalem.

The God who was Adam's and Eve's Obstetrician
is to Jesus not only a Father
Who saw him through birth and mission
but, at Joe's and Mary's behest, his wise Pediatrician.

A Meaningful Trip
(Matthew 2:13-15)

When they had departed, behold, the angel of the Lord appeared to Joseph in a dream and said, "Rise, take the child and his mother, flee to Egypt, and stay there until I tell you. Herod is going to search for the child to destroy him." Joseph rose and took the child and his mother by night and departed for Egypt. He stayed there until the death of Herod, that what the Lord had said through the prophet might be fulfilled, "Out of Egypt I called my son."

How significant it is
he was counted among fugitives—
signaling the harvest he's destined to reap'll
embrace affrighted, in-flight people!

The Deliverer's Deliverer
(The donkey's angle, part 3[45])
(Matthew 2:14)

"Then Joseph got up, took the child and his mother by night, and went to Egypt... "

> I bore God on my back
> from Bethl'em's welcoming shack
> across the hostile sand
> to refuge in Egypt land.
>
> When the Lord helps His own find redress
> it's not a matter of worthiness
> but one wherein the most humble steed
> can be called to perform a crucial deed.

The Savior's Surrogates
(Matthew 2:16-18)

Herod was furious on realizing that he had been fooled by the wise men, and in Bethlehem and its surrounding district he had all the male children killed who were two years old or less, reckoning by the date he had been careful to ask the wise men. (NJB)

> It was surely not God's will!
> It gives our spines a chill
> when one of Herod's cruelest mandates
> engulfs our Savior's surrogates!
>
> Should those teaching atonement by substitution
> not honor Herod in a resolution?
> By his decree many died for the One
> so that before His work was done
> the One could die for the many, not excepting any.
>
> We can imagine long waits
> for some at the pearly gates
> but against our conscience it harshly grates
> to think that could have happened to the surrogates.

Boys Will Be . . .
(Luke 2:52)

And Jesus advanced (in) wisdom and age and favor before God and man.

Surely he was a typical boy
with a favorite toy
who played with typical boys,
sharing their snits and joys.

It probably gave him pleasure
to engage in hunts for treasure.
Whether as champ or challenger
he'd have played with zeal the role of scavenger.

There were probably even coals
for his parents to rake. . .
and an occasional correction
for a childish mistake.

Perhaps he enjoyed a serenity
that accompanied his divinity
but, given his human identity,
he must also have wrestled envy and enmity,

The Ro(u)te to Wisdom
(Luke 2:39-40, 52)

When they had fulfilled all the prescriptions of the law of the Lord, they returned to Galilee, to their own town of Nazareth. The child grew and became strong, filled with wisdom; and the favor of God was upon him . . . And Jesus advanced (in) wisdom and age and favor before God and man.

It's outré today to learn by rote
but in antiquity, we should note,
in matters curricular the student's vote
mattered little in the way things were done.

In *shul* elective courses were non-flyers;
rabbis didn't consult students' desires;
texts, not texting, lit talmidim's[46] fires
and they mastered those texts one by one.

Much of Jesus' remarkable human wisdom
likely came from Nazareth's *shul* system,
where, beneath the eyes of learned rabbis,
he was given text after text to memorize.

The Virgin
(Matthew 1:18-25, 13:55; Mark 3:31, 6:3; Luke 1:26-31; John 7:3-5; Acts 1:14)

Who is this woman, that God should so adorn her?
What made her seemingly betrayed betrothed
decide not to scorn her?
What's required to complete her true picture?
Is it completed by natural motherhood
or by virginity that's a fixture?

On one hand we have the texts
speaking of Jesus' brothers and sisters,
on the other a tradition,
taught us by fathers and sisters,
that she remains sexually alone,
never biblically known.

Tides ebb and flow theologically
on the subject of Mary's destiny:
Does she so partake of her Son's divinity
as to remain a virgin through eternity,
or does she attest to his full humanity
by ans'ring nature's call to maternity?[47]

Launching the Ministry

The Terms of a Trade
(Mark 1:2-6)

As it is written in Isaiah the prophet: "Behold, I am sending my messenger ahead of you; he will prepare your way. A voice of one crying out in the desert: 'Prepare the way of the Lord, make straight his paths.'" John (the) Baptist appeared in the desert proclaiming a baptism of repentance for the forgiveness of sins. People of the whole Judean countryside and all the inhabitants of Jerusalem were going out to him and were being baptized by him in the Jordan River as they acknowledged their sins. John was clothed in camel's hair, with a leather belt around his waist. He fed on locusts and wild honey.

He was dressed in camel's hair
and had about him the air
of a hermit who'd shed secular care
to retreat to a desert pass
all but bare of plants and grass.

The place had him so seduced
that for food he was reduced
to a menu set by creatures of modest diet—
bees exhausted by searches for pollen
and locusts fed on the fruit of a Garden fallen.

The camel that had lent him its skin
died, likely, serving a desert denizen,
a caravanning wanderer in wilderness wastes
ignorant entirely of fashionable tastes
but arrested beside the river's water
by the words of this spiritual marauder.

The preacher had bartered with him, perhaps,
for the dead camel's skin
by offering, in exchange,
freedom from the yoke of sin.

Awe
(Matthew 3:11-12; cf. Isaiah 52:7)

"I am baptizing you with water, for repentance, but the one who is coming after me is mightier than I. I am not worthy to carry his sandals. He will baptize you with the holy Spirit and fire. His winnowing fan is in his hand. He will clear his threshing floor and gather his wheat into his barn, but the chaff he will burn with unquenchable fire."

Who is this who fans the flames,
who knows people's hearts as well as their names,
who sees not only the deed but the motivating desire
and from the wheat sifts chaff for the unquenchable fire?

John sees in him far more than a peer,
one who stirs an awe surpassing fear
and whose shoes cover feet of such astounding beauty
they convince him he's not worthy of shoe-toting duty.

The Coo of the Dove
(Matthew 3:13-17)

After Jesus was baptized, he came up from the water and behold, the heavens were opened (for him), and he saw the Spirit of God descending like a dove (and) coming upon him. And a voice came from the heavens, saying, "This is my beloved Son, with whom I am well pleased." 16–17

Adam, Eve, and I went with Him into the river's bed
and rose soon after from the dominion of the dead,
resurrected by the Dove circling His head.

Up 'til then we'd lived in the shadows of other birds,
hawks, eagles, and vultures who sensed in our empty words
the choking scent of death haunting every breath.

When He came up from the waters our hopes came up too
as we heard our marching orders in the Dove's coo
that drowned the cries of the scavengers
and armed us to face creation's vile and noxious challengers.

The Scapegoat and the Lamb
(Matthew 4:5-7; Leviticus 16:6-10)

Then the devil took him to the holy city, and made him stand on the parapet of the temple, and said to him, "If you are the Son of God, throw yourself down. For it is written: 'He will command his angels concerning you and 'with their hands they will support you, lest you dash your foot against a stone.'" Jesus answered him, "Again it is written, 'You shall not put the Lord, your God, to the test.'"
Matthew

Did the spirit of Azazel haunt his trail?
Both scapegoat and Lamb bear the sins of the people,
the goat to a cliff, the Lamb to a steeple,
but can the atoning mission they're assigned to keep
best be accomplished by a flying leap?

The goat bound for Azazel
had done its job well
if, borne on its back,
Israel's sin fell,
sating the lust of a minion of hell.

Was that the route for the atoning Lamb too?
Was falling for Satan all He had to do
to deliver His people from their sins
and see His mission through?

Deeds and Interactions

So much for Jesus the Teetotaler. . .
(John 2:1-11)

Jesus told them, "Fill the jars with water." So they filled them to the brim. Then he told them, "Draw some out now and take it to the headwaiter." So they took it. And when the headwaiter tasted the water that had become wine, without knowing where it came from . . . , the headwaiter called the bridegroom and said to him, "Everyone serves good wine first, and then when people have drunk freely, an inferior one; but you have kept the good wine until now." 2:7–10

"Some think I could never party,
much less partake of strong wine,
but take a hard look at Cana, me hearty—
that should change your mind.

"Some who read my story most literally
in this case oppose such reading bitterly,
insisting my sober state of mind
approved only the fresh juice of the vine.

"None are so blind
as those who will not see:
blind indeed are those
who'd make a teetotaler of me."

A Roof-Raising Tale
(Mark 2:2-12)

When Jesus returned to Capernaum after some days, it became known that he was at home. Many gathered together so that there was no longer room for them, not even around the door, and he preached the word to them. They came bringing to him a paralytic carried by four men. Unable to get near Jesus because of the crowd, they opened up the roof above him. After they had broken through, they let down the mat on which the paralytic was lying. When Jesus saw their faith, he said to the paralytic, "Child, your sins are forgiven." Now some of the scribes were sitting there asking themselves, "Why does this man speak that way? He is blaspheming. Who but God alone can forgive sins?" Jesus immediately knew in his mind what they were thinking to themselves, so he said, "Why are you thinking such things in your hearts? Which is easier, to say to the paralytic, 'Your sins are forgiven,' or to say, 'Rise, pick up your mat and walk'? But that you may know that the Son of Man has authority to forgive sins on earth"—he said to the paralytic, "I say to you, rise, pick up your mat, and go home." He rose, picked up his mat at once, and went away in the sight of everyone. They were all astounded and glorified God, saying, "We have never seen anything like this."

> The jamb was jammed,
> the door in effect slammed,
> but they were only slowed
> in reaching Jesus with their suffering load.
>
> His home was open, his welcome theirs,
> and, despite the lack of outside stairs,
> he lifted not a word to stop
> the lifting of their burden to his rooftop.
>
> The insurance adjuster would not be pleased
> but their thoughts were on a friend diseased;
> of that we have sufficient proof
> in their eagerness to break through the low-pitched roof.
>
> Soon at his feet the patient lay,
> thrilled to hear the Doctor say,
> "Be grateful for your faithful friends!
> Their faith's helped win you release from your sins!"
>
> Thereupon a murmur rose:
> he'd stepped again on the elders' toes.
> How dare he assume the role of God
> and dare to forgive this pitiful clod.
>
> In face of their doubt he was quick to say,
> "Suppose we take another way
> to prove pains that make us writhe and bend
> may stem from sin deep within."
>
> To the prone man he then said,
> "Rise, take up your bed,
> depart;
> God can heal your body by healing your heart."

Nicodemus
(John 3:1-17, 19:38-42)

After this, Joseph of Arimathea, secretly a disciple of Jesus for fear of the Jews, asked Pilate if he could remove the body of Jesus. And Pilate permitted it. So he came and took his body. Nicodemus, the one who had first come to him at night, also came bringing a mixture of myrrh and aloes weighing about one hundred pounds. They took the body of Jesus and bound it with burial cloths along with the spices, according to the Jewish burial custom. Now in the place where he had been crucified there was a garden, and in the garden a new tomb, in which no one had yet been buried. So they laid Jesus there because of the Jewish preparation day.... 19:38–42a

> The first time, he'd approached self-protectively,
> under cover of darkness.
> Now, retrospectively,
> he moved boldly and effectively,
> in the light released by the cross's starkness.
>
> If we ask what intervenes
> between the two scenes
> we may discover the new birth
> that's shifted his allegiance
> to heaven from earth.

The Nabi's[48] Choice
(Luke 7:36-50)

A Pharisee invited him to dine with him, and he entered the Pharisee's house and reclined at table. Now there was a sinful woman in the city who learned that he was at table in the house of the Pharisee. Bringing an alabaster flask of ointment, she stood behind him at his feet weeping and began to bathe his feet with her tears. Then she wiped them with her hair, kissed them, and anointed them with the ointment. When the Pharisee who had invited him saw this he said to himself, "If this man were a prophet, he would know who and what sort of woman this is who is touching him, that she is a sinner." Jesus said to him in reply, "Simon, I have something to say to you." "Tell me, teacher," he said. "Two people were in debt to a certain creditor; one owed five hundred days' wages and the other owed fifty. Since they were unable to repay the debt, he forgave it for both. Which of them will love him more?" Simon said in reply, "The one, I suppose, whose larger debt was forgiven." He said to him, "You have judged rightly." Then he turned to the woman and said to Simon, "Do you see this woman? When I entered your house, you did not give me water for my feet, but she has bathed them with her tears and wiped them with her hair. You did not give me a kiss, but she has not ceased kissing my feet since the time I entered. You did not anoint my head with oil, but she anointed my feet with ointment. So I tell you, her many sins have been forgiven; hence, she has shown great love. But the one to whom little is forgiven, loves little." 36–47

Who's this, who dares barge in on dinner?
An uninvited guest! A known sinner!
Of all places, in the house of a Pharisee
who lives near virtue's apogee!

Who's this, who shares the great man's table?
A hill-country commoner who's hard to label . . .
Of all places, in the house of a Pharisee,
a pairing off you'd not expect to see . . .

She came because of stories she'd heard
of things he'd done just by saying a word—
of a centurion's slave and a widow's son at Nain
whose master's and mother's prayers hadn't been in vain.

Ignoring the house's master,
who stared at, then past her,
she went straight to his strange guest's feet
to offer homage entire, complete.

Capture the picture on your mind's screen:
the holy man towering and glowering above,
the sinner cowering below, in fear and love,
with the object of both's attention sitting between.

To which of them would he pay heed—
to the one he'd be smart to please, or the one in obvious need?

> Ignoring the one with virtue in the bank,
> he attends the one on whom his host pulls rank.
>
> "Simon, Simon," said he,
> "you've shown me but slight hospitality;
> but this woman, with her perfume,
> refreshes not just me but the whole room.
>
> "Accused of vice and vagrancy,
> she's responded as humbly as she has fragrantly,
> and now, to be freed of her enormous sense of debt,
> she must be forgiven for what she yearns to forget."

Holes in Kipling's Case
(Luke 10:38-42)

The Lord said to her in reply, "Martha, Martha, you are anxious and worried about many things, There is need of only one thing. Mary has chosen the better part and it will not be taken from her. . . ."   41–42

> "because . . . [Martha] lost her temper once,
> and because she was rude to the Lord her guest,
> Her Sons must wait upon Mary's Sons,
> world without end, reprieve, or rest."
> —Lines 3 and 4, Rudyard Kipling's "The Sons of Martha"
>
> As they sit dreaming of pie in the sky
> do Mary's kids on Martha's rely?
> A Lamarckian would likely say so,
> but whoa, Mr. Kipling, whoa:
> The Darwinian majority would surely say No.
>
> That this tale of Kipling's Just *Ain't* So
> is what other evidence also seems to show:
> Though M and M be sweet
> as their namesake candy,
> there's no hint they were wooed by anyone manly . . .

A Broad-Minded Walk along the Narrow Way
(Matthew 7:13-14; Mark 2:16; 1 Corinthians 9:19-22; 2 Corinthians 5:21)

"Enter through the narrow gate; for the gate is wide and the road broad that leads to destruction, and those who enter through it are many. How narrow the gate and constricted the road that leads to life. And those who find it are few."   Matthew 7:13–14

Some scribes who were Pharisees saw that he was eating with sinners and tax collectors and said to his disciples, "Why does he eat with tax collectors and sinners?"   Mark 2:16

Although I am free in regard to all, I have made myself a slave to all so as to win over as many as possible. To the Jews I became like a Jew to win over Jews; to those under the law I became like one under the law—though I myself am not under the law—to win over those under the law. To those outside the law I became like one outside the law—though I am not outside God's law but within the law of Christ—to win over those outside the law. To the weak I became weak, to win over the weak. I have become all things to all, to save at least some.   1 Corinthians 9:19–22

The funny-paradoxical thing about Jesus' counsel regarding the narrow way is that his behavior contradicts—or, more accurately, redefines—what many of us would take his words to mean. When it comes to life-practices it is the Pharisees, not Jesus, who seem to walk the narrow way. Jesus walks an apparently care-free but actually care-driven way among outcasts and untouchables. How are we to reconcile such a walk with his talk about a narrow way? Obviously, his Pharisaic critics weren't able to do so.

    Christianity's greatest teacher this side of Jesus helps us out here. "[God] made him to be sin . . . who knew no sin," Paul writes,[49] and he then emulates his Lord's strategy of becoming all things to all sorts of people that he might by all means save some.

> They're almost one,
> the Lord and His servant,
> the latter of the former's way
> devoutly observant—

each in his place and time
intently single-minded,
using all available means
to reach the sin-blinded.

Even Winds and Waves Obey Him . . .
(Matthew 8:23-27; Mark 4:35-41; Luke 8:22-25)

He got into a boat and his disciples followed him. Suddenly a violent storm came up on the sea, so that the boat was being swamped by waves; but he was asleep. They came and woke him, saying, "Lord, save us! We are perishing! He said to them, "Why are you terrified, O you of little faith?" Then he got up, rebuked the winds and the sea, and there was great calm. The men were amazed and said, "What sort of man is this, whom even the winds and the sea obey?"
Matthew

The shortest verse in Scripture
says simply, "Jesus wept;"
another, far more alarming,
that, during a storm, Jesus slept.

"Lord," cried the apostles,
"how can you sleep,
leaving us to struggle alone
with the demons of the deep?"

"Oh ye of little faith,
why do you disturb my slumber,
adding to my burdens,
already of sufficient number?

"How many of you are fishermen here?
How many know how to tuck sail and steer,
keeping your bark afloat through the stoutest wind shear?"
Then, in a voice as soothing as Gilead's finest balm,
He spoke to his friends, the winds—and they grew calm.

A Call for Health Reform?
(Mark 5:25-26)

There was a woman afflicted with hemorrhages for twelve years. She had suffered greatly at the hands of many doctors and had spent all that she had. Yet she was not helped but only grew worse.

Perhaps we should assign proctors
to assess the work of doctors.
Whatever the verdict of the statisticians,
Lord deliver us from the hands of *"many physicians."*

The Last Laugh
(Mark 5:21-43)

And they laughed at him.   5:40a (*NRSV*)

The first laugh, derisive,
luckily wasn't decisive
as the Christ's powers of healing
broke through their faith's low ceiling
to exceed the bounds of the medical craft
and educe a hearty and happy last laugh.

The Bellwether of Sin? Or a Stand-in?
(John 8:2-11)

Jesus straightened up and said to her, "Woman, where are they? Has no one condemned you?" She replied, "No one, sir." Then Jesus said, "Neither do I condemn you. Go, [and] from now on do not sin any more."   10-11

Blake presumed she was the Mary
whose loves were known to vary.[50]
True or no, Jesus made her accusers wary
lest lookers-on be allowed to see
their own unchastity.

But should we take her for the Magdalen,
that bellwether of sin,
or better hold her anonymous,
a stand-in for all adulterers
who keep a gossipy world aspin?

In any case she was down and out
'til Jesus turned her fortunes about,
saving her, with the grace that saves the world,
from the stereotype of Naughty Girl,
and enjoining her to choose the Way
that arrived with His new day.

An Unobserved Precedent?
(Matthew 8:14, 16:17-19; Mark 1:30; Luke 4:38)

Jesus entered the house of Peter, and saw his mother-in-law lying in bed with a fever.   Matthew 8:14

Was Peter the only pope
ever to wear the marital rope?
Have all popes since had to choose
between wearing the good noose
and serving as Prime Bearer of the good news?

Such Company!
(Matthew 9:10-13; Mark 2:14-17; Luke 5:27-28)

While he was at table in his house, many tax collectors and sinners came and sat with Jesus and his disciples. The Pharisees saw this and said to his disciples, "Why does your teacher eat with tax collectors and sinners?"   Matthew 9:10-11

How could he be so lax
as to consort with those who tax!
Did he mean to condone
sins for which these turncoats
surely would have to atone?

Polls would have suggested there was adequate data
to prove collecting Rome's taxes made you a traitor
or at the very least a very poor Jew—
yet the job still managed to seduce quite a few.

It was bad enough that he ate with the hicks:
now he was messing in politics!
All roads lead to Rome, it was said,
but should they take with them your family's bread?

Yet to all this he turned a deaf ear,
a course hardly designed to endear
him to patriots of the super sort,
'specially zealots who killed Romans for sport.

He thus proved his mission was not to please
pursuers of kosher identities
but instead to live out a gospel of love
that embraced even enemies.

The Aquathon
(Matthew 14:22-33)

Then he made the disciples get into the boat and precede him to the other side, while he dismissed the crowds. . . . Meanwhile the boat, already a few miles offshore, was being tossed about by the waves, for the wind was against it. During the fourth watch of the night, he came toward them, walking on the sea. 22, 24a

As people of the desert, the children of Israel developed a decidedly ambivalent attitude toward water—one combining gratitude for its often rare availability with terror before large quantities of it. This ambivalence colored their view of the Sea of Galilee. As Palestine's largest freshwater lake (7 miles wide, 13 long) it was the region's main source of drinking water and seafood. On the other hand, its frequent thunder storms, popularly blamed on demons in the depths, were a source of great dread.

In the fourth watch of the night
the Twelve became consumed with fright,

cast into throes of pathos
by demons of marine chaos.

Several miles from each shore,
tossed from portside, starboard, aft, and afore,
they frantically worked to lower sail,
hugging for dear life mainmast and rail.

Half a millennium before, Pheidippides
mastered much land but no stormy seas
from the jubilant town of Marathon
to announce to Athens that the Greeks had won.

But none before or since has walked or run
anything like this night's Aquathon,
treading through the squalls of the Galilee
and rendering it, miraculously, demon-free.

At least 3K he must have strode
as if on a smooth, hard-surface road,
to bring timely rescue
to the Ship of Faith's despairing crew.

Today's seas are often stormy too
and when we wonder if we can see them through
it's good to know we can depend upon
th' Inventor of the Aquathon.

Pete's Propensity
(Matthew 14:22, 24-33)

When the disciples saw him walking on the sea they were terrified. "It is a ghost," they said, and they cried out in fear. At once (Jesus) spoke to them, "Take courage, it is I; do not be afraid." Peter said to him in reply, "Lord, if it is you, command me to come to you on the water." He said, "Come." Peter got out of the boat and began to walk on the water toward Jesus. But when he saw how (strong) the wind was he became frightened; and, beginning to sink, he cried out, "Lord, save me!" Immediately Jesus stretched out his hand and caught him, and said to him, "O you of little faith, why did you doubt?"

25-31

With two main principles of action—
impulse and dread—
Simon Peter made a habit
of getting in over his head.

Getting out of the boat
hadn't seemed hard
as long as he'd kept Jesus
as the focus of his regard.

But whenever he failed to go
where his Lord led,
Pete's impulse gave way quickly
to consuming dread.

Many things must happen
before he'll understand
how important it is
to hang on to Jesus' hand.

The Bitter and the Sweet
(Luke 10:15)

"And as for you, Capernaum, did you want to be raised high as heaven? You shall be flung down to hell." (KJV)

"In every religion, there has been a Tartarus as well as an Elysium, a place provided for the punishment of the wicked, as well as one for the reward of the just." —Adam Smith, *The Theory of Moral Sentiments*, p. 110.

Less separable than hands and feet,
those ultimate forms of bitter and sweet,
Elysium and Tartarus, Heaven and Hell,
seem indispensable to the stories we tell.

How could we cope if,
amid all the things we go through,
there were no Heaven to wish our friends,
no Hell to tell foes to go to.

Mixed Feelings
(Mark 6:17-29)

Herod feared John, knowing him to be a righteous and holy man, and kept him in custody. When he heard him speak he was very much perplexed, yet he liked to listen to him. 20

> Funny, isn't it, how opposites attract,
> so even porcine Herod
> could like lean John's act—
> at least 'til he fell under the sway
> of the seductive Salomé.

Headhunters
(Matthew 14:1-11; Mark 6:17-29; Judges 4:1-23; Judith 1:1-16:25)

. . . at a birthday celebration for Herod, the daughter of Herodias performed a dance before the guests and delighted Herod so much that he swore to give her whatever she might ask for. Prompted by her mother, she said, "Give me here on a platter the head of John the Baptist." Matthew 14:6-8

> Was it because they got tired of dealing
> with the proverbial glass ceiling
> that Jael, Judith, and Salomé
> attacked male authority in a violent way?
>
> Each uses a woman's strength—
> an alluring hospitality,
> a flirtatious rascality,
> a seductive musicality—
> to probe for her target's flaws at length.
>
> Jael took Sisera into her tent
> hiding cleverly her malicious intent,
> 'til, after lulling him to sleep,
> she could assassinate the creep.

Judith flirted her way into Holofernes' tent
where, after getting him drunk,
she could her feelings vent
and behead him as he slept on his bunk.

Salome's methods were less direct,
one could even say circumspect:
she used Herod, the royal jerk,
to do her and her mother's dirty work.

Neither heroines Jael and Judy
nor Sal the villainess
are at all hesitant their aims to press;
each, far from shrinking back in dread,
goes straight for her chosen target's head.

A Unique Résumé
(John 11:1–12:11)

And the chief priests plotted to kill Lazarus too, because many of the Jews were turning away and believing in Jesus because of him   12:10–11

We may imagine Sheol's warden
posts guards by the Jordan
lest, in some strange way,
traffic should become two-way.

But the guards' worst fears are realized
and their escape-free record drastic'ly revised
when, just as Lazarus starts to turn to dust,
Jesus lends his weight to the oar
to bring his friend back to the nearer shore.

Stunned by the much-bruited sensation
of this amazing resuscitation,
enemies of the man from Nazareth
plot both the raised and the Raiser's death.

> Whether the raised one later died
> of other causes or homicide
> we are not privileged to know—
> only that on his second dying day
> he completed a unique résumé.

How Big is the House?
(Matthew 12:22-29; Mark 3:22-27; Luke 11:14-22; 1 Peter 3:18-19)

Then they brought to him a demoniac who was blind and mute. He cured the mute person so that he could speak and see. All the crowd was astounded, and said, "Could this perhaps be the Son of David?" But when the Pharisees heard this, they said, "This man drives out demons only by the power of Beelzebul, the prince of demons." But he knew what they were thinking and said to them, "Every kingdom divided against itself will be laid waste, and no town or house divided against itself will stand. And if Satan drives out Satan, he is divided against himself; how, then, will his kingdom stand? And if I drive out demons by Beelzebul, by whom do your own people drive them out? Therefore they will be your judges. But if it is by the Spirit of God that I drive out demons, then the kingdom of God has come upon you. How can anyone enter a strong man's house and steal his property, unless he first ties up the strong man? Then he can plunder his house.   Matthew

For Christ also suffered for sins once, the righteous for the sake of the unrighteous, that he might lead you to God. Put to death in the flesh, he was brought to life in the spirit. In it he also went to preach to the spirits in prison. . . .   1 Peter

> Our Lord's analogy implies imperiously
> that He has the "strong man" under arrest,
> and perhaps it's an analogy we should take more seriously
> if we want justice for *everyone* Satan's oppressed.

> Beelzebul's well known as the prince of this world
> but there's a nether world too, says popular lore,
> and that's where his banner's more fully unfurled,
> a fact a just God wouldn't likely ignore.

> So a question Jesus' analogy brings into view
> asks if 'Bul's house has one story, or two:
> *How many* of Satan's goods is the Christ sent to plunder?
> Just those on grade level, or also those down under?

Teachings

Questions re Destiny
(Matthew 5:22,29,30; 10:28; 18:9; 23:15; Mark 9:43,45,47; Luke 12:5)

The word translated "hell" in English renderings of Jesus' teachings is *Gehenna*,[51] the name of Jerusalem's "unquenchably"[52] aflame solid waste dump. Located in the Valley of Hinnom just outside the city, the site was considered accursed not just for its gruesome work of destruction but also as the legendary site of Manasseh's sacrifice of his firstborn to the horrendous appetite of Moloch in the eighth century B.C. As Jerusalem was considered close enough to Heaven to be deemed God's footstool, so the neighboring valley was widely viewed as the point farthest removed from paradise.

> Proud, greedy, wrathful, lazy,
> gluttonous, envious, and unchaste—
> a life so described wouldn't just be crazy
> but a perfect example of solid waste.

> If a single one of these
> is enough to condemn you,
> will adding more take you
> to a more hellish venue?

> And does assignment to Gehenna
> mean loss of all hope?
> Or is it only your life-wasting sins
> that'll go up in smoke?[53]

How Now, "Perfect"?
(Matthew 5:43-48)

"So be perfect, just as your heavenly Father is perfect."   Matthew 5:48

If we're to detect
the aim of Matthew's text
we'll have to respect
its informing context.

Though we're far from God
in every conceivable respect
there's one divine trait
we're *required* to reflect.

As drops of rain and rays of the sun
fall plentifully on everyone,
so God, in His bounteous grace,
enfolds saint and sinner in a single embrace.

It's fitting then that our Lord requires
that we temper our impulses and desires
with an all-embracing charity
that shoots at making us as perfect as (S)He.

My Forte
(Matthew 6:3)

. . . when you give alms, your left hand must not know what your right is doing. . . .   (NJB)

As a model of uncoordination
I can say without reservation
that this rule's for me—
or, metaphorically,
that it's my cup of tea.

Right from left I can hardly tell
and though I might think it swell

> for my left to inform my right,
> I could never bring it off,
> try though I might.

Accessory to a Prior Crhyme
(Matthew 6:9-13; Luke 11:2-4)

In this book's prequel the following verses appeared:

> For creatures of habit the surprising thing
> when they read the Lord's Prayer
> isn't found in what's in it but in what *isn't* there.
>
> Look as carefully as you'd like and you'll still never see
> the prayer's Composer ending it
> "In the name of Me."

Having since reflected on possible *whys* for the noted omission, the best I've been able to come up with is the following:

> Though the Lord's name is a thing to relish
> He didn't intend to make it a fetish;
> He must consider sadly tragic
> efforts to use it like an instrument of magic.

A Splendor Greater than Solomon's
(Matthew 6:28-30)

"Why are you anxious about clothes? Learn from the way the wild flowers grow. They do not work or spin. But I tell you that not even Solomon in all his splendor was clothed like one of them. If God so clothes the grass of the field, which grows today and is thrown into the oven tomorrow, will he not much more provide for you, O you of little faith?"

> Wildflowers' season of glory is short
> but neither Solomon nor any in his court
> could inspire poets to render
> praise adequate to such splendor.

Unlike you and me,
the flowers live worry-free,
yet reflect magnificently
the Lord's creativity.

Which, then, is the greater wonder,
the glory kings build via loot and plunder
or the Providence simple creatures
constantly live under?

Uncommon Wisdom and Common Sense
(Matthew 5:38-39; Mark 6:12; Luke 6:27)

"You have heard that it was said, 'An eye for an eye and a tooth for a tooth.' But I say to you, offer no resistance to one who is evil. When someone strikes you on (your) right cheek, turn the other one to him as well."   Matthew

"But to you who hear I say, love your enemies, do good to those who hate you . . ."   Luke

"Whatever place does not welcome you or listen to you, leave there and shake the dust off your feet in testimony against them."   Mark

"The best way to be rid of an enemy is to make him a friend."
—Abraham Lincoln

Soon after beginning to speak,
in a message for the strong, not the weak,
He said, "When struck on one,
turn the other, cheek."

We wonder what he meant by this.
It puts all our natural ways at risk:
Why extend a second cheek
instead of a fist?

Perhaps the answer's to be found by reaching
deeper into our Lord's teaching,
where we'll learn the likely answer is
"Cheek-turning's proof of love for enemies."

But how literally does our Lord mean to be taken?
Is common sense to be entirely forsaken?
Perhaps His rule's meaning lies in its intended end:
"To those who'd make you a foe, insist on being a friend."

"You mustn't, though, become a constant loser;
to do so could enable a wanton abuser.
Before taking abuse for days or weeks,
remember God only gave you four cheeks."

Wit-nessing: The Serpent's Part
(Matthew 10:16)

"Behold, I am sending you like sheep in the midst of wolves; so be shrewd as serpents *and simple as doves. . . ."*

The first ingredient of witness is wit,
and Jesus tells us to exercise it
not just to jostle and tease
but the way to a hearing to ease.

As the craftiest of creatures
the serpent offers a model for preachers,
or so Jesus seems to say
as he advises those who'd preach *his* way.

As we learn from events in the Garden,
the snake used blandishments and wit
lest Eve's defenses should harden
and prevent it from testing her grit.

So: in spreading the good news too
the first thing you want to do
is to make it easy as possible
for the message to get through.

With the snake's crafty wit
paving the way

the innocent Dove
may get its say.

Wit-nessing: The Dove's Role
(Matthew 10:16)

"Behold I send you out as sheep in the midst of wolves; so be wise as serpents and innocent as doves...." (RSV)

Once burned, twice shy,
so trust must be re-earned
from the gal or guy
who's been duped by a snake
with mischief in its eye.

So, though the serpent's wise,
it may not be able
to win again a seat
at Eve's bargaining table.

Yet p'r'aps it may regain
some of Eve's lost love
if it finds an ally
in the innocent dove.

Tickled to Death
(Luke 6:25b)

"Woe to you who laugh now, for you will grieve and weep...."

Whether you're speaking in prose or rhyming
everything seems to depend on timing.
Great as laughter is as a gift to our race,
each laugh seems to have its own time and place.

Laughter at those cast down
or a smile in response to a frown

that would to God's honor redound
might make you the prey of Heaven's hound.

Overmatched
(Luke 11:20)

But if it is by the finger of God that [I] drive out demons, then the kingdom of God has come upon you.

Let demons do their best
to offend, then malinger,
they must be nonplussed
when God gives them the finger.

As through Jesus God's dawning kingdom
kills the roots evils spring from
we see a potent example of what can be done
by the Spirited work of the Father through the Son!

The Seed of Greatness
(Matthew 13:31–32)

He proposed another parable to them. "The kingdom of heaven is like a mustard seed that a person took and sowed in a field. It is the smallest of all the seeds, yet when full-grown it is the largest of plants. It becomes a large bush, and the birds of the sky come and dwell in its branches."

In what way "great," the mustard plant's seed?
Is it at all superior to that of a common weed?
Is it plausible to claim that this humble herb
can in any way at all be deemed superb?

Or is the parable, perchance, a comment on size?
Does our Lord want anything more than that we realize
that judging by quantitative impressions
might lead us to setbacks and depressions?

Hot dog relishers might quickly concede
that there's merit to the fruit of the mustard seed.

> And, as long as the dog was made of beef,
> Jesus might have accepted that as part of his brief.
>
> But the great thing about the mustard seed,
> the thing we could swear to under oath,
> is, it doesn't let others' impressions of it
> slow down or impede its growth.

Seeing as the Lord Sees
(Luke 10:25-36)

There was a scholar of the law who stood up to test him and said, "Teacher, what must I do to inherit eternal life?" Jesus said to him, "What is written in the law? How do you read it?" He said in reply, "You shall love the Lord, your God, with all your heart, with all your being, with all your strength, and with all your mind, and your neighbor as yourself." He replied to him, "You have answered correctly; do this and you will live." But because he wished to justify himself, he said to Jesus, "And who is my neighbor?" Jesus replied, "A man fell victim to robbers as he went down from Jerusalem to Jericho. They stripped and beat him and went off leaving him half-dead. A priest happened to be going down that road, but when he saw him, he passed by on the opposite side. Likewise a Levite came to the place, and when he saw him, he passed by on the opposite side. But a Samaritan traveler who came upon him was moved with compassion at the sight. He approached the victim, poured oil and wine over his wounds and bandaged them. Then he lifted him up on his own animal, took him to an inn and cared for him. The next day he took out two silver coins and gave them to the innkeeper with the instruction, 'Take care of him. If you spend more than what I have given you, I shall repay you on my way back.' Which of these three, in your opinion, was neighbor to the robbers' victim?"

"God, who alone is true and righteous and powerful in himself, wants to be such also outside himself, namely, in us, in order that he may thus be glorified (for this is the glory of any good that is in anyone, that it must pour itself out beyond itself among others). . . .   Martin Luther[54]

> Why does Jesus change the question
> at the end of the story?

Was he making the suggestion
that true neighbors mightn't be
those who want most to bask in God's glory?

No one could have wanted more
to shine in God's sight
than the pious priest
and the kosher Levite.

Yet so priggish was their piety
they couldn't imagine that what God might see
would focus not on "the righteous"
but on people in misery.

Was God through Christ then saying,
"Those who'd see as I see
must learn that seeing the desperate
is the best way to see me"?

Music to Our Ears
(Luke 12:32)

"Do not be afraid any longer, little flock, for your Father is pleased to give you the kingdom."

The Maker of all must surely take pleasure
in the abundance of Heaven's treasure,
but as frightened sheep we love to hear Christ say
that God takes pleasure too in giving it away.

Looking the Wrong Direction
(Luke 17:20-33)

Asked by the Pharisees when the kingdom of God would come, he said in reply, "The coming of the kingdom of God cannot be observed, and no one will announce, 'Look, here it is,' or, 'There it is.' For behold, the kingdom of God is among you." 20–21

And a Suspicion, like a Finger / Touches my Forehead now and then
That I am looking oppositely / For the site of the Kingdom of Heaven
—Emily Dickinson

"Where's the Kingdom?"
the Pharisees asked,
and the Teacher offered
an answer at last:

"Those who think it's to be found by treadin'
historical trails toward Armageddon
are looking in the wrong direction;
it's not at a terrestrial intersection.

"Nor is the Kingdom so much a place 'within,'
though that's often the site of our battle with sin;
instead it's the neighbors we live '*among*'
from whom we may hear Kingdom anthems sung.

"So it's futile to assign it a street address
or to seek it using a GPS;
the Kingdom's not a place you get to,
but letting the cries of your neighbors
help the God of grace rule you."

A Prognostication about Prognosticators
(Matthew 24:11, 35-36)

Many false prophets will arise and deceive many; ... Heaven and earth will pass away, but my words will not pass away. But of that day and hour no one knows, neither the angels of heaven, nor the Son, but the Father alone.

When he who embodies the Word
says he doesn't know
should we infer he's deferred
to a preacher on a TV show?

The Goats' Point of View
(Matthew 25:31-46)

"When the Son of Man comes in his glory, and all the angels with him, he will sit upon his glorious throne, and all the nations will be assembled before him. And he will separate them one from another, as a shepherd separates the sheep from the goats. He will place the sheep on his right and the goats on his left."   31–33

What's so wrong with us goats?
Can we help it 'cause we're good at seeing the motes
at home in the sheep's eyes?
Should that exclude us from Paradise?

We're horny sorts, that's sure,
and our breath and b. o. are hard to endure,
but why should becoming God's pet
be a matter of hygiene and etiquette?

Should God care how we smell,
and even if (S)He does, how could we tell?
Sheep smell pretty bad too, you know:
one whiff of sweaty wool can exert sufficient pull
to make tear and nose ducts overflow.

What's wrong with us then?
Is it our fault the Lord hears only baa-d from and about us
or that the sheep's p. r. folk can outshout us?
Should we be blamed when, again and again,
our normal habits are construed as sin?

Do you s'pose if we changed our ornery ways
or found a less destructive way to graze,
then, by the beards of our chinny-chin-chin,
the Shepherd would let us in
the Pastures for those forgiven of sin?

Whatever it may take
we'll be glad to do, for Heaven's sake,
to feel included instead of bereft
and win a transfer to Right from Left.

Salvation from Silliness
(Matthew 28:19; Romans 6:3-4; Ephesians 2:4-10)

"Go, therefore, and make disciples of all nations, baptizing them in the name of the Father, and of the Son, and of the holy Spirit...."   Matthew

A funny thing happens as some people make their way through these and other texts about God's grace and Christian baptism. Though these readers insist that salvation has nothing to do with what we do and depends entirely on what God has done and does, they also say that it depends in the last analysis on *how* we do something. Only if we baptize people a certain way, they say, can those baptized become full members of God's family.

Though theology, like any other human enterprise, cannot save us from sin, it can save us from the silliness of thinking that *what* we do can't save us but *how* we do certain things is a prerequisite of right standing with God.

Sound theology can teach us that there are two very meaningful ways of baptizing people: the immersion of believers, and the christening of infants and children. The immersion of declared believers is most effective in symbolizing baptism's *meaning*. It effectively represents our dying to sin (burial) and rising to new life with Christ, which is our way into unity with Him. (Romans 6:3-4 expresses baptism's meaning in these terms.) The christening of infants is the clearest possible expression of baptism's *basis*: the gospel that God accepts us into His family before we choose Him. Since infants are helpless to do anything toward their own salvation, baptizing of this kind expresses most powerfully that salvation is God's doing, not ours. (Ephesians 2:4-10 undergirds this mode of baptism.)

Eastern Orthodox churches combine the two meanings by practicing threefold immersion of infants, the first time in the name of the Father, the second in the name of the Son, and the third in the name of the Spirit. Here as in other regards the Eastern Church conforms its liturgical practice to sound theological principles.

Who's Saved—and How?, or The Long Reach of the Word
(John 1:3b-5, 9)

What came through him was life, and this life was the light of the human race; the light shines in the darkness, and the darkness has not overcome it. . . . The true light, which enlightens everyone, was coming into the world.

In every time and every clime
there's a single source of sunshine.
But how much it enables people to see
isn't determined by you or me
or anybody's theology.

Whether we live in the open air of the public square
or by the dark hearth of a shy Cinderella
one thing we can do
to let the light shine through
is avoid raising a dogmatic umbrella.

Words not in the Word
(John 3:8)

The wind blows where it pleases; you can hear its sound, but you cannot tell where it comes from or where it is going . . .

Sneeze, wheeze, frieze, trapeze,
dental, rental, brindle, swindle,
diddle, daddle, fiddle, faddle,
noodle, poodle, ishkadoodle;
capsule, molecule, miniscule, drool . . .

These words and countless more
that help us keep life's score
didn't make it into the Word,
reminding us that those who'd confine
God's truth to a biblical party line
are peddlers of the absurd.

The Thirteenth Man
(Matthew 26:30; John 17:24)

I tell you, from now on I shall not drink this fruit of the vine until the day when I drink it with you new in the kingdom of my Father." Then, after singing a hymn, they went out to the Mount of Olives.   Matthew

Father, they are your gift to me. I wish that where I am they also may be with me . . .   John

> "And Christ he stude i' the middle there
> And was the thirteenth man,
> And sang the bonniest song that e'er
> Was sung since Time began."
> —Hugh MacDiarmid, "I heard Christ Sing," Stanza 3

It may help ya get over ya
triskaidekaphobia
to know the fate portended
by your end amount
depends on where you end your count.

Isn't it possible that the thirteenth man
within this tiny band,
thirteen centuries before the superstition
acquired its own tradition,[55]
wasn't the infamous Also-ran?

Having declared again and again
that the first should be last,
the Drama's Hero would willingly
have counted himself last.

Sound Footing
(John 13:1-20)

Then he poured water into a basin and began to wash the disciples' feet. . . . Peter said to him, "You will never wash my feet." Jesus answered him, "Unless I wash you, you will have no inheritance with me."   5, 8

Did He wash Judas' feet?
The scribe doesn't say,
but the one called Iscariot
had walked their dusty way.

Once, Peter's faltering feet
had mounted the rolling wave;
now, He who'd saved him as his Lord
acted like his slave.

Sons of Thunder James and John
likely preferred to keep their sandals on;
even their mother's ambitious drumbeat
hadn't prepared them to watch Him wash their feet.

Like Peter and the Sons of Thunder,
others of the Twelve, also filled with wonder,
may have murmured dissents left and right
till He set the matter in the proper light.

Death and Resurrection

Lazarus' Dream
(John 11:1-44)

When Jesus arrived, he found that Lazarus had already been in the tomb for four days.   11:17

Dreamt I, in my dark tomb:
"If I could re-enter my mother's womb,
should I join Nicodemus in such an attempt
or hold such efforts in just contempt?"

"The issue, after all, is moot,
its goal a target at which I dare not shoot:
it lies beyond my capacity
to accomplish reborn reality. . . .
Still, there's that lingering memory.

> "He loved to drop by and lounge
> with Mary, Mart, and me in our wayside house.
> Mightn't I dream He'll do that here too
> and, portending greater things to come,
> my spent body rouse?"

At a Loss
(John 13:16-25)

When he had said this, Jesus was deeply troubled and testified, "Amen, amen, I say to you, one of you will betray me." The disciples looked at one another, at a loss *as to whom he meant. One of his disciples, the one whom Jesus loved was reclining at Jesus' side. So Simon Peter nodded to him to find out whom he meant. He leaned back against Jesus' chest and said to him, "Master, who is it?" Jesus answered, "It is the one to whom I hand the morsel after I have dipped it." So he dipped the morsel and [took it and] handed it to Judas, son of Simon the Iscariot.* 21–25

> How unaware they were,
> when first *at a loss,*
> of how slight a down payment it was
> toward the Next Day's awful cost.
>
> They cast furtive glances,
> sorting out the chances
> as to which among them
> would be the wasp who stung him.
>
> In a moment he'd never forget,
> the Teacher's personal favorite
> learned, surely to his later shame,
> the future traitor's name.
>
> That he (and Peter too, privy to the same)
> did nothing to intervene,
> to abort a plot so vile and mean,
> must have brought remorse relentlessly keen.

> Yet these same culpable men
> stuck it out to the end,
> to shout, once Easter'd dawned,
> a "Hallelujah, Amen!"

Garden Lessons
(Genesis 3:10, 4:13; Matthew 26:39, Mark 14:36; Luke 22:42; 23:46a)

> "I heard your voice; I was afraid; I hid myself."
> "My punishment is greater than I can bear."
> "Nevertheless not my will but thine be done."
> "Father into thy hands I commit my spirit."

"There are only two kinds of people in the end: those who say to God 'Thy will be done,' and those to whom God says, in the end, 'Thy will be done.'"
—C. S. Lewis, *The Great Divorce*, p. 72

As philosopher Georg W. F. Hegel set out to show, community and individuality, authority and liberty, depend in each instance on each other for fulfillment. Runaway liberty and rootless individuality end in anarchy; heavy-handed authority and stifling community, in tyranny.

Hegel's great Teacher in this was the Holy Trinity, in whom the Father (representing for the philosopher community or family authority) and the Son (filial, individual liberty) find unity (co-operative co-fulfillment) in the Holy Spirit.

The Bible illustrates and elaborates on this essential co-dependency in many ways, one of the most instructive of which is via its Garden stories:

> Adam and Cain left home,
> never to return,
> each thinking his Father
> excessively stern.
>
> Jesus and the Prodigal
> left home with their Fathers' blessing
> and show us two ways of dealing
> with paternal testing.

Adam and Cain succumb to exile;
Jesus (willy)
and the Prodigal (nilly)
become subject to conditions vile.

Adam, Cain, and the Prodigal
each ruined a garden.
The soil of their fields did only harden,
providing only grudging yields to them.

Jesus used a garden
to win Adam, Cain, and the Prodigal a pardon,
not by striving to be outstanding in his field
but by producing the Garden of History's greatest Yield.

The Snake and the Rooster
(Matthew 26:69-75; Mark 14:66-72; Luke 22:54-62; Genesis 3:1-7)

Now the snake was the most cunning of all the wild animals that the LORD God had made. He asked the woman, "Did God really say, 'You shall not eat from any of the trees in the garden'?"   Genesis 3:1

And immediately a cock crowed a second time. Then Peter remembered the word that Jesus had said to him, "Before the cock crows twice you will deny me three times." He broke down and wept.   Mark 14:72

Both worked at dawn—the serpent to wake Eve
from her dreaming innocence,
the cock to shake from slumber Peter's moral sense.

The snake, not the rooster, was the ego booster.
The cock, like a clock, alerted Pete to the time,
in doing so calling his cowardice to mind.

When Eve later sees the snake it's hard for her not to shake
as she shouts to Adam,
"Quick! Bring the hoe and rake!"

When he hears the cock crow Pete begins to sicken
as he hears in it a welcome
to the Order of the Chicken.

From the Diary of A Practical Man
(Matthew 27:11-26)

When Pilate saw that he was not succeeding at all, but that a riot was breaking out instead, he took water and washed his hands in the sight of the crowd, saying, "I am innocent of this man's blood. Look to it yourselves." 24

It all seemed ironic.
Though the situation was chronic—
Jews laying curses on Jews—
here the object of shame
chose a course unique
and, refusing to play their game,
turned his cheek—
signaling readiness, as 't were,
to take another verbal bruise.

Though they cursed him and charged him
with threatening Caesar's throne
he refused to respond with a curse of his own,
and as they shouted "Crucify him!"
he turned a benevolent eye on them.

As a *practical* man no such eye had I.
My job, as it happens, is mainly to keep order,
so, washing my hands in a basin of water
and scorning the crowd's affronts,
I solemnly declared my innocence
while consenting to an innocent's slaughter.

The Happy Exchange
(John 2:7-11a, 19:28-30)

Jesus told them, "Fill the jars with water." So they filled them to the brim. Then he told them, "Draw some out now and take it to the headwaiter." So they took it. And when the headwaiter tasted the water that had become wine, without knowing where it came from (although the servers who had drawn the water knew), the headwaiter called the bridegroom and said to him, "Everyone serves good wine first, and then when people have drunk freely, an inferior one; but you have kept the good wine until now." Jesus did this as the beginning of his signs in Cana in Galilee and so revealed his glory.
. . .   2:7-11a

After this, Jesus knew that everything had now been completed and, so that the scripture should be completely fulfilled, he said: I am thirsty. A jar full of sour wine stood there; so, putting a sponge soaked in the wine on a hyssop stick, they held it up to his mouth. After Jesus had taken the wine he said 'It is fulfilled'; and bowing his head he gave up his spirit.   19:28-30 (NJB)

The most profound and insight-laden concept of the atonement propounded among the Church Fathers was the one Martin Luther dubbed "the happy Exchange" (*der froehliche Wechsel*[56]) between God and us sinners, whereby our sin and death become Christ's and His righteousness and immortality become ours. This exchange is well illustrated biblically by the contrast between St. John's description of the launching of Christ's ministry and the descriptions of how it ended found in his, Matthew's, and Mark's gospels.

> He had served them
> the best wine last;
> now they thanked Him
> with the spoils
> of their ruinous past.
>
> The sop was meant to slake his pain
> but was a gesture largely vain.
> 'Twas mostly a taunt,
> its smell lingering to haunt
> and render his last hour even more sour.

> The world for whom he'd saved
> the best wine 'til last
> now offered him the dregs
> of its befouled kegs
> for his final repast.
>
> Yet He'd once more hear
> His mother's prayer
> and bring forth,
> from his blood and the surrounding air,
> a wine that forever bears His saving care.

Cross Fire
(Matthew 27:38-44)

Two revolutionaries were crucified with him, one on his right and the other on his left. Those passing by reviled him, shaking their heads and saying, "You who would destroy the temple and rebuild it in three days, save yourself, if you are the Son of God, [and] come down from the cross!" Likewise the chief priests with the scribes and elders mocked him and said, "He saved others; he cannot save himself. So he is the king of Israel! Let him come down from the cross now, and we will believe in him.... The revolutionaries who were crucified with him also kept abusing him in the same way. 38–42, 44

> On that Cross hangs the answer
> to many a historic riddle.
> Among them:
> The way to be doubly crucified
> is to be caught in the Middle.

Redeeming Wounds
(John 19:33-37; Genesis 2:20-24)

But when they came to Jesus and saw that he was already dead, they did not break his legs, but one soldier thrust his lance into his side, and immediately blood and water flowed out. John

Twice Scripture mentions a riven side,
once when Eve was born,
once when her greatest child died.
Great was humanity's gain
from both occasions of pain:
From the first we got the first father's wife
and the whole race's mother,
from the second a heaven-bound life
and blood kinship with our Savior-Brother.

How Long, O Lord . . .
(Luke 23:39-43)

Now one of the criminals hanging there reviled Jesus, saying, "Are you not the Messiah? Save yourself and us." The other, however, rebuking him, said in reply, "Have you no fear of God, for you are subject to the same condemnation? And indeed, we have been condemned justly, for the sentence we received corresponds to our crimes, but this man has done nothing criminal." Then he said, "Jesus, remember me when you come into your kingdom." He replied to him, "Amen, I say to you, today you will be with me in Paradise."

How great a wait will there be at the Gate?
Among those who've dared to estimate,
the one immune to rebuke
would seem to be St. Luke.

Among Scripture's scribes
he may lack seniority,
but he clearly cites
the highest authority.

Where We Least Expect
(John 20:1-9)

Then went in also that other disciple, which came first to the sepulcher, and he saw, and believed. For as yet they did not know the scripture, that he must rise again from the dead.   8–9 (KJV)

"In the Nuremburg War Crime Trials a witness appeared who had lived for a time in a grave in a Jewish grave-yard, in Wilna, Poland. It was the only place he, and many others, could live, when in hiding after they had escaped the gas chamber. During this time he wrote poetry, and one of the poems was a description of a birth. In a grave nearby a young woman gave birth to a boy. The eighty-year-old gravedigger, wrapped in a linen shroud, assisted. When the newborn child uttered his first cry, the old man prayed: 'Great God, hast Thou finally sent the Messiah to us? For who else than the Messiah Himself can be born in a grave?'" —Paul Tillich[57]

> When the Jews sought direction
> toward *Ha Mashiah*'s identity,
> no one thought a resurrection
> would provide a key.

> Then too who'd have thought to look
> for the One who'd Isr'el save
> in an out-of-the-way nook,
> least of all a grave?

A New Dawn in the Garden of Good and Evil
(John 20:11-16; compare Genesis 3:1-19)

But Mary stayed outside the tomb weeping. And as she wept, she bent over into the tomb and saw two angels in white sitting there, one at the head and one at the feet where the body of Jesus had been. And they said to her, "Woman, why are you weeping?" She said to them, "They have taken my Lord, and I don't know where they laid him." When she had said this, she turned around and saw Jesus there, but did not know it was Jesus. Jesus said to her, "Woman, why are you weeping? Whom are you looking for?" She thought it was the gardener and said to him, "Sir, if you carried him away, tell me where you laid him, and I will take him." Jesus said to her, "Mary!" She turned and said to him in Hebrew, "Rabbouni," which means Teacher.

> At least as errant as Eve she was—
> probably even more than she because
> she'd learned not just from Eve but from later exiles
> and had succumbed often to the serpent's wiles.

To make matters worse, the Garden she was in
remained the very one ruined by sin—
Eve's, Adam's and her own,
with thorns and thistles overgrown.

For her as for Eve the Garden
offered occasion to grieve,
she for the One Who'd granted her pardon,
Eve for the reason she'd had to leave.

In Eden the Lord came to seek Eve out;
here, seeker and sought are turned about
as, confronted with an empty tomb,
Mary seeks the One for whom
the sin-wracked Garden hadn't had room.

Eve and Mary, prime witness each to a crucial dawn,
symbolize hinges all history hangs on:
Eve, the dawn of moral consciousness,
Mary, the resurrection of righteousness.

Keeping Count
(John 21:1-13; Matthew 4:17-19)

So Simon Peter went over and dragged the net ashore full of one hundred fifty-three large fish. John 21:11a

He [Jesus] said to them, "Come after me, and I will make you fishers of men." Matthew 4:19

There's one in every crowd,
a calculator counting,
quietly or aloud.

Was it Matthew né Levi,
the tax collector guy,
who felt compelled to
compute the catch's future value
and the taxes that would be due?

Or was it one of the anglers,
Jim, John, Pete, or 'Drew,
who kept count of the long day's catch,
slave to the habit of the crew
of making sure the haul and their needs would match.

Or maybe it was Pete in particular,
he whose soul bore the scar
of a betrayal so vast
he'd do anything to stay busy
in hopes the memory wouldn't last.

Whoever did it and whatever its cause
the counting should give us a moment's pause:
When the Lord sends us out to fish
and we wonder what He'll later ask, it's
that we give an account of what's in our baskets.

For 94 more reflections on humor in the four Gospels, see the first volume of *Funny Things*, pp. 213–81.

6-Acts of the Apostles

The 1-2-3 on Sapphira and Ananias
(Acts 5:1-10)

A man named Ananias, however, with his wife Sapphira, sold a piece of property. He retained for himself, with his wife's knowledge, some of the purchase price, took the remainder, and put it at the feet of the apostles. But Peter said, "Ananias, why has Satan filled your heart so that you lied to the holy Spirit and retained part of the price of the land? While it remained unsold, did it not remain yours? And when it was sold, was it not still under your control? Why did you contrive this deed? You have lied not to human beings, but to God." When Ananias heard these words, he fell down and breathed his last, and great fear came upon all who heard of it. The young men came and wrapped him up, then carried him out and buried him. After an interval of about three hours, his wife came in, unaware of what had happened. Peter said to her, "Tell me, did you sell the land for this amount?" She answered, "Yes, for that amount." Then Peter said to her, "Why did you agree to test the Spirit of the Lord? Listen, the footsteps of those who have buried your husband are at the door, and they will carry you out." At once, she fell down at his feet and breathed her last. When the young men entered they found her dead, so they carried her out and buried her beside her husband.

One thing we know about her
is that they had his funeral without her.
And in *two* things they were co-sharers:
an intentional lie and the same pallbearers.

They died only *three* hours apart,
each brought to a stop with a start,
by their selfish natures so accurst
that their only way out was feet first.

Custodian of the Cloaks
(Acts 7:55-58)

But he [Stephen], *filled with the holy Spirit, looked up intently to heaven and saw the glory of God and Jesus standing at the right hand of God, and he said, "Behold, I see the heavens opened and the Son of Man standing at the right hand of God." But they cried out in a loud voice, covered their ears, and rushed upon him together. They threw him out of the city, and began to stone him. The witnesses laid down their cloaks at the feet of a young man named Saul. . . .*

As Heaven threw off its cloak,
opening to Stephen an amazing view,
the bearers of Torah's yoke
threw off their cloaks too.

For what Stephen said he saw
stuck in their craw,
violating as it did
their reading of the Law.

Closing their ears
to what Steve had to say
and aboil with anger to the point of dismay,
they piled their rage-heated cloaks in the way.

The wraps fell at the feet
of a stern-jawed man named Saul
who, as a rain of stones began to fall,
looked approvingly on it all.

None in the crowd more relished Torah's yoke
nor stood readier fiery tempers to stoke
than this smug Saul,
whose eyes would yet a while wear a cloak.

Defying the NIMBY Gremlin
(Acts 10:1-9)

Now in Caesarea there was a man named Cornelius, a centurion of the Cohort called the Italica, devout and God-fearing along with his whole household, who used to give alms generously to the Jewish people and pray to God constantly. One afternoon about three o'clock, he saw plainly in a vision an angel of God come in to him and say to him, "Cornelius." He looked intently at him and, seized with fear, said, "What is it, sir?" He said to him, "Your prayers and almsgiving have ascended as a memorial offering before God. Now send some men to Joppa and summon one Simon who is called Peter. He is staying with another Simon, a tanner, who has a house by the sea." 1–6

By boarding with Simon the tanner
Peter all but hung out a banner
that, with the force of a stentorian call,
cried "The gospel of the Christ is for all!"

Your art too would likely go unsung
if your media, like a tanner's, were hides, urine, and dung;
so we can know with some certainty
why the tanner's house was *by the sea,*
apart from the polite community.

The tanner's life, then, was far from an easy one;
it was, indeed, a life easy to shun.
'Twas especially hard for him to win a spouse,
for where's the girl who'd wish to build
her family's nest in an outhouse?

Our response to the building of a tannery
would probably be just as unmannerly
as, lacking Peter's grace, we'd frown on such a place,
finding it not in the least hard
to say "Not in my back yard."

That Peter consented to abide
in Simon's humble, despised abode
signaled his willingness to ride
the lowly path Jesus rode.

Bound by the Light
(Acts 16:16-33)

As we were going to the place of prayer, we met a slave girl with an oracular spirit, who used to bring a large profit to her owners through her fortune-telling. She began to follow Paul and us, shouting, "These people are slaves of the Most High God, who proclaim to you a way of salvation." She did this for many days. Paul became annoyed, turned, and said to the spirit, "I command you in the name of Jesus Christ to come out of her." Then it came out at that moment. When her owners saw that their hope of profit was gone, they seized Paul and Silas and dragged them to the public square before the local authorities. They brought them before the magistrates and said, "These people are Jews and are disturbing our city and are advocating customs that are not lawful for us Romans to adopt or practice." The crowd joined in the attack on them, and the magistrates had them stripped and ordered them to be beaten with rods. After inflicting many blows on them, they threw them into prison and instructed the jailer to guard them securely. . . . About midnight, while Paul and Silas were praying and singing hymns to God as the prisoners listened, there was suddenly such a severe earthquake that the foundations of the jail shook; all the doors flew open, and the chains of all were pulled loose. When the jailer woke up and saw the prison doors wide open, he drew (his) sword and was about to kill himself, thinking that the prisoners had escaped. But Paul shouted out in a loud voice, "Do no harm to yourself; we are all here." He asked for a light and rushed in and, trembling with fear, he fell down before Paul and Silas. Then he brought them out and said, "Sirs, what must I do to be saved?" And they said, "Believe in the Lord Jesus and you and your household will be saved." So they spoke the word of the Lord to him and to everyone in his house. He took them in at that hour of the night and bathed their wounds; then he and all his family were baptized at once.   16–23, 25

For Paul and Silas
life for a while was
precarious as could be.

Stripped naked, then beaten,
soon they found their feet in
stocks proscribing their liberty.

Yet, though their bodies were bound,
their spirits weren't cast down,
and they made their prison resound
with the joy of faith's hymnody.

Though the ensuing earthquake
opened the doors for a jailbreak,
they chose instead to witness where they were
and show life contains better things
than getting out of stir.

When we examine their story carefully,
the most surprising thing we see
is not that Paul and Silas stayed put,
but that none of their fellow prisoners
seized the chance to hotfoot.

What held them in thrall
is not clear at all—
'til their jailer is moved, in his desperate plight,
to ask for and see the spell-binding Light.

The Unknown God
(Acts 17:16-34)

While Paul was waiting for them in Athens, he grew exasperated at the sight of the city full of idols. So he debated in the synagogue with the Jews and with the worshipers, and daily in the public square with whoever happened to be there. Even some of the Epicurean and Stoic philosophers[4] engaged him in discussion. Some asked, "What is this scavenger trying to say?" Others said, "He sounds like a promoter of foreign deities," because he was preaching about 'Jesus' and 'Resurrection.' They took him and led him to the Areopagus and said, "May we learn what this new teaching is that you speak of? For you bring some strange notions to our ears; we should like to know what these things mean." Now all the Athenians as well as the foreigners residing there used their time for nothing else but telling or hearing something new. Then Paul stood up at the Areopagus and said: "You Athenians, I see that in every respect you are very religious. For as I walked around looking carefully at your shrines, I even discovered an altar inscribed, 'To an Unknown God.' What therefore you unknowingly worship, I proclaim to you. The God who made the world and all that is in it, the Lord of heaven and earth, does not dwell in sanctuaries made by human hands, nor is he served by human hands because he needs anything. Rather it is he who gives to everyone life and breath and everything. He made from one the whole human race to dwell on the entire surface of the earth, and he fixed the ordered seasons and the boundaries of their regions, so that people might seek God, even perhaps grope for him and find him, though indeed he is not far from any one of us. For 'In him we live and move and have our being,' as even some of your poets have said, 'For we too are his offspring.' Since therefore we are the offspring of God, we ought not to think that the divinity is like an image fashioned from gold, silver, or stone by human art and imagination. God has overlooked the times of ignorance, but now he demands that all people everywhere repent...." 16–30

> Athenians used the public square
> to discuss matters of common care
> under the watchful eye
> of their gods.
>
> To guarantee no god was neglected
> they made sure their piety was reflected
> in idols hon'ring all
> on the city's quads.
>
> Paul couldn't help but observe this
> and quickly resolved to disturb this,
> even in the face
> of formidable odds.
>
> "Of gods, Athenians, you have many
> and you're obviously afraid to offend any;
> yet the one you've labeled 'Unknown'
> is the One you dearly need to be shown.
>
> "Clearly, you must come to know
> that no smith or sculptor can show,
> by means of metal or stone,
> what *this* god wants known.

"You need to know, in the second place,
that the true God's a god you needn't chase
but the One who's here
and in every place.

"Any knowledge of this God
must remain impossibly dim
'til we realize (S)He's the Being
in which we and our world swim.

"Your own poets speak of this encompassing God,
the sole valid one of the kind,
but, if you're to be spared His chastening rod,
you'll need a change of heart and mind."[58]

An Ode to Paul from Eutychus
(Acts 20:7-9)

On the first day of the week when we gathered to break bread, Paul spoke to them because he was going to leave on the next day, and he kept on speaking until midnight. There were many lamps in the upstairs room where we were gathered, and a young man named Eutychus who was sitting on the window sill was sinking into a deep sleep as Paul talked on and on. Once overcome by sleep, he fell down from the third story . . .

You know so well the ethereal,
you can make the vibrancy of the ether real
and usually when you do
I appreciate you
and the way you make me feel.

But ether has two senses:
in channeling one
you pierce my heart's defenses,
but the other has the effect
of sheep leaping fences.

Ananias the Third[59]
(Acts 23:1-10)

Paul looked intently at the Sanhedrin and said, "My brothers, I have conducted myself with a perfectly clear conscience before God to this day." The high priest Ananias ordered his attendants to strike his mouth. Then Paul said to him, "God will strike you, you whitewashed wall. Do you indeed sit in judgment upon me according to the law and yet in violation of the law order me to be struck?" The attendants said, "Would you revile God's high priest?" Paul answered, "Brothers, I did not realize he was the high priest. For it is written, 'You shall not curse a ruler of your people.'"

Paul was aware that some were Sadducees and some Pharisees, so he called out before the Sanhedrin, "My brothers, I am a Pharisee, the son of Pharisees; [I] am on trial for hope in the resurrection of the dead." When he said this, a dispute broke out between the Pharisees and Sadducees, and the group became divided. For the Sadducees say that there is no resurrection or angels or spirits, while the Pharisees acknowledge all three. A great uproar occurred, and some scribes belonging to the Pharisee party stood up and sharply argued, "We find nothing wrong with this man. Suppose a spirit or an angel has spoken to him?" The dispute was so serious that the commander, afraid that Paul would be torn to pieces by them, ordered his troops to go down and rescue him from their midst and take him into the compound.

After watching him provoke Paul
to call him a whitewashed wall
we'd hardly want the third Ananias
to be among those who try us.

But if we were as shrewd as Paul,
we'd mount, as he did, an attempt
to avoid getting pinned to a judicial wall
and elude charges of contempt.

On learning of the priest's legitimate authority,
Paul quickly offers a sincere apology,
adroitly adopts a change of strategy,
and sets up a debate about theology.

>Before Ananias can give him the third degree
>he recalls the high priest is a Sadducee,
>then exploits the differences in eschatology
>between that school and his own as a Pharisee.
>
>Playing this game of cat and mouse
>he manages to divide the house
>and light a fire
>Ananias can't douse.

The More Things Change...
(Acts 28:17-22)

"... *we know that this sect is denounced everywhere....*"   22

> He went from home to homeland
> to assume the name Saul.
>
> He went from homeland to Rome
> where he'd become known as Paul.
>
> In the homeland he persecuted
> a sect spoken against everywhere.
>
> In Rome he died for...
> a sect spoken against everywhere.

For 29 more reflections on humor in *Acts*, see *Funny Things*, volume one, pp. 282–99.

7-Letters of Paul

Romans

The Case of I v. Me
(Romans 2:1, 7:7–12)

Therefore, you are without excuse, every one of you who passes judgment. For by the standard by which you judge another you condemn yourself, since you, the judge, do the very same things.   2:1

Apart from the law sin is dead. I once lived outside the law, but when the commandment came, sin became alive; then I died, and the commandment that was for life turned out to be death for me. For sin, seizing an opportunity in the commandment, deceived me and through it put me to death.   7:8b–11

Be careful how you throw judgments around
lest they destroy your pedestal on the rebound.
The Law of which Pharisee Paul liked to jaw
lived on in Christian Paul to nag and gnaw.

Though deep down he could see
how the Christ had set him free,
splits in his moral consciousness
impeded his new liberty.

"Self," said he,
"I don't trust you and maybe you shouldn't trust me,
for I have a civil war raging inside—
an I that's eager Me to deride and a Me avid I to chide."

The Match
(Romans 5:18-21; I Corinthians 15:21-22; Genesis 32:24-32)

For since death came through a human being, the resurrection of the dead came also through a human being. For just as in Adam all die, so too in Christ shall all be brought to life.   1 Corinthians

Perhaps it's possible
the gist of Scripture to catch
by viewing it as an account
of a perennial wrestling match.

Our father Jacob was reborn
when on his way home, conscience-torn,
he met a Stranger on the way
who wrestled with him 'til break of day.

His spiritual children, ever since,
haven't had the option of riding the fence.
With him they've been pulled into the ring
to grapple with One on whom hangs everything.

Whatever comes, Paul reminds us,
we never wrestle alone,
and then th' apostle goes out of his way
to make possible tagteam mates known:

In one corner there's Adam,
whose holds are Sin and Death,
in the other the One from whose hold
we catch the Kingdom's Second Breath.

For five more humorous reflections on *Romans*, see the first volume of *Funny Things*, pp. 300–304.

1 and 2 Corinthians

The Wise Fool's Conundrum
(1 Corinthians 1:18–31)

Where is the wise one? Where is the scribe? Where is the debater of this age? Has not God made the wisdom of the world foolish? For since in the wisdom of God the world did not come to know God through wisdom, it was the will of God through the foolishness of the proclamation to save those who have faith. 20–21

During an excavation of Rome's Palatine Hill in 1857, an etching and a piece of graffiti known as the *Alexemenos graffito* were uncovered on a plaster wall. Some authorities believe it to be the earliest depiction, albeit a mocking one, of Jesus' crucifixion. In it an early believer named Alexemenos looks up at a crucified figure, presumably representing Jesus, who bears the head of a donkey. The etching likely reflects a belief among cynical Romans that Christians were *onolaters*—"donkey worshippers"—and the inscription is translated loosely, "Alexemenos worshipping [his] god." Taken together, they illustrate the position of the "wise fool" Paul puts down in 1 Corinthians, a position a latter-day wise fool might express in something like the following crhyme:

> What in tarnation
> can be made of an incarnation?
> That stuff went out with Socrates.
> (As well picture God wearing BVDs!)
>
> A god who rides an ass
> appears to lack class,
> so small wonder an early crucifix,
> properly mocking gullible hicks,
> portrayed the one who did just that
> wearing the head of an ass
> where most people wear a hat.

If the Avon bard's Bottom
chose to wear such a head for a top,
mightn't a god fool enough to take a body
find a similar place to stop?

(Yet wouldn't it be quite wonderful
if the One who filled the world so full
loved fallen creation to such a degree
(S)He'd take up the cause of asses like me!)

Paul's Rule of Thumb
(1 Corinthians 9:18-22)

What then is my recompense? That, when I preach, I offer the gospel free of charge so as not to make full use of my right in the gospel. Although I am free in regard to all, I have made myself a slave to all so as to win over as many as possible. To the Jews I became like a Jew to win over Jews; to those under the law I became like one under the law—though I myself am not under the law—to win over those under the law. To those outside the law I became like one outside the law—though I am not outside God's law but within the law of Christ—to win over those outside the law. To the weak I became weak, to win over the weak. I have become all things to all, to save at least some.

"Use all the means you must
to save people from sin
even if it means you must
become all things to all men."
This, says Paul, is his rule of thumb
as he beats the Gospel drum.

'Twas a rule he learned from Jesus
as he did all he could to release us
from the grip of sin—
employing various tactics to win
various sorts of women and men.

The Fundamentals
(1 Corinthians 15:35-50)

But someone may say, "How are the dead raised? With what kind of body will they come back?"

You fool! What you sow is not brought to life unless it dies. And what you sow is not the body that is to be but a bare kernel of wheat, perhaps, or of some other kind; but God gives it a body as he chooses, and to each of the seeds its own body. Not all flesh is the same, but there is one kind for human beings, another kind of flesh for animals, another kind of flesh for birds, and another for fish. There are both heavenly bodies and earthly bodies, but the brightness of the heavenly is one kind and that of the earthly another. The brightness of the sun is one kind, the brightness of the moon another, and the brightness of the stars another. For star differs from star in brightness. So also is the resurrection of the dead. It is sown corruptible; it is raised incorruptible. It is sown dishonorable; it is raised glorious. It is sown weak; it is raised powerful. It is sown a natural body; it is raised a spiritual body. If there is a natural body, there is also a spiritual one. So, too, it is written, "The first man, Adam, became a living being," the last Adam a life-giving spirit. But the spiritual was not first; rather the natural and then the spiritual. The first man was from the earth, earthly; the second man, from heaven. As was the earthly one, so also are the earthly, and as is the heavenly one, so also are the heavenly. Just as we have borne the image of the earthly one, we shall also bear the image of the heavenly one. This I declare, brothers: flesh and blood cannot inherit the kingdom of God, nor does corruption inherit incorruption.

Believe it or not the nineteenth century
didn't define eternity.
What happened in 1895[60]
neither made God more alive
than (S)He'd been before
nor ushered inerrant truth,
infallibly, through the door.

To consider fundamentalist beliefs typical
of what Christians held in faith's Age Umbilical
is to stretch credulity.
Far from speaking in the spirit irenical

of the Ur-Church ecumenical,
the "Fundamentals" were highly selective
and expressed an extremely despotic perspective.

As defenders of an inerrant text
they leave us bemused, perplexed,
and draw hearty, appropriate laughs
by claiming such perfection solely
for the initial (lost!) autographs.

Fundies assure us of a physical resurrection,
rejecting Paul's Spirit-guided perception
that to believe flesh and blood can the kingdom inherit
is to endorse an idea totally without merit.

And by granting exclusive enthronement
to one of many ideas of atonement
they ignore theological history's
wiser approach to faith's mysteries—
one of inquiry, discourse, and judicious postponement.

What's the Veil For?
(2 Corinthians 3:12-16; cp. Exodus 34:29-35)

Therefore, since we have such hope, we act very boldly and not like Moses, who put a veil over his face so that the Israelites could not look intently at the cessation of what was fading. Rather, their thoughts were rendered dull, for to this present day the same veil remains unlifted when they read the old covenant, because through Christ it is taken away. To this day, in fact, whenever Moses is read, a veil lies over their hearts, but whenever a person turns to the Lord the veil is removed.   2 Corinthians

As Moses came down from Mount Sinai with the two tablets of the covenant in his hands, he did not know that the skin of his face had become radiant while he spoke with the LORD. When Aaron, then, and the other Israelites saw Moses and noticed how radiant the skin of his face had become, they were afraid to come near him.   Exodus 34:29–30

Was it because he feared abusing it,
or instead was on the verge of losing it
that, a la the Exodus tale,
Moses, bearing God's radiance, donned a veil?

However you're inclined, Paul's of a mind
that the veil story's designed
to usher Covenanters from Moses' way
to reflect fully the light of Christ's new day.

The Weight of Glory
(2 Corinthians 4:16-18)

Therefore, we are not discouraged; rather, although our outer self is wasting away, our inner self is being renewed day by day. For this momentary light affliction is producing for us an eternal weight of glory beyond all comparison, as we look not to what is seen but to what is unseen; for what is seen is transitory, but what is unseen is eternal.

Who among us can say
how much glory might weigh?
Is it a weight assigned by gravity
or by that counterweight known as levity?

St. Paul, with atypical brevity,
lauds the value of focusing steadily
on the glory to be found above
where earthly afflictions yield, conquered by love.

The ways we're changed
will be profound
when glory begins to throw
its weight around.

When Giving, Laughing Does Matter
(2 Corinthians 9:5-7)

I thought it necessary to encourage the brothers to go on ahead to you and arrange in advance for your promised gift, so that in this way it might be ready as a bountiful gift and not as an exaction. Consider this: whoever sows sparingly will also reap sparingly, and whoever sows bountifully will also reap bountifully. Each must do as already determined, without sadness or compulsion, for God loves a cheerful giver.

In Scripture giving is generally no laughing matter. The greatest gift of all, indeed, involved the sacrifice of the noblest life ever lived. Because of that greatest of gifts, however, all other gifts may be made freely, gratefully, joyfully. In a sense, indeed, they do become "laughing matters," so that, when Paul speaks of being cheerful in giving, the Greek word he uses for "cheerful" is *hilaron*, from which comes our word "hilarious."

> I don't want to pressure you, says Paul,
> but I'm hoping for a sufficient haul,
> as you take your offering for the poor of Jerusalem,
> to justify my boasts about you to them.

> So please! As you bring your abundant harvest in,
> do it without a dragging chin,
> no trace of a gloomy Gail or Gus
> but with a spirit abounding, even hilarious!

God's Way
(2 Corinthians 12:9)

... [the Lord] said to me, 'My grace is sufficient for you, for my power is made perfect in weakness...'

> The Bible speaks not so often of a plan
> as of a Providence.
> Least of all is its God like a man
> who peddles life and health insurance.

Even St. Luke's "blueprint,"[61]
applied to what's to happen hence,
expresses faith in no pre-set plan
but in a Providence—
a faith providing no details
of how the Kingdom's to come to birth
but declaring firmly that it's bound
to reach "the ends of the earth."[62]

A Will and Intention God clearly has,
but one less like a set plan than like a piece of jazz—
an inspired and inspiring work of improvisation,
patient with detours, even procrastination,
but aimed in all cases at restoring creation.

So beware the preacher who's always right,
who substitutes a "must happen" for every "might"—
the one whose "God with a plan"
comes not from the fresh market but out of a can.

For ten more humorous reflections on *1 and 2 Corinthians*, see *Funny Things*, volume one, pages 304–10.

Galatians and Ephesians

Equality in Christ
(Galatians 3:26-28)

. . .through faith you are all children of God in Christ Jesus. For all of you who were baptized into Christ have clothed yourselves with Christ. There is neither Jew nor Greek, there is neither slave nor free person, there is not male and female; for you are all one in Christ Jesus.

Those who'd use Eve's role in the original sin
to justify subordinating women to men
undervalue the effects of the very great price
God paid in the coming and dying of Christ.

How sad that Adam and Eve's becoming one in marriage
is ignored by those willing to disparage
Eve's claim to equality with Adam thereafter
and treat it, to their shame, with mockery and laughter.

Even more to be pitied are those
who in so doing expose
the effects of Christ's deeds of ministry
and of his death on Calvary
to similarly absurd calumny.

Time Redeemed and Redeeming
(Galatians 4:4-5; Ephesians 5:15-16)

But when the fullness of time had come, God sent his Son, born of a woman, born under the law, to ransom those under the law, so that we might receive adoption.   Galatians

Watch carefully then how you live, not as foolish persons but as wise, making the most of the opportunity [KJV: redeeming the time; Greek: *exagoratsomenoi ton kairon*]. . . .   Ephesians

There's a time we are to redeem
and a time that redeems us;
the latter's the pie's filling,
the former its crust.

In the fullness of the latter
we reach the heart of the matter
as the Christ's impact on time
produces history at its most sublime.

This special time, called *kairos* in Greek,
sees the proud give place to the meek,
as overpowering love sends waves of shock
to redeem the time of calendar and clock.

Our job's neither to watch the clock
nor to bide our time

but to build on the Rock
of God's Gift sublime.

In Him All Holds Together
(Ephesians 2:19-22)

So then you are no longer strangers and sojourners, but you are fellow citizens with the holy ones and members of the household of God, built upon the foundation of the apostles and prophets, with Christ Jesus himself as the capstone. Through him the whole structure is held together and grows into a temple sacred in the Lord; in him you also are being built together into a dwelling place of God in the Spirit.

Its language tends to make us suspect
Ephesians is the work of an architect.
As a tentmaker, Paul might qualify,
though the building the author seems to descry
is not, like the Tent of Meeting, simple,
but something grander, like the Temple.

Whether or not its blueprint
is Paul's formulation,
his message is a key part
of this temple's foundation,
for it's built by him and other prophets and apostles,
reliable witnesses to the Truth in the gospels.

At the heart of the blueprint One stands alone
as the Temple's cap- and corner-stone;
it is He who holds together
this household of God,
disciples and martyrs who the *via crucis*
now tread or once trod.

Filling All Things
(Ephesians 4:7-10)

But grace was given to each of us according to the measure of Christ's gift. Therefore, it says: "He ascended on high and took prisoners captive; he gave gifts to men." What does "he ascended" mean except that he also descended into the lower (regions) of the earth? The one who descended is also the one who ascended far above all the heavens, that he might fill all things.

> Why'd He have to die
> to ascend on high?
> Could the answer to such a "why"
> relate to His living as we live
> to bring us the grace He'd give?
>
> And why'd He go below
> if not Hell's fields to plow and the Word to sow,
> inspiring Hell's captives to grow—
> when their prospects are starkest!—
> into a mighty harvest?
>
> In taking captivity captive
> was He simply being reactive
> or did He do it a-purpose, our Captor to plunder,
> accomplishing thus the wonder
> of filling all things—here, above, and under.

For three further reflections on *Galatians* and *Ephesians*, see volume one of *Funny Things*, pp. 310-12.

Philippians

Be Wary of Deceivers!
(Philippians 3:2-3; Galatians 6:15)

Beware of the dogs! Beware of the evil workers! Beware of the mutilation! For we are the circumcision, we who worship through the Spirit of God, who boast in Christ Jesus and do not put our confidence in flesh.   Philippians

For neither does circumcision mean anything, nor does uncircumcision, but only a new creation.   Galatians

Because they fail to show patience
toward God-fearers from Gentile nations
Paul counts ultra-kosher Galatians
among the kin of Dalmatians.

Those who consider every course unwise
that doesn't insist converts be circumcised
are victims, Paul implies,
of the father of lies.

On Not Becoming Fill-upians . . .
(Philippians 3:19b; cf. I Corinthians 8:7–13)

Their god is their stomach . . . (NAB; NRSV reads "belly" for "stomach.")   Philippians 3

If a god's defined as a being to whom we adhere,
whom we follow inseparably far and near,
then we don't need theologs of pulpit or telly
to tell us our god is often our belly.

Should we be surprised, then,
that St. Paul's advice is
to avoid off'ring our stomachs
unwarranted sacrifices?

Sound Advice
(Philippians 4:5)

Let your good sense be obvious to everybody. The Lord is near.   (NJB)

In a day when raging passion
is the ruling fashion,
it's good to hear the Apostle engage our ear
with a plea intense
lauding the use of simple good sense.

> As Plato said, it's only by using our head
> that we can tame the rambunctious steeds
> of appetites, passions, and needs
> that can overturn our chariot-souls[63]
> and make us miss our goals.
>
> As Paul goes on to say, the Lord's not far away
> where good sense is found.
> The Logos that translates "Word"
> may sometimes appear absurd
> but is at bottom *logic*ally sound.

For another reflection on humor in *Philippians*, see *Funny Things*, volume one, p. 313.

Colossians

Countering Counterfeiters
(Colossians 2:5-19)

... as you received Christ Jesus the Lord, walk in him, rooted in him and built upon him and established in the faith as you were taught, abounding in thanksgiving. See to it that no one captivate you with an empty, seductive philosophy according to human tradition, according to the elemental powers of the world and not according to Christ. For in him dwells the whole fullness of the deity bodily, and you share in this fullness in him, who is the head of every principality and power.   6–10

> Pirating copyrights
> is not a new venture,
> and we learn as much here
> in St. Paul's censure.
>
> The brand name "Christ" has been abused—
> falsely and fraudulently used.
> Star-deities known as *stoicheia*[64]
> are claiming credit for His career
> and asserting He's at most their peer.

> Against such blatant counterfeiting
> Paul suggests a response quite fitting:
> derailing deceivers' self-promotion
> by off'ring the Brand Name total devotion.

For an additional humorous reflection on *Colossians*, see the first volume of *Funny Things*, pp. 312–13.

1 and 2 Thessalonians

Could TL Be the Beast and JJ his Prophet?
(2 Thessalonians 2:8-10; Revelation 19:20 et passim)

And then the lawless one will be revealed, whom the Lord (Jesus) will kill with the breath of his mouth and render powerless by the manifestation of his coming, the one whose coming springs from the power of Satan in every mighty deed and in signs and wonders that lie, and in every wicked deceit for those who are perishing because they have not accepted the love of truth.
. . .   2 Thessalonians

The beast was caught and with it the false prophet who had performed in its sight the signs by which he led astray those who had accepted the mark of the beast and those who had worshiped its image.   Revelation

> It's a sin to defame
> and even hinting at it should make us blush with shame,
> but it may occasionally be good to remind
> those who're quick to assign
> all evil to a single source
> that they too should blush with remorse.

> The greatest irony of all may be
> the use of Beast imagery
> to induce a smug sense of security
> that smacks of Satanic impurity.

> And how does a putative prophet avoid the 'witching spell

    and gain the insight to tell
    authentic truth received
    from being self-deceived?

What if fear of being left behind
renders people spiritually blind,
  unable to distinguish a prophet
    who brings true treasure
from one for whom popular appeal
  constitutes truth's measure?

What if the language of hate and rejection
is a product of inadvertent projection
    by which we cast our sin,
our pact with Old Ned, hid within,
  onto an object we find detestable,
a *bête noire* who's media-accessible.

    Three cheers for LaHaye
    would be a very quick way
      to arrive at 666—
and is there a holy man in our whole land
with greater proven power to create addicts?

For another reflection on humor in *1 and 2 Thessalonians*, see the first volume of *Funny Things*, p. 314.

1 and 2 Timothy

Zero Sum Game
(1 Timothy 6:3-10)

We brought nothing into the world, and we can take nothing out of it.
...
                                                          7 (*NJB*)
    Into the world we came
    without a stitch to our name,

and though we attain wealth and fame
we'll leave as well with nothing to claim.

So it's a zero sum game
we're playing on this orb,
though, to our brain's chagrin and shame,
that's something we can't seem to absorb.

It's true you can't take it with you,
but should you really care?
Perhaps the answer depends
on what you're expecting There.

The Most Abused Text
(2 Timothy 3:16-17)

All scripture is inspired by God and is useful for teaching, for refutation, for correction, and for training in righteousness, so that one who belongs to God may be competent, equipped for every good work.

This very important text
is abused far more than whichever's next,
and, to make matters worse,
its abusers invoke a curse
on truer readings that leave them vexed.

How ironic this is,
for if we read the text as is,
its list of Scripture's proper uses
seems designed to prevent abuses.

Whence comes the aberrancy
that finds here a claim of inerrancy,
denies interpreters malleability,
and grants a favored reading infallibility?

In the text itself we read
that Scripture's aim is to meet human need
and to equip us
for every good work;

> it's not there to anoint some specious claim
> that abuses the Trinity's name
> and makes a bullying tyrant
> of many a half-literate jerk.

Titus

The Task in Crete
(Titus 1:12-13a)

One of them, a prophet of their own, once said, "Cretans have always been liars, vicious beasts, and lazy gluttons." That testimony is true.

> This assessment of the Cretans
> as the worst among the worst
> obviously comes from a philosopher,[65]
> not Crete's chamber of commerce.
>
> Living among beasts and liars is hardly what a pastor desires,
> so as pastor of the church in Crete, Titus must be discreet,
> civilizing the flock with the milk of faith[66]
> before trusting them with its red meat.

Philemon

Getting Personal
(Philemon 10-19a)

I urge you on behalf of my child Onesimus, whose father I have become in my imprisonment, who was once useless to you but is now useful to (both) you and me. I am sending him, that is, my own heart, back to you. I should have liked to retain him for myself, so that he might serve me on your behalf in my imprisonment for the gospel, but I did not want to do anything without your consent, so that the good you do might not be forced but voluntary.

Perhaps this is why he was away from you for a while, that you might have him back forever, no longer as a slave but more than a slave, a brother, beloved especially to me, but even more so to you, as a man and in the Lord. So if you regard me as a partner, welcome him as you would me. And if he has done you any injustice or owes you anything, charge it to me. I, Paul, write this in my own hand: I will pay.

> If you wonder how much
> Onesimus meant to Paul,
> note the personal touch
> from one who wrote in his own hand scarcely at all.

> Though he rarely wrote himself, perhaps because of poor sight,[67]
> he takes pains here to do so to be sure things are done right,
> promising to pay Philemon whatever he's due
> and personally signing his IOU.

For four more reflections on humorous aspects of 1 and 2 Timothy, Titus, and Philemon, see the first volume of *Funny Things,* pp. 315–17.

8—Letters General and Catholic

Hebrews and James

A Cure for the Fear of Falling
(Hebrews 10:28-31; Matthew 27:48, Mark 15:34)

It is a fearful thing to fall into the hands of the living God.   Hebrews 10:31

And at three o'clock Jesus cried out in a loud voice, "Eloi, Eloi, lema sabachthani?" which is translated, "My God, my God, why have you forsaken me?"
Mark 15:34

But must falling into the living God's hands
terrify one who understands
that by submitting to be Crucified
God knows what it means to be terrified?

Only the One who comes from above,
straight from the sea of unconditional love,
adequately understands that, especially for the devout,
falling into the living God's hands is far better than falling out.

Faith
(Hebrews 11:1-3)

Faith is the realization of what is hoped for and evidence of things not seen. Because of it the ancients were well attested. By faith we understand that the universe was ordered by the word of God, so that what is visible came into being through the invisible.

Darwinists admit as evidence
only what's seen
and tell us it explains sufficiently
all that is or's been.

Yet every event and its effects
are shrouded in mystery,
little of which is lifted
by our power to see.

Pushing On toward the Mark
(Hebrews 11:1-40)

What more shall I say? I have not time to tell of Gideon, Barak, Samson, Jephthah, of David and Samuel and the prophets, who by faith conquered kingdoms, did what was righteous . . . Yet all these, though approved because of their faith, did not receive what had been promised. God had foreseen something better for us, so that without us they should not be made perfect.
32–33, 39–40

They bore such a heavy load on such a short leash,
these writers of holy writ, of conscience replete,
that they despaired of serving the whole feast,
struggle though they might their task to complete.

Time and space were far too short
to tell the stories of the entire cohort
of faithful souls who'd run the race—
yet the Spirit pushed these scribes on, full apace.

Why this sense of urgency, absent an obvious emergency?
It seems the Hebrews' scribe believes that,
unless their full story's told,
the venerable saints' work may fall short of its goal.

For an additional reflection on *Hebrews*, see *Funny Things*, volume one, pp. 318–19.

Temptation's Whence
(James 1:12-15)

No one experiencing temptation should say, "I am being tempted by God"; for God is not subject to temptation to evil, and he himself tempts no one. Rather, each person is tempted when he is lured and enticed by his own desire. Then desire conceives and brings forth sin, and when sin reaches maturity it gives birth to death.   13–15

    Are good and evil Siamese twins
  and virtues, siblings of grievous sins?
    And is the Author of all creation
  Source also of the pull of temptation?

  In some slight sense that may be true:
Because created goodness is attractive to you,
    its force as an occasion for trial
      seems beyond denial.

    But to think good depends on evil
  or that the bad's presence primeval
    as a target for moral resistance
    is essential to good's existence
      goes a step too far.

  "And God saw that it was good"
before evil entered the neighborhood,
so the claim that good on evil depends
  arises from assumptions bizarre.

    In a calm, matter-of-fact voice
the Garden's Tester only poses a choice
while the Desert's Tempter, a champion of vice,
    is clearly out to lure and entice.
Neither determines what you do; that's entirely up to you.

    The source of temptation, then,
      is not without but within—
not in God's Spirit nor anything near it;
    it shows up exclusively when
we take the God-good border and blear it.

Break the Restless Bronco!
(James 1:26)

If anyone thinks he is religious and does not bridle his tongue but deceives his heart, his religion is vain.

> A bridle is a strip of leather
> usually employed as a horse's tether
> but also a pertinent metaphor
> re training the tongue to do what it's for.
>
> What it's for is the service of grace and truth,
> but unless it's trained during childhood and youth
> to express an honest, undeceived heart,
> it'll be ill-suited, grace and truth to impart.

For another humorous reflection on James, see the first volume of *Funny Things*, p. 319.

1 and 2 Peter

Aiming High
(1 Peter 2:18-20)

Slaves, be subject to your masters with all reverence, not only to those who are good and equitable but also to those who are perverse. For whenever anyone bears the pain of unjust suffering because of consciousness of God, that is a grace. But what credit is there if you are patient when beaten for doing wrong? But if you are patient when you suffer for doing what is good, this is a grace before God.

> It's asking a lot of a slave
> to insist (s)he behave,
> but when modeling yourself
> after the Master of Class
> it's important to shoot
> for a grade higher than Pass.

The Courageous Chameleon
(2 Peter 3:1-9)

This is now, beloved, the second letter I am writing to you; through them by way of reminder I am trying to stir up your sincere disposition, to recall the words previously spoken by the holy prophets and the commandment of the Lord and savior through your apostles. Know this first of all, that in the last days scoffers will come (to) scoff, living according to their own desires and saying, "Where is the promise of his coming? From the time when our ancestors fell asleep, everything has remained as it was from the beginning of creation." They deliberately ignore the fact that the heavens existed of old and earth was formed out of water and through water by the word of God; through these the world that then existed was destroyed, deluged with water. The present heavens and earth have been reserved by the same word for fire, kept for the day of judgment and of destruction of the godless. But do not ignore this one fact, beloved, that with the Lord one day is like a thousand years and a thousand years like one day. The Lord does not delay his promise, as some regard "delay," but he is patient with you, not wishing that any should perish but that all should come to repentance.

Second Peter had a hard time making it into the canon because, first, its vocabulary differs strikingly from that of First Peter and, second, 2 Peter 3:2 speaks of the apostles in the third person, as though the writer was not to be counted among them. Since apostleship or "apostolicity" (evidence of close acquaintance with an apostle) was a prerequisite for inclusion in the canon, doubts about the author's identity and a vocabulary more appropriate to the second century than to the first led some to resist classifying the letter as holy writ. All of which adds to the already pervasive mystery, from very early on, about the identity of the impulsively courageous but chameleonic character for whom the book was named.

Who is Peter anyway?
Though he's appointed to lead us on The Way
he struggles to keep his impulses at bay
and sometimes displays feet of clay.

The Big Fisherman's fortunes so often shine,
then plunge precipitously into decline,
yoyoing him into and then out of trouble,
making some wonder if he has an evil double.

Thus it's not so surprising that in a later day
two letters purport his views to convey,
one pointing one,
the other a different way.

The first deals with issues sociological:
how can Christians keep their heads above water
in an alien and hostile social order?
The second's focus is more theological:
whether history will or won't prove wrong
the belief it's soon to hear its swan song.

In the two letters as in life, "Peter" searches for direction,
showing in both that, though our heads need correction,
when all is done and said,
sound faith's a matter more of heart than head.

For more reflections on humor in *1-2 Peter*, see *Funny Things*, volume one, pp. 319-21.

1, 2, and 3 John

The Gold Standard and Fool's Gold
(1 John 1:8, 2:3-9, 4:2-3)

If we say, "We are without sin," we deceive ourselves, and the truth is not in us. 1:8

Whoever says, "I know him," but does not keep his commandments is a liar, and the truth is not in him.... This is the way we may know that we are in union with him: whoever claims to abide in him ought to live (just) as he lived.... the darkness is passing away, and the true light is already shining. ...Whoever says he is in the light, yet hates his brother, is still in the darkness. 2:4, 5b-6, 8b-9

This is how you can know the Spirit of God: every spirit that acknowledges Jesus Christ come in the flesh belongs to God, and every spirit that does not acknowledge Jesus [as enfleshed] does not belong to God. 4:2-3

Heresy literally means "wrong choice" and heterodoxy, "strange teaching." The so-called Johannine School, out of which came the letters of John and perhaps the gospel and apocalypse as well, alerts us (even as St. Paul had) to the presence of both within the missionary churches of the first and early second centuries. The letters emerging from this school are especially concerned with identifying, avoiding, and eradicating heresies. But there is a peculiar irony in this: the Johannine community itself is probably a product of a move within Jewish synagogues of a slightly earlier time to purge themselves of what orthodox Jews labeled a "messianist" heresy—the belief that in Jesus of Nazareth the Messiah had come.

The heresies the letters of John specifically hone in on are, first, an assumed sinless perfection in true believers and, second, a belief that Jesus' body was only apparent—i.e., that in him God did not assume (i.e., save by taking upon Himself) *full-bodied* humanity.

> It's not pure ego or fear of rejection,
> that leads some to seek and claim perfection:
> John's opponents have made perfection attainable
> by denying a doctrine they think unsustainable.
>
> If our job (they taught) is to emulate Jesus
> the good news is that God would never tease us
> by doing something as dotty
> as make Himself at home in a frail, mortal body.
>
> No. The gospel is that God's been so kind
> as to make perfection just a matter of mind.
> To move from darkness into light
> it'll be enough to get our *minds* right.
>
> To live as Christ lived (John's foes taught)
> it'll be enough just to pray and talk;
> 'tis the inward path that opens doors
> to a perfect, purely spiritual walk.
>
> But people who think thus, says John,
> can't belong to the Johannine school,
> and to follow what they teach
> is to play the fool.

'Tis not enough to say "Lord, Lord,"
and neglect the body's part in bearing the Word;
the God who accepted our bodily fate
must again in us become incarnate.

Anticipation
(1 John 3:1-2)

Beloved, we are God's children now; what we shall be has not yet been revealed. We do know that when it is revealed we shall be like him, for we shall see him as he is.   3:2

It's not a matter of physical proximity
but one of spiritual intimacy:
because God creates us with miens like mirrors
we're bound to reflect what's spiritually near us.

And because our Lord's been born one of us,
a richer mix of deity and dust,
by looking to Christ alone will we see
what all of us are meant to be.

Rejecting the miracle—that He's drawn so near,
our befogged mirrors progressively to clear—
we yearn, squirming, to be left alone
as His approach impacts our comfort zone.

As our mirrors reflect Him only dimly
what we see's largely fancy and whimsy:
it doth not yet appear what we shall be,
but the closer He comes the better we'll see.

Mending Fences...
(2 John 7-11)

Many deceivers have gone out into the world, those who do not acknowledge Jesus Christ as coming in the flesh; such is the deceitful one and the antichrist. Look to yourselves that you do not lose what we worked for but may receive a full recompense. Anyone who is so "progressive" as not to remain in the teaching of the Christ does not have God; whoever remains in the teaching has the Father and the Son. If anyone comes to you and does not bring this doctrine, do not receive him in your house or even greet him; for whoever greets him shares in his evil works.

The "teaching of the Christ" to which the author refers in 2 John 9 means not only the doctrine of unconditional love the Christ taught but also the Church's teaching about the expression of that love through the Incarnation. In the Incarnation (i.e., the Word's expression of itself in a complete human being) and in it alone, the Apostles taught, can we see the full height and depth, width and breadth—in a word, the cosmic scope—of God's love for us.

> "Don't offer the truth as a sacrifice
> to the worthless conceits of an antichrist.
> They who'd have you skip the bother
> of going through the Son to the Father
> are not your friends as they'd have you think
> but would send you and your faith over the brink.
>
> "'Spiritualists,' they call themselves,
> but in size of spirit they're at best elves
> who in denying the Incarnation
> deny the fullness of salvation;
> for, unless God's Lord of body as well as mind,
> we'll foolishly think His work's
> to some spirit-world confined.

... and Tearing One Down
(3 John 9-10)

I wrote to the church, but Diotrephes, who loves to dominate, does not acknowledge us.

Therefore, if I come, I will draw attention to what he is doing, spreading evil nonsense about us. And not content with that, he will not receive the brothers, hindering those who wish to do so and expelling them from the church.

> Having to send this postscript
> must have hit John hard
> when, after he warned the church to keep up its guard,
> a congregational leader
> paid his gospel no regard.
>
> Doing what he must, th' Elder uses an end run
> to get around Diotrephes, a mean son of a gun
> who's barred John's letters and legates
> from the beloved congregation,
> kindling in the Elder intense frustration.
>
> "You're a dear friend," writes he to fellow elder Gaius—
> "one who, unlike Diotrephes, will never betray us.
> I'm sorry to hear he's giving your members hard times
> and can't wait for the day he'll pay
> full measure for his crimes."

For more reflections on humor in *1, 2, and 3 John*, see the first volume of *Funny Things*, pp. 321–22.

Jude

Gut Check Time in the Faith Community
(Jude 1-20)

... complainers ... utter bombast as they fawn over people to gain advantage. But you, beloved, remember the words spoken beforehand by the apostles of

our Lord Jesus Christ, for they told you, "In (the) last time there will be scoffers who will live according to their own godless desires." These are the ones who cause divisions; they live on the natural plane, devoid of the Spirit. But you, beloved, build yourselves up in your most holy faith 16–20a

>Jude calls the roll
>of sinners who've taken a toll
>on the covenant's health over time.
>
>He's also quick to scold
>folks who'd let a poll
>the Church's mission define.
>
>Sin comes in all shapes and sizes
>and it's way past time the church realizes
>it'll be known by the company it keeps.
>
>Unless the community recants
>and is careful hereafter with the seeds it plants
>it'll greatly regret the crop it reaps.

For another reflection about humor in *Jude*, see volume one of *Funny Things*, p.323.

9—The Apocalypse

Perspective

A Book Misnamed?
(Revelation 1:1-22:21)

Why, if "apocalypse" means "revelation,"
do many treat it as occult speculation?
And how come it names a book
that only fuzzily *reveals*
the secrets behind its seven seals?

Our Lord, it turns out, is a master of disguise
who with our expectations rarely complies,
much less countenances false prophets' lies
or readings of His Revelation
whose main fruit is frustration.[68]

Grand Refusals
(Revelation 3:14-16; Matthew 27:24; Luke 18:18-23)

To the angel of the church in Laodicea, write this: . . ."I know your works; I know that you are neither cold nor hot. I wish you were either cold or hot. So, because you are lukewarm, neither hot nor cold, I will spit you out of my mouth." Revelation

When Pilate saw that he was not succeeding at all, . . .he took water and washed his hands in the sight of the crowd, saying, "I am innocent of this man's blood. Look to it yourselves." Matthew

An official asked him this question, "Good teacher, what must I do to inherit eternal life?"Jesus answered him, "Why do you call me good? No one is good but God alone. You know the commandments, 'You shall not commit adultery; you shall not kill; you shall not steal; you shall not bear false witness;

honor your father and your mother.'" And he replied, "All of these I have observed from my youth." When Jesus heard this he said to him, "There is still one thing left for you: sell all that you have and distribute it to the poor, and you will have a treasure in heaven. Then come, follow me." But when he heard this he became quite sad, for he was very rich.   Luke

> Futures of ill consequence await Indifference:
> The man of wealth unusual, guilty of the grand refusal,
> the governor of Judea, and the denizens of Laodicea
> earn trips south, spat from Christ's mouth,
> proving it's bad form
> to become and stay lukewarm.

A Tree-Hugger's Prayer
(Revelation 7:3)

"Hurt not the . . . trees."

> The logging trucks roam
> and groan everywhere—
> brute muses of
> a tree-hugger's prayer:

> "You've shown us, Lord,
> in Your description of Eden,
> that it's a crime to kill
> when we should be seedin'.

> "Yet we, in our stupidly flippant way,
> pay no attention to what You say,
> even to Your ultra-urgent decrees,
> including Your call to "Hurt not the . . . trees."

> "Harder than hardwoods are these heads of ours.
> Pray, let Your seal make real our alliance
> with the friendly sheltering giants
> who populate Your beloved forests and bowers."

Life-saving Badges
(Revelation 7:1-3; cf. Genesis 3:8-10, 4:15-16)

"Hurt not the earth, neither the sky, nor the trees, till we have sealed the servants of God on their foreheads."   Revelation 7:3

. . . the man and his wife hid themselves from the LORD God among the trees of the garden.   Genesis 3:8b

So the LORD put a mark on Cain, so that no one would kill him at sight.   Genesis 4:15b

> Their excuses were sadly lame
> as they sought to cast the blame
> for their irresponsibilities
> on the overarching trees.
>
> Trees, though used as shields of shame,
> are in no way fit objects of blame,
> nor was earth or sky
> in our Trespass a willing ally.
>
> There must be for them another seal
> than the one imposed for Abel's ordeal—
> that wrathful storm he'd had to sustain
> that led to the banishment and mark of Cain.
>
> Borne by Adam's ilk, each and all,
> that mark of our race's corporate fall
> will be ours alone 'til, at Grace's table,
> it's removed by the blood of the second Abel.

The Pits
(Rev. 9:1-6)

Then the fifth angel blew his trumpet, and I saw a star that had fallen from the sky to the earth. It was given the key for the passage to the abyss.[69] It opened the passage to the abyss, and smoke came up out of the passage like smoke from a huge furnace. The sun and the air were darkened by the smoke from the passage. Locusts came out of the smoke onto the land, and they were given the same power as scorpions of the earth. They were told not to harm the grass of the earth or any plant or any tree, but only those people who did not have the seal of God on their foreheads. They were not allowed to kill them but only to torment them for five months; the torment they inflicted was like that of a scorpion when it stings a person. During that time these people will seek death but will not find it, and they will long to die but death will escape them.

    Like a spray of cherries
    the Bible's with pits replete,
    though the "pit" theme widely varies,
    expressing many a poetic conceit:

From Sarah, Abe, and Jake, in Macpelah interred,
to Joseph who, facing one, surely must have demurred
  to David who found in one a refuge from Saul
and the one of a heroic trio[70] whose faith proved a firewall.

  Daniel showed in his pit the courage of a lion,
and David's troops crawled through one in order to capture Zion.
  Scriptural pits, caves, and tunnels with significance abound,
  belying their lowly status as mere holes in the ground.

  In the New Testament too we find quite a few,
  the most important surely being the one they lay Jesus in
    in the futile campaign to hem him in
    in his to-the-death battle against the curse of sin.

Now, stretching to the breaking point the reach of our wit
  the Seer brings into view a *bottomless* pit,
challenging as vigorously our strength of mind and soul
  as the modern physicist's concept of the black hole.

But though the two pits seem similar in some respects,
  the Seer's receives and retains but also ejects;
it spews smoke, locusts, scorpions, and for all we know weevils,
  to visit on the damned a host of harsh evils.

Eve and the Snake, Round Fifteen
(Revelation 12:1-6)

Then the dragon stood before the woman about to give birth, to devour her child when she gave birth. She gave birth to a son, a male child, destined to rule all the nations with an iron rod. Her child was caught up to God and his throne. 4b–5

Are the celestial woman and child
creatures only of a fancy run wild?
Or do they throw open the finite mind's door
to reveal what a provident God has in store?

M(Adam) Eve stands, clothed only by the sun,
Queen Regent o'er the moon, crowned by the stars,
pregnant with many, but with only One who bears,
Deo a se volente,[71] salvation's scars.

The Great Serpent too lurks insidiously there,
coveting as in Eden all Eve's womb will bear.
But the Greatest of her children escapes its predation
and ushers Eve and her ruin'd Eden to final regeneration.

The Queen Astride the Beast
(Revelation 17:1-5, 18:1-2; cf. 12:1-6)

Then he carried me away in spirit to a deserted place where I saw a woman seated on a scarlet beast that was covered with blasphemous names, with seven heads and ten horns. The woman was wearing purple and scarlet and adorned with gold, precious stones, and pearls. She held in her hand a gold cup that was filled with the abominable and sordid deeds of her harlotry. 17:3–4

Upon the Beast of scarlet
sits the spry, resplendent Harlot
in robes adorned in gold, gems, and pearl—
an abomination to all the world.

From dawning east to dusky west
the Beast pursues with cruel zest
the Woman of the Wilderness,
adorned in sun-bright dress.

To the seer on his isle
the rider, envious as the whore of Solomonic lore,
pursues, unrelenting, her rival's Child,
intent on consuming Him forevermore.

The Beast, seven-headed and ten-horned,
goes before the Whore to earn Earth's scorn,
pimping her services to all the nations,
arranging trysts and assignations.

Her ancient name was Babylon, her current alias Rome,
and she uses her wanton charms
to lure the world into her arms
and make of it her home.

But her days are numbered as she becomes encumbered
with devils, foul spirits, and vultures
who take frightened flight from the light now dawning
on the world's benighted cultures.

First and Last
(Revelation 20:4-6; cf. Matthew 20:16)

Then I saw thrones; those who sat on them were entrusted with judgment. I also saw the souls of those who had been beheaded for their witness to Jesus and for the word of God, and who had not worshiped the beast or its image nor had accepted its mark on their foreheads or hands. They came to life and they reigned with Christ for a thousand years. The rest of the dead did not come to life until the thousand years were over. This is the first resurrection. Blessed and holy is the one who shares in the first resurrection. The second death has no power over these; they will be priests of God and of Christ. . . . Revelation

"*. . . the last will be first, and the first will be last.*" Matthew

> Shall the first-raised too
> be in their way last?
> Shall they henceforth know only the future,
> never recall the past?
>
> Yes and No!
>
> If they're to be priests as Christ was
> they'll have to remain first by putting themselves last
> and they'll have to do so by continuing to care
> about people they knew in the past.

For five more humorous reflections on or about *Revelation*, see the first volume of *Funny Things,* pp. 324–27.

End Notes

Preface

1. On the other hand, "*A verse too polished will not stick at all:/ the worst back-scratcher is a billiard ball.*"—Verse attributed to Oliver Wendell Holmes by Matthew Pearl in *The Dante Club* (New York: Random House, 2003), p. 33.

Introduction

2. *The Princess and the Goblin; The Princess and Curdie*. (Middletown, CN. American Educational Publications, 1970), p. 18.
3. Though fundamentalism and modernism appear to be arch foes, in reality the read-Scripture-as-literal-history approach of traditional fundamentalism finds its mirror image in the mine-Scripture-to-find-the-true-history-behind-it line of inquiry modernist scholars pursue. Though their conclusions may differ as much as dogs differ from cats, both require that the pots they seek at the end of their respective rainbows be filled with historically demonstrable (or at least cogent) facts before valid religious and theological meanings may be drawn from them.
4. For a more extensive, suggestive but still sketchy treatment of various Christian canons, see Philip Jenkins, "Which Bible, whose canon?," in *The Christian Century*, Vol. 128, No. 18, September 6, 2011, p. 45.

Chapter 1: Torah

1. Cf. Psalm 36:10b: ". . . in your light we see light."
2. So St. Paul: "the letter kills, but the Spirit gives life" (2 Corinthians 3:6).
3. The use of *adam* in the Genesis creation stories appears to be exclusively generic, though some translators have chosen to add an additional element of drama to the story by rendering it as a personal name in Genesis 2 and 3. It is doubtful that the Hebrew original intends the term as a proper name earlier than Genesis 4:25 and 5:3. Cf. the Wikipedia entry for "Adam" (January 14, 2010), and compare as well the evidence for early belief in a pre-fall bisexual version of humankind represented in Plato's myth of the androgyne,

Symposium, pages 189c–193e, *Great Books of the Western World*, ed. R. M. Hutchins, Vol. 7. (Chicago, London, Toronto: Encyclopedia Britannica, Inc., 1953).

4. *The Problem with Pain*. (New York: Macmillan Publishing Co., Inc., 1962), p. 83.
5. The notion of the reptilian soul has long been a motif in the theories of evolutionary psychologists. According to Dr. Peter Whybrow, a neuroscientist at UCLA, "Human beings are wandering around with brains that are fabulously limited. . . . We've got the core of the average lizard." Cit. *Boomerang: Travels in the New Third World*. (New York and London: W. W. Norton Co., 2011), p. 146.
6. Jacob Brackman, "The Graduate," July 27, 1968.
7. Robert Atwan and Lawrence Wieder are among the host of literary critics who concur: "Poetry inspired by classical Greek and Latin models has dominated the poetic landscape for so many centuries that most readers now consider it the only literary tradition. Although the Scriptural tradition in the English language is every bit as venerable as the classical, it has never received the attention accorded its chosen twin. Like Ishmael and Esau, it has led a shadow existence." *Chapters into Verse: Poetry in English Inspired by the Bible*. Vol. 1 (Oxford and New York. Oxford University Press, 1993), p. xxv.
8. See Genesis 22:1–2.
9. See Genesis 19:6–8.
10. A name meaning "wrestler with God."
11. J. Edgar Park, Exposition for the Book of Exodus, *The Interpreter's Bible*, ed. G. A. Buttrick. (New York and Nashville: Abingdon-Cokesbury Press, n.d.), Vol. 1, p. 972.
12. Exodus 4:24–26. See the crhyme paraphrasing the story in the first volume of *Funny Things Can Happen*, pp. 54–55.
13. Edmond Fleg, *The Life of Moses*, tr. S.H. Guest. (New York: E.P. Dutton & Co., 1928), p. 102.
14. The name Orthodox Jews use to invoke God, fearful that the use of *YHWH* (the tetragram which, vocalized, becomes Y(a)HW(e)H or Y(a)H(o)W(a)H), would violate the third commandment. (Note that the first three vowels in Adonai are the vowels in Yahowah, the German sounding of the name Jehovah.)
15. New York: Penguin Books, 2009. (Orig. Edinburgh, 1759).
16. Numbers 21:9.

Chapter 2: History

17. NRSV.
18. John Greenleaf Whittier, "King Solomon and the Ants."
19. William Butler Yeats, "Solomon and the Witch."
20. So J. G. Whittier in "The Song of the Ants": "*Comely, but black withal, To whom, perchance belongs, That wonderful Song of songs, Sensuous and mystical . . .*"
21. See "Elisha I: Going Elijah One Better" in this book's prequel, *Funny Things Can Happen*, p.133.
22. Deriving its name from this incident, ". . . the 'Abana and Pharpar Syndrome' . . . [is] the angry rejection of a physician's advice, because it contradicts a patient's expectations, or is not delivered in a manner considered appropriate." "An English Physician," kataphusin.blogspot.com/2010/03/abana-and-pharpar-syndrome.html.
23. "Introduction to 1 Chronicles," www. usccb.org/nab/bible... (Web site of the United States Conference of Catholic Bishops).
24. 1 Chronicles 1:35, Numbers 16:1–49.
25. The order followed here conforms to the Greek original as translated in *The New Oxford Annotated Bible* (NRSV), ed. Bruce M. Metzger and Roland E. Murphy (New York: Oxford University Press, 1991) instead of the order devised by St. Jerome for his Latin *Vulgate* and preserved in Stephen Langton's division of the Bible into chapters. ("Churchmen Archbishop Stephen Langton and Cardinal Hugo de Sancto Caro determined different schemas for systematic division of the Bible in the early 13th century. It is the system of Archbishop Langton on which the modern chapter divisions are based. . . . The first Bible in English to use both chapters and verses was the Geneva Bible published shortly afterwards in 1560. These verse divisions soon gained acceptance as a standard way to notate verses, and have since been used in nearly all English Bibles." "Chapters and Verses of the Bible," *Wikipedia.com*. (February 2010)
26. 2:18.
27. Some have surmised that the great irony in this is that the king's loss of sleep resulted from the hammering of Haman's carpenters as they constructed a gallows on which to hang Mordecai, Haman's nemesis.
28. The literal meaning of Maccabeus is "hammer."

Chapter 3: Wisdom and Poetry

29. Ezra 10:10–11.

30. The quotes, descriptive respectively of the book and person of Job, are from David Dendy, *Great Books: My Adventures with Homer, Rousseau, Woolf and Other Indestructible Writers.* (New York: Simon and Schuster, 1996), p. 167.

31. I had no idea until, while composing this crhyme, I researched the phrase "come a cropper," that it had become so rare in recent usage, According to the web site *phrases.org,uk*, "The phrase is first cited in Robert S. Surtees' *Ask Mamma*, 1858: [He] 'rode at an impracticable fence, and got a cropper for his pains.' By the time John C. Hotten published his *A Dictionary of Modern Slang, Cant, and Vulgar Words* in 1859, the phrase has come to refer to any failure rather than just the specific failure to stay on a horse: 'Cropper,' 'to go a cropper', or 'to come a cropper', i.e., to fail badly." (A similar broadening of meaning seems to have occurred in the usage of the quaintly archaic phrase, "hoist on his own petard," used elsewhere in this volume. It too refers to ironic reversals of intentions beyond that of a fuse-lighter's destruction by the very explosive [s]he ignites, to which the original use referred.)

32. Cf. Genesis 1:27 and 2:19.

33. Numbers 27:1–8 ; see the first volume of *Funny Things*, pp. 70–71.

34. *Pensees* 347–48, in *Pensees and the Provincial Letters,* trans. W.F. Trotter and Thomas M'Crie. (New York: Random House, 1941), p. 116. Copyright@ E.P. Dutton & Co.

35. *The Great Divorce.* (New York: Macmillan Publishing Co., Inc., 1946), p. 71.

36. The literal meaning of Luther's Latin term, *carcer theologicus.*

37. I Kings 3:11–12: *So God said to him: "Because you asked for this. . . I now do as you request. I give you a heart so wise and discerning that there has never been anyone like you until now, nor after you will there be anyone to equal you."*

38. One such scheme involved the priestly clan's practice of allowing grown children to avoid the obligation to support their parents by declaring assets *corban*—dedicated to God (i.e., Temple support). This practice draws Jesus' ire in Mark 7:9–13.

39. Italicized phrases in this stanza are from the NAB renderings of Lamentations 1:4, 1:6b, and 3:8; those in subsequent stanzas from 3:10, 3:22, 3:24a, and 3:24b.

Chapter 4: The Prophets

40. The Book of Job may be said to share this honor with Habakkuk, but the issue in Job is more personal, those in Habakkuk more social, political, international. In Job too the main question has to do with *Job's* righteousness, not God's, and at issue is the justification of God's faith in Job, not Job's in God. See Job 1:8–11 and *Funny Things*, first volume, pp. 150–51.
41. American slang for "a small surprise" or "gift for no reason." (OnlineSlangDictionary.com)

Chapter 5: The Gospels

42. Garden City, N.Y.: Doubleday, 1977, p. 114. Cit. E.H. Peterson, *Christ Plays in Ten Thousand Places* (Grand Rapids: Wm. B. Eerdmans, 2005), p. 65.
43. The Hebrew term in Genesis 1:2, typically translated "formless and void."
44. It was Origen of Alexandria who baptized for Christian use what I call here "history's frontispiece"—viz., Plato's myth of the transhistoric Fall in which the human consciousness of Time and Estrangement originated. William Blake's painting, *The Temptation and Fall of Eve*, uses the images of Genesis 3 to depict just such a transaction. (The painting currently resides in the Boston Museum of Fine Arts.)
45. For two previous treatments of biblical donkeys' perspectives, see the first volume of *Funny Things*, p. 216.
46. Hebrew for "students, disciples."
47. "The official Roman Catholic and Eastern Orthodox doctrine is that Mary was a perpetual virgin; this view was also held by many of the early Protestants, including Luther and Zwingli, as well as John Wesley, the 18th century Methodist leader. Indeed, the majority of early Christians seem to have left this doctrine completely unquestioned. The Roman Catholic Church, following Jerome, conclude (*sic*) that the *adelphoi* were Jesus' cousins, but the Eastern Orthodox, following Eusebius and Epiphanius, argue that they were Joseph's children by his (unrecorded) first wife. . . . Some modern Protestants generally regard the *adelphoi* as Mary's biological children, by Joseph; since these churches usually view Jesus as the son of God, rather than of Joseph, the *adelphoi* are seen as Jesus' half-brothers. . . . A modern proposal has these men as the sons of Clopas (Joseph's brother according to Hegesippus) and *Mary, the Wife of Cleopas* (not necessarily referring to Jesus' mother's sister)." From the article *Desposyni* (the relatives of Jesus), in Wikipedia, the free online encyclopedia, May 8, 2012.

48. *Nabi* = Prophet.
49. 2 Corinthians 5:21 (*KJV*).
50. Cf. William Blake's poem, "The Everlasting Gospel."
51. According to Wikipedia, Jesus refers to Gehenna as a destination to be dreaded and avoided eleven times:

    Matt.5:22: whoever calls someone "you fool" will be liable to Gehenna.
    Matt.5:29, 30: better to lose one of your members than that your whole body go into Gehenna.
    Matt.10:28: fear him who can destroy both soul and body in Gehenna.
    Matt.18:9, Mark 9:47: better to enter life with one eye than with two eyes to be thrown into Gehenna.
    Matt.23:15: Pharisees make a convert twice as much a child of Gehenna as themselves.
    Matt.23:33: Jesus to Pharisees: you brood of vipers, how are you to escape being sentenced to Gehenna?
    Mark 9:43: better to enter life with one hand than with two hands to go to Gehenna.
    Mark 9:45: better to enter life lame than with two feet to be thrown into Gehenna.
    Luke 12:5: Fear him who, after he has killed, has authority to cast into Gehenna.

52. Dante and tradition notwithstanding, the idea that individuals will sustain *eternal* punishment rests on fragile foundations. In Jesus' teaching it is the fire, not the duration of individual souls and bodies, that is everlasting and unquenchable. Moreover, note Matthew 10:28's dire warning that the lord of Gehenna can *destroy* (presumably put an end to) body and soul in Gehenna.
53. The Wikipedia article on the topic notes that in the rabbinical Judaism of Jesus' time (particularly in Sanhedrin 7), "Gehenna is considered a Purgatory-like place where the wicked go to suffer until they have atoned for their sins. It is stated that the maximum amount of time a sinner can spend in Gehenna is one year, with the exception of five people who are there for all of eternity...."
54. Martin Luther, *Lectures on Romans (1515)*. Volume XV. Library of Christian Classics. Trans. and ed. Wilhelm Pauck. (Philadelphia: Westminster Press, 1961), p. 79.
55. "Friday the 13th has been considered an unlucky day since the year 1307 . . . , as a combination between an unlucky day, Friday, and the number 13. Another theory as to why the date and number 13 is considered unlucky is that, on the day of Friday the 13th after the final Crusade the pope had sent out men to capture and burn alive the last 13 Knights Templar in order to put an end to the Crusades. Another theory states that the number 13 is un-

lucky because, when in years where there were 13 full moons instead of 12, it made it difficult for the monks who were in charge of the calendars. "This was considered a very unfortunate circumstance, especially by the monks who had charge of the calendar of thirteen months for that year, and it upset the regular arrangement of church festivals. For this reason thirteen came to be considered an unlucky number." *Wikipedia* as of January 12, 2011,

56. Luther's typically free translation of the ancient Latin phrase for it, *communicatio idiomatum,* or "communication of attributes."

57. *The Shaking of the Foundations.* (New York: Charles Scribner's Sons, 1948), p. 165.

Chapter 6: Acts of the Apostles

58. "Change of mind" is the literal meaning of the Greek term for repentance, *metanoia.*

59. The first two Ananiases' stories are related in Acts 5:1–11 and 9:10–19. For whimsical rhyming paraphrases of these stories, see the first volume of *Funny Things,* pp. 284 and 289–90.

60. "A few years after the Civil War, Christians who would later be called fundamentalists began to hold Bible conferences and prophecy conferences. These were held in such places as Chicago, Illinois, Swampscott, Massachusetts, Watkins Cove, New York, Old Orchard, Maine, and Mackinac Island, Michigan. They attracted famous pastors and Bible teachers from throughout America. For 14 years the Bible Conference near the famous Niagara falls boasted the teaching and preaching of such luminaries as A. J. Gordon, A. C. Dixon, Hudson Taylor and A. T. Pierson. As an outgrowth of this popular yearly conference, in 1895 there was adopted a Statement of Belief that listed 14 articles as essential truths to be spread. Five of them, the inspiration of the Bible, the depravity of man, redemption through Christ's blood, the true church made up of all believers and the second coming of Christ to reign on this earth, have been called the Magna Carta of Fundamentalism, but the Niagara conference listed 14." Mike Randall, "Introducing the Fundamentals," *www.breadandlentils.org/?p=126.*

Chapter 7: The Letters of Paul

61. *Boule* is the Greek term favored by St. Luke. It is usually translated "blueprint" or "groundplan."

62. Acts 1:8.

63. *Phaedrus,* sections 246a-254e.
64. *Stoicheia* (sing. *stoicheion)* is the Greek term translated "elemental powers of the world" in Colossians 2:8. Such powers presumably ruled heavenly spheres or star kingdoms sometimes referred to as "principalities."
65. Epimenides, Cretan philosopher of the sixth century B.C., has been credited with this saying.
66. I Corinthians 3:2, Hebrews 5:2, 13.
67. This is a conclusion reached by some in explanation of Galatians 6:11: "See with what large letters I am writing to you in my own hand!"

Chapter 9: The Apocalypse

68. I am indebted to Barbara Brown Taylor, whose sermon "Apocalyptic Figs" in the book *Bread of Angels* (Cambridge-Boston, Mass. Cowley Publications, 1997), pp. 156–160, evoked the imagery in this crhyme.
69. Other translations read "bottomless pit."
70. Daniel 3:1–30.
71. Latin: "God Himself willing it."

An Eschatological Appendix

Surely Heaven must contain a salvation salon—
a recital hall poets of all sorts may count on—
a room presided over by some penitent like Peter
who turns to the Lord's praise
poor diction and hobbled meter.

Veterans like Dante, Goethe, and Shakespeare
surely must win and tickle God's ear
but poetic ingenues
may require a change of muse.

If justice there be, George Herbert will be there,
and surely Miss Dickinson—
William Blake to add spice and flair,
and Ogden Nash, master of the non-metrical pun.

The venerable Dr. Seuss, the creators of Mother Goose,
(virtually all anonymous)
will be there too, leading a guild of poets pseudonymous—
contrivers of funny and nonsense rhymes
who carry into Heaven's courts laugh-filled earthly times.

Appendix 2

Biblical "Funnies": A Brief Typology

How is the Bible funny?
Let me count the ways!
First, instead of taking aeons,
creation happens in days....

But it's not just in its account of cosmic beginnings that Scripture hits the modern, scientific mindset in its silly plexus. The fact is, holy writ can be funny in virtually every sense of the word.

If you're looking for *funny-jocular*—as in jokes featuring generic irony or the recreational, practical, mischievous, and even malicious sub-types of the genre—there's the tale of Tamar and Judah (Genesis 38:11-30) or, even more blatantly— in a sub-type of malicious irony one could call the vengeful— of the revenge Dinah's brothers wrought on Shechem (Genesis 34:1-11). In the New Testament (NT), meanwhile, there are, among many examples, the depictions of Jewish mothers (John 2:1-11 and Mark 10:25-35) and a side, perhaps even snide, comment on Paul's preaching (Acts 20:7-12).

If it's *funny-strange* you're after, in the Original or Old Testament there's the teasing tale of the Nephilim (Gen. 6) or that of the demonic attack on Moses on his trek back to Egypt to rescue the house of Israel (Exodus 4:24-26), while in the NT, there're the similarly weird cases of the sons of Sceva (Acts 19:11-20) and of the Maltan serpent (Acts 28:1-6).

Looking for the *funny-odd*—sub-type, perhaps, of the funny-strange—try the descriptions of King Saul's flirtations with spirits, mediated (through the Witch of Endor—1 Samuel 28:3-25) or unmediated (same book, 19:9–24). Or for the *funny-quaint,* sub-category of the funny-odd distinguished by some charming or exotic quality: the First Couple's flight to the woods (Genesis 3:8–24), Abraham's dickering with God over the fate of Sodom (Genesis 18:16–33), or David's negotiation with Yahweh over who should provide housing for whom (2 Samuel 5:1–12, 7:1–29). As for the New Testament, consider Peter's choice of Simon the Tanner as a friend and landlord (Acts 10:1–9) and the behavior of Paul, Silas, and the other inmates of an earthquake-shattered jail (Acts 16:16–33) after the quake.

The *funny-punny* deserves a category all to itself. Despite the scorn intellectuals heap on it as the least respectable gift of wit, word play is a popular favorite both in the Bible and out. In Scripture it is such, I think, because it is a handy instrument of revelation as well as a good friend of memory. And one need look no further in the Bible, of course, than to the naming of Adam (Genesis 2:7) or the renaming of Abram ben-Terah (Genesis 17:5) and Simon bar-Jonah (Matthew 16:17) for examples of its use.

The *funny-ethnic* is an all too familiar feature of the scriptural narrative. In the Hebrew Bible it targets, for the most part, Israel's foes and rivals, especially Edom (Numbers 20:14–21, e.g.), Moab (Balaam and his ass, Numbers 22:21–24:25), and Syria (Naaman and Elisha, 2 Kings 5:1–19), with an occasional racial overtone (e.g., re Moses' Cushite wife—Numbers 12:1–14). And despite Jesus' ethic of all-comprehending love it shows up occasionally in the New Testament as well (e.g., Matthew 15:21–28, John 4:1–42, Acts 10:9–35).

Finally, there's plenty of the *funny-ribald* too, from the mild and Platonic (see the deathbed test of David's chances of hanging on, 1 Kings 1:1–4) to the downright raunchy (Lot and his daughters, Genesis 19:1–26, David's most famous romp, 2 Samuel 11:1–27, and Solomon's escapades, 1 Kings 11:1–4).Though somewhat muted in the NT it rears its head gently in the stories of Salome in Herod's court (Matthew 14:3–12), traditions surrounding Mary Magdala (Luke 7:37–48, 8:2, and John 8:1–11), and the anonymous streaker in Mark 14:51–52.

www.ingramcontent.com/pod-product-compliance
Lightning Source LLC
Chambersburg PA
CBHW071237230426
43668CB00011B/1480